Fictions of Autonomy

Modernist Literature and Culture

Kevin J. H. Dettmar and Mark Wollaeger, Series Editors

Fictions of Autonomy

Modernism from Wilde to de Man

Andrew Goldstone

OXFORD
UNIVERSITY PRESS

OXFORD
UNIVERSITY PRESS

Oxford University Press is a department of the University of Oxford.
It furthers the University's objective of excellence in research, scholarship,
and education by publishing worldwide.

Oxford   New York
Auckland   Cape Town   Dar es Salaam   Hong Kong   Karachi
Kuala Lumpur   Madrid   Melbourne   Mexico City   Nairobi
New Delhi   Shanghai   Taipei   Toronto

With offices in
Argentina   Austria   Brazil   Chile   Czech Republic   France   Greece
Guatemala   Hungary   Italy   Japan   Poland   Portugal   Singapore
South Korea   Switzerland   Thailand   Turkey   Ukraine   Vietnam

Oxford is a registered trademark of Oxford University Press
in the UK and certain other countries.

Published in the United States of America by
Oxford University Press
198 Madison Avenue, New York, NY 10016

Library of Congress Cataloging-in-Publication Data
Goldstone, Andrew, 1982–
    Fictions of autonomy : modernism from Wilde to de Man / Andrew Goldstone.
    p. cm. — (Modernist literature & culture)
    Includes index.
    ISBN 978-0-19-986112-5
    1. Literature, Modern—20th century—History and criticism—Theory, etc.
    2. Modernism (Literature)   3. Autonomy (Philosophy)   4. Aestheticism
    (Literature)   I. Title.
    PN771.G65 2013
    809'.9112—dc23
    2012017544

9 8 7 6 5 4 3 2 1

Printed in the United States of America
on acid-free paper

Contents

Acknowledgments

Writing about literary autonomy has made me particularly conscious of the ways my own writing has depended on a great many people and institutions. But then the only varieties of autonomy real enough to be worth pursuing are those which are fostered by meaningful relationships with others. So I am very happy to record my gratitude to those who have made this work possible even as they allowed me to chart my own course.

Langdon Hammer and Amy Hungerford nurtured this project from its earliest days as a dissertation idea and have continued to improve it as it has become a book. They have been generous with encouragement and equally generous with necessary criticism. They have been kind, wise, and patient over many conversations and rereadings and e-mails. I could never have undertaken this project without their support.

Many colleagues, teachers, and friends have worked with me on all or part of what follows. Pericles Lewis has been particularly generous with his time and his thoughtful suggestions, from an early independent study course to the dissertation and beyond. Barry McCrea's reading has also been a great boon. Jill Campbell is more responsible than she probably knows for the shape of the final project. Tanya Agathocleous, Caleb Smith, Victoria Rosner, and Douglas Mao all read long sections and offered me their incisive readings. I could never have begun this work without Helen Vendler, Philip Fisher, and John Parker, the college mentors who launched me into graduate school and planted the seeds of this book long before I knew I would write it. Before even that, Mary Burchenal of Brookline High School made poetry a real subject for me.

The two readers for Oxford University Press were as insightful, scrupulous, and generous as any first-time author could have hoped. It's been a pleasure and a privilege to work with the Modernist Literature & Culture series editors, Mark Wollaeger and Kevin Dettmar, as well as the editors at the press, Brendan O'Neill and Shannon McLachlan. I am grateful to Laura Poole and Sravanthi Sridharan for their work in editing and production.

Portions of chapter 1 first appeared in my "Servants, Aestheticism, and 'The Dominance of Form,'" *ELH* 77.3 (2010): 615–643, ©2010 by The Johns Hopkins University Press; they are reprinted with permission by The Johns Hopkins University Press. My graduate work at Yale University was supported by fellowships in the names of Richard J. Franke, John F. Enders, and Mrs. Giles F. Whiting; at Stanford University I was the beneficiary of a Mellon Fellowship in the Humanities.

The making of this book depended heavily on open-source software produced and maintained by volunteer communities. I am grateful indeed for LaTeX, XꟼLaTeX, Philipp Lehman's biblatex, and David Fussner's biblatex-chicago.

In my two years in Stanford's quasi-paradisal environs, I was very fortunate in friends and colleagues. Lanier Anderson and J. P. Daughton have made the Mellon Fellowship of Scholars in the Humanities a wonderful institution in which to begin academic life after grad school; they and all the Mellon Fellows of 2009–2011 worked patiently over long pieces of this book with me. My redoubled gratitude to Lanier Anderson for his willingness to lend his brilliance to improving my arguments (and those of everyone else who comes his way). Blakey Vermeule, Nick Jenkins, Saikat Majumdar, Hannah Sullivan, Harris Feinsod, Roland Greene, and Ramón Saldívar have been excellent friends to this book as well as to me.

I have learned much by sharing my ideas in many forums. I have profited from discussions at the Yale Twentieth Century Colloquium, the Modernist Studies Association, and the American Comparative Literature Association. At Stanford it was a great pleasure to be part of the Working Group in Poetics and to have gained in my turn from that group's energetic commentary. All those who gave their time to the Yale Using Theory Brown Bag Lunches, session leaders and participants, may not have known that they were helping me in my struggles over methods — but they were. Chief among these was my fellow theory user Colin Gillis, but that barely begins to cover the thanks I owe him for many kinds of collaboration, coordination, co-conspiracy, and friendship over the past eight years.

Other dear friends have helped this book by supporting me through many ups and downs. I cannot possibly mention all the friends I have been lucky to have in the years in which I have been writing this book, but I cannot possibly not mention Philip Zeyliger, Jordan Zweck, and Erica Levy McAlpine.

My partner, Anne DeWitt, is a continually amazing presence, an inspiration, a brilliant interlocutor, and much more than I can say. She has hashed over every page of this book with me multiple times. Autonomous or not, this book is a product of our life together.

Above all: with love and gratitude, I dedicate this book to my parents, Roberta Gordon and Jeffrey Goldstone.

Series Editors' Foreword

In everyday life, most of us take for granted that autonomy is always a relative concept. What seems to stand alone, be it a book or a business, always depends on multiple forms of relatedness. But as Andrew Goldstone points out, the issue has played out differently in literary studies, especially in modernist studies. For the most part, literary studies deems autonomy a passé topic and ignores it; modernist studies may shy away from it altogether. When autonomy is addressed, formulations tend to gravitate toward extremes. Thus, instead of granting a complex dialectic between claims to autonomy and social embeddedness, critics who choose to keep autonomy on the table as a key term either embrace it as the guarantor of the literary or, far more often, reject it as a politically suspect ideology, where "ideology" equates to false consciousness. Both extremes are misguided, Goldstone argues, because they fail to recognize that the doctrine of autonomy advanced by so many modernists constituted an effort to free literature as a practice from a particular form of constraint, and that effort provided insight into the social relations that made autonomy seem desirable.

Few modernist writers, moreover, embraced the philosophically dubious notion of absolute aesthetic autonomy for their work, and not all versions postulated autonomy as "an essential, axiomatic quality of art." Many modernists, including T. S. Eliot, self-consciously "sought to secure relative, worldly forms of independence for literature in society," and even delusory beliefs in absolute aesthetic autonomy ended up producing "representations of a socially embedded autonomy for literature." The literary-historical study of autonomy that Goldstone undertakes therefore does not lead back into the apolitical formalism that is the bugbear of long-standing critics of modernism, whether Marxian or militantly postmodern, but ultimately outward into what some have called contextual study but which Goldstone (following Bourdieu in *The Rules of Art*, not in *Distinction*) thinks of as the sociology of literary production. In this model, the goal is not to "bring in" extraliterary determinations but to treat style itself as a social practice.

What, then, are the forms of worldly relative autonomy that Goldstone explores? There are four: autonomy from labor, personality, political community, and linguistic reference (though he also comments acutely on the more established critical conversation about the marketplace). These correspond to four chapters. The first focuses on servants and domestic labor, from late nineteenth-century aesthetes (Villiers de l'Isle-Adam, Huysmans, and Wilde) to the canonical modernist Proust, and examines servants as charged nodal points in which social and aesthetic conventions meet. Of the unlikely pairing of aesthetes and servants, Goldstone remarks that "such characters work to reveal the inextricable connection between a 'dominant' aesthetic form and social domination." Key here is the argument that the works of these writers dwell knowingly on the insight that "servants challenge the purity of the aesthetic even as they serve it." Thus, instead of presenting as a revelation the notion that modernists wanted to make money with their work and were implicated in the very social issues they criticized—we can all agree to that—Goldstone teases out the subtle ways these texts explore the sometimes troubling social entanglements entailed by their aspirations to autonomy.

This is not to say that Goldstone's aim is to exonerate modernists—see, for example, his searching treatment of anti-Semitism in Djuna Barnes. What he wants to do is escape the false dichotomy in which modernists either sought to escape from history through formal autonomy or aimed to transform social reality by the same means. He takes up the argument for the transformative political effects of modernist formal innovations in his third chapter, on Barnes, Joyce, and exile. Still influential early accounts of modernist exile emphasized it as a strategy of aesthetic transcendence: Joyce leaves Ireland for the world of art. More recently, accounts of cosmopolitanism tend to attribute political effects to the exilic position, most often through the invention of a critical cosmopolitan subjectivity that makes possible new forms of transnational community. Goldstone troubles such assertions by showing how Barnes, like Stephen Dedalus in Joyce's *Portrait*, associates expatriation with formal innovations that foster "a liberating distance from national and other group identities." Neither completely detached aesthetes nor fully engaged in communal projects (such as queer identity or transnational sol-idarity), Joyce and Barnes understand and depict "cosmopolitanism as an always imperfect, socially specific practice" that favors "a relatively autonomous aesthetic practice" over "political community." By attending to *versions* of autonomy, we can avoid either-or formulations and the ascription of social roles that do not match up accurately, Goldstone argues, with the lived experience of the writ-ers or the dialectical meditations on autonomy versus engagement that shape their works.

Chapter 2 aims straight at the heart of modernist theories of autonomy by pairing Eliot and Theodor Adorno as related proponents of freedom from person-ality, which is to say as theorists of impersonality. Even though both writers were concerned with high-cultural formalism, their conjunction may seem surprising, given that Eliot is associated with a conservative social and cultural program, and Adorno is generally understood as a defender of the socially transformative power of aesthetic autonomy. Yet Goldstone argues that the concept of late style, which Adorno derived from his study of Beethoven, helps us see how both Eliot and Adorno practice a style that insists on the impersonality of aesthetic forms while also preserving a sense of the personal that is bound up with intimations of mortality.

The fourth and final chapter (followed by a brief epilogue) takes on the most extreme form of modernist autonomy: freedom from reference. Goldstone's last pairing focuses on the shared investment in tautology—the trope of autonomy par excellence—in Wallace Stevens and Paul de Man. Both poet and critic-theorist are read as exemplary modernists concerned with defending literature's right to autonomy as a free-standing field of study within the modern American uni-versity. This struggle partly took the form of asserting the claims of literature against those of philosophy and through the paradoxical acknowledgment of the reader in the denial of reference: "The stuttering, nearly nonsensical sound of tau-tological formulae becomes an essential reminder that literary autonomy, even autonomy from reference, is a social arrangement made by and for real-world audiences."

One suspects de Man would not have been keen to find himself linked to Stevens in quite this way, but you can judge Goldstone's case for yourself. That the real-world audience for nonreferential literary practice and theories of language could only be the university suggests the degree to which the university itself, especially the liberal arts, remains indebted to modernist principles of autonomy. This, in turn, suggests why the study of autonomy as a socially embedded practice remains an urgent project, not only for literary studies but for the university, both of which, as we all know, are facing challenges to their legitimacy from those with the power to defund them. In addition to a deeply engaging return to a foundational concept of modernism, *Fictions of Autonomy* is an important contribution to the project of thinking through what is at stake in questions of autonomy today.

—Mark Wollaeger and Kevin J. H. Dettmar

Fictions of Autonomy

Introduction

In literary studies, we regard aesthetic autonomy as an idea whose time has passed. Once an influential doctrine among writers, artists, and critics, the belief that art—including literature—is a law unto itself, neither governed by nor responsible to extra-aesthetic concerns, has few defenders among scholars today. Contemporary scholarship rejects the notion of the freestanding literary artwork, concentrating instead on the ways literature participates in history.[1] Autonomy's disrepute casts its greatest shadow on the twentieth century's most strident advocates of aesthetic autonomy for literature: the writers and critics of literary modernism. In 1923, T. S. Eliot could confidently proclaim, "I have assumed as axiomatic that a creation, a work of art, is autonomous."[2] At the time, he spoke as an innovator, asserting the right of his and others' literary practice to dictate its own terms. Now such a doctrine seems to represent the most hopelessly deluded aspect of modernism. We who wish to understand literature in and through its contexts can no longer share Eliot's belief in the entire independence of the artistic "creation."

This book argues that ideas of aesthetic autonomy are nonetheless central to both the history of modernist literature and the discipline of literary studies. These

1. In *Practicing New Historicism*, Catherine Gallagher and Stephen Greenblatt denounce the practice of "ignoring the cultural matrix out of which [artistic] representations emerge," and they scorn the "culturally conservative point of view" that "the art object, ideally self-enclosed, is freed not only from the necessities of the surrounding world (necessities that it transforms miraculously into play) but also from the intention of the maker." Catherine Gallagher and Stephen Greenblatt, *Practicing New Historicism* (Chicago: University of Chicago Press, 2000), 9, 11–12.

2. T. S. Eliot, "The Function of Criticism," *Criterion* 2, no. 5 (October 1923): 38.

ideas exerted a transformative force on the literature of the modernist period. They have a real existence as emerging norms, central aspirations, and abiding problems for modernism—and for present-day readers of literature. Though some of the most familiar conceptions of aesthetic autonomy are philosophically questionable, modernism developed many versions of autonomy, not all of which suppose autonomy to be an essential, axiomatic quality of art. Modernist writers, Eliot included, also sought to secure relative, worldly forms of independence for literature within society. Sometimes this pursuit of partial autonomy was self-conscious. At other moments, the very belief, delusory though it might have been, in the absolute autonomy of the artistic work led modernist writers to produce representations of a socially embedded autonomy for literature. Given this range of possibilities for modernist beliefs in and practices of autonomy, literary historians cannot simply dismiss the concept as a relic of modernism and New Criticism. We should treat autonomy claims with skepticism, and we must reject hyperbolic assertions that all literature is intrinsically autonomous, but we must take the forms of relative autonomy seriously as a genuine and significant aspect of modernist literature's engagement with its world. We must undertake the literary-historical study of autonomy itself.

My contribution to this scholarly endeavor concentrates on British, American, and French aestheticist literary modernism. I examine the "high" modernism of Henry James in his late period, Marcel Proust, T. S. Eliot, Djuna Barnes, James Joyce, and Wallace Stevens, together with their precursors in nineteenth-century decadence and aestheticism, Auguste Villiers de l'Isle-Adam, Joris-Karl Huysmans, and Oscar Wilde, and their successors in mid-twentieth-century modernist theory, Theodor Adorno and Paul de Man. These writers made aesthetic autonomy a central theme of their work in narrative, poetry, and criticism. Ideas of aesthetic and literary autonomy predate the late nineteenth century, of course, and the problems of the independence of artists and their work appear in many times and places. But the period of canonical modernism created distinctive versions of autonomy that persist both within academic literary studies and in the larger field of literary production. I discuss four of these versions of autonomy that have been particularly consequential for twentieth-century literary and cultural history: the refusal of social realism through literary form, artistic impersonality, apolitical artistic exile, and linguistic nonreferentiality. Modernist literary autonomy is historically distinctive because aesthetic and literary laws like these also became the principles of a new social formation for literature: a world of specialized and professionalized writers, publishers, and readers with their own particular rules of description and evaluation, their own claims to independence.

Crucially, this world overlapped with a nascent academic approach to literature. The kind of modernism discussed in this study provided both the principles and the occasions for the new discipline of academic literary criticism that came to dominate English and other language departments in North American and British universities over the course of the century.[3] The autonomy of literature could be invoked to justify academic literary criticism as a distinctive discipline with an isolable object of study; at the same time, a specialist mode of interpretation and appreciation served to buttress modernism's claim to autonomy. The continuities between an aestheticist writer like Wilde, a poet-critic like Eliot, and a critic-theorist like de Man exemplify this modernist genealogy of the contemporary literature department.[4] Nor has the academic influence of high modernism waned even if the canonical modernist period has long been over. The modernism I discuss set the terms in which literary scholars, and literary readers in general, still debate fundamental questions about literature in society, aesthetic form, and literary meaning. Chief among these debates is the ongoing contention over the relations between literary production and its historical contexts, a debate in which the very nature of the subject matter of literary study is at stake. Yet the apparent alternatives in dispute—historical context or the autonomous artwork—are both rendered problematic by the reexamination of modernism I undertake in this book, which shows, surprisingly, that literary practices of autonomy draw on and engage with the social world.

I seek to address these basic theoretical and disciplinary questions by means of a literary-historical analysis of the varieties of aesthetic autonomy in modernism. I show that autonomy is at stake, either explicitly or as an inescapable subtext, in an unexpectedly diverse range of modernist practices, from the representation

3. The standard account of this academic history is Gerald Graff, *Professing Literature: An Institutional History*, 20th anniversary ed. (Chicago: University of Chicago Press, 2007). On modernism and the American university, see also Gail McDonald, *Learning to Be Modern: Pound, Eliot, and the American University* (Oxford: Clarendon, 1993).

4. Though I do not discuss the New Criticism extensively in this book, of course it belongs to this history; indeed, perhaps the exemplary statement of the connections between literary autonomy and the departmental autonomy of literary studies can be found in one of the New Criticism's most important manifestos, John Crowe Ransom's "Criticism, Inc.," in *The World's Body* (New York: Scribner, 1938), 327–50. For important reflections on New Criticism, autonomy, and institution-building, see Graff, *Professing Literature*, esp. chap. 9, and John Guillory, "Ideology and Canonical Form: The New Critical Canon," chap. 3 in *Cultural Capital: The Problem of Literary Canon Formation* (Chicago: University of Chicago Press, 1993). Stephen Schryer places the New Criticism in a broader history of U.S. academic professionalism in "Fantasies of the New Class: The New Criticism, Harvard Sociology, and the Idea of the University," *PMLA* 122, no. 3 (May 2007): 663–78.

of domestic servants to the poetic use of the figure of tautology. By tracing the importance of autonomy across a range of modernist themes and genres, we will see that practices of autonomy themselves vary according to their contexts—according, that is, to what modernist writers, in particular times and places, most urgently seek autonomy *from*. Discussions of literary autonomy have tended to limit themselves to a singular concept of the self-regulating or self-contained artwork, which is then either dismissed or (less frequently) celebrated. My aim here is to argue for treating modernist autonomy as a complex, ramified family of practices, evolving across a transnational literary field. Indeed, autonomy has been a challenging subject in part because of its protean nature; autonomy arguments and practices change shape under varying pressures.

The four cases studied in *Fictions of Autonomy* lay out the basic possibilities as a sequence of ever-more-extensive claims for literary autonomy: elevating the cultivation of aesthetic form over mimetic realism; distinguishing the autonomous artistic work from the less independent artist who makes it; rejecting any political or communal affiliation for artist and artistic practice alike; or, finally, disavowing reference to reality altogether. I do not offer this as a definitive typology—not least because, as we will see repeatedly in the detailed analyses, these strategies can flow into one another—but as a set of orienting landmarks: they indicate the range of modernist autonomy practices. This range allows me to discuss the differing ways modernist attempts to secure autonomy in fact confront and make use of the artist's and the artwork's embeddedness in social life. Seemingly nonaesthetic aspects of the author's class position, biography, habits of affiliation, and rhetorical aims can become essential to the meaning of a literary practice that still insists on autonomy. This diversity of forms of autonomy constitutes an argument for my overarching thesis: the pursuit of autonomy leads modernist writers to take account of, and seek to transform, the social relations of their literary production. Sometimes, it is true, the pursuit of autonomy leads writers into blindness about their work's social embeddedness. But I emphasize the decisive importance of those moments in which, instead of denying its social relations, literary art for art's sake is capable of unique insights about them; I argue that those insights depend on the distinctive vantage point that relative autonomy gives particular writers on their works' constraints and freedoms.

My analysis constitutes an alternative to standard historicizing approaches to modernism, which describe modernist literature as *responding*, often with political critique, to historical circumstances—as though modernism needed to be saved from its own aestheticist tendencies by the work of contextualist scholarship. Pericles Lewis's *Cambridge Introduction to Modernism* sums up the new scholarly consensus about the "historical understanding of modernism": rather than "isolating the 'great works,'" this understanding "emphasizes the immersion of modernist literature in a culture of experiment . . . the distinctively literary solutions that they found for the central problems of their time."[5] I also differ in emphasis from those works of the New Modernist Studies which, though properly taking modernism's aesthetic orientation seriously, still grant those aesthetics direct political effects. I am thinking, here, of Jed Esty's argument about the cultural work performed by the "anthropological turn" of British late modernism in *A Shrinking Island*; Rebecca Walkowitz's defense of the politics of *Cosmopolitan Style*; and Douglas Mao's history of theories of the developmental power of the aesthetic in *Fateful Beauty*.[6] Whereas work like Esty's, Walkowitz's, and Mao's continues to look for an extraliterary social program behind modernist aesthetics, my approach treats the aestheticist practices of modernism *as* its social program. I show that it is by pursuing relative autonomy as a *mode of relation* between literature and the social world of its emergence that modernism's engagements with its contexts come about. Indeed, these engagements make the word *context* misleading, because seemingly nonliterary concerns and materials become essential to modernism's claims for literary autonomy; the literary work seeks self-governance even as it extends its relations in a great variety of directions.[7] To think about autonomy *is* to think about literature's social embeddedness in the distinctive way the modernist period permits.

Distinctive though the modernist versions of autonomy are, scholars have also recently shown renewed interest in the problem of autonomy in other literary-historical periods. Mary Poovey's *Genres of the Credit Economy* gives a history of the differentiation of "Literary" value from economic value over the course

5. Pericles Lewis, *The Cambridge Introduction to Modernism* (Cambridge: Cambridge University Press, 2007), xx. A very clear overview of present-day modernist studies in relation to the history of the field may be found in Douglas Mao and Rebecca L. Walkowitz, "Introduction: Modernisms Bad and New," in *Bad Modernisms*, ed. Douglas Mao and Rebecca L. Walkowitz (Durham, NC: Duke University Press, 2006), 1–17.

6. Jed Esty, *A Shrinking Island: Modernism and National Culture in England* (Princeton, NJ: Princeton University Press, 2004); Rebecca Walkowitz, *Cosmopolitan Style: Modernism beyond the Nation* (New York: Columbia University Press, 2006); Douglas Mao, *Fateful Beauty: Aesthetic Environments, Juvenile Development, and Literature, 1860–1960* (Princeton, NJ: Princeton University Press, 2008). Here is a typical statement, from Mao's discussion of Joyce's *Portrait*: "For some inhabitants of the late nineteenth and early twentieth centuries, the meaning of art was associated with the possibility that beauty might shape beneficially the souls of those exposed to it, might usher in a better society" (138).

7. For a provocative argument against the reductive tendencies implicit in an overly simplistic notion of "social context" invoked in studies of artistic, scientific, and many other domains, see Bruno Latour, *Reassembling the Social: An Introduction to Actor-Network-Theory* (Oxford: Oxford University Press, 2005).

of the eighteenth and nineteenth centuries. Moving into the late nineteenth century and the political rather than the economic field, Leela Gandhi has analyzed the potentially "radical" discourse of aesthetic autonomy in late-nineteenth-century Britain in *Affective Communities*. Scholarship on literature of the later twentieth century has also started to make much of aspirations to autonomy, as it has become clear just how consequential the institutionalization of modernism's autonomy concerns has been to subsequent literature. Mark McGurl's history of *The Program Era* goes so far as to wonder whether "the whole enterprise of literature as we have known it in modern times [hasn't] been driven by an impulse to artistic autonomy." On an even grander scale, Pascale Casanova, by putting the concept of a specifically literary capital at the heart of her model of the worldwide competition among authors and nations in *The World Republic of Letters*, has provoked widespread interest in the question of literature's autonomy in work on world literature.[8] All of this scholarship gravitates toward early twentieth-century modernism as the decisive moment of crystallization for the social forms and practices of aesthetic autonomy, but modernist studies itself has become shy of mentioning autonomy except to dismiss it. *Fictions of Autonomy* aims to provide a fuller, socially situated account of the pivotal modernist era in the literary history of autonomy.

An Institutional Approach

My approach to modernist autonomy draws on a tradition of studies of modernism as a social formation. The landmarks of this tradition are Peter Bürger's *Theory of the Avant-Garde*, Lawrence Rainey's *Institutions of Modernism*, and—most significantly for this book—Pierre Bourdieu's *The Rules of Art*.[9] Since the apex of modernism, most accounts have described it either art-internally, as a break

8. Leela Gandhi, *Affective Communities: Anticolonial Thought, Fin-de-Siècle Radicalism, and the Politics of Friendship* (Durham, NC: Duke University Press, 2006), 146; Mary Poovey, *Genres of the Credit Economy: Mediating Value in Eighteenth- and Nineteenth-Century Britain* (Chicago: University of Chicago Press, 2008); Mark McGurl, *The Program Era: Postwar Fiction and the Rise of Creative Writing* (Cambridge, MA: Harvard University Press, 2009), 325; Pascale Casanova, *The World Republic of Letters*, trans. M. B. DeBevoise (Cambridge, MA: Harvard University Press, 2004).

9. Peter Bürger, *Theory of the Avant-Garde*, trans. Michael Shaw (Minneapolis: University of Minnesota Press, 1984); Lawrence Rainey, *Institutions of Modernism: Literary Elites and Public Culture* (New Haven, CT: Yale University Press, 1998); Pierre Bourdieu, *The Rules of Art: Genesis and Structure of the Literary Field*, trans. Susan Emanuel (Cambridge: Polity Press, 1996). Also important are Jonathan Freedman, *Professions of Taste: Henry James,*

with old artistic forms, or contextually, as a response to changing historical circumstances—with the latter account dominating the scholarship of recent years.[10] Bürger, Rainey, and Bourdieu, by contrast, emphasize the emergence of a social grouping of people and practices around the idea of artistic and aesthetic autonomy; autonomy, in this sense, is shorthand for the specialized institutions in which modernist cultural production and reception proceed in a self-consciously distinctive manner, pursuing newly independent artistic goals not necessarily endorsed by the broader culture. This sociologically informed perspective can encompass both alternative explanations of modernism. It describes the social practices through which purely aesthetic or formal innovations *become* goals in themselves for certain specialist artists. At the same time, this perspective allows us to see why modernists might appear to gain a critical purchase on the life of modernity in general, because their institutional autonomy, though variable and never more than relative, can encourage the feeling that artists observe ordinary life from the outside. More fundamental than either the modification of forms or the response to history, however, is the pursuit of a relative autonomy within society for literature and other arts—a pursuit that, as we shall see, both gives a social content to the putative purity of aesthetics and imposes aesthetic constraints on the relationship between art and social modernity at large.[11]

Despite their usefulness, descriptions like Bürger's, Rainey's, and Bourdieu's sometimes threaten to reduce autonomy to an ideology, in the disparaging sense of a cover story that attempts to disguise art's complicity with the dominant

---

British Aestheticism, and Commodity Culture* (Stanford, CA: Stanford University Press, 1990) and Raymond Williams, *The Politics of Modernism: Against the New Conformists*, ed. Tony Pinkney (London: Verso, 1989).

10. The degree to which these alternate theories continue to hold the field is indicated by their codification as a hybrid in Lewis's *Cambridge Introduction to Modernism*: "In English the word [modernism] refers primarily to the tendency of experimental literature of the early twentieth century to break away from traditional verse forms, narrative techniques, and generic conventions in order to seek new methods of representation appropriate to life in an urban, industrial, mass-oriented age" (xvii). For useful surveys of these conceptual alternatives, see Astradur Eysteinsson, *The Concept of Modernism* (Ithaca: Cornell University Press, 1990) and Rita Felski, "Modernity and Feminism," chap. 1 in *The Gender of Modernity* (Cambridge, MA: Harvard University Press, 1995).

11. The idea of an institutional approach to literature as a compromise between historicism and formalism dates at least to Harry Levin's call for studies of "literature as an institution" in *The Gates of Horn: A Study of Five French Realists* (New York: Oxford University Press, 1963). But the sociological approach taken here is not a compromise of this kind, because it insists that literature can become a relatively autonomous institution only in particular historical settings and only by dint of artistic practices that are both social and formal at once.

powers. Bürger explicitly carries out this reduction: aesthetic autonomy, he says, is an "ideological category" of bourgeois society; the idea that art is essentially autonomous obscures the historical emergence of artistic institutions.[12] He then goes on to argue that the historical avant-gardes attempted, though unsuccessfully, to correct this earlier modernist tendency by "reintegrat[ing] art into the praxis of life."[13] But the distinction between modernist and avant-garde does not seem to me of much use. It applies at best awkwardly to Britain, the United States, and elsewhere outside Bürger's Franco-German field of reference. In the years since his *Theory* first appeared, *modernism* has become the broader term, equally applicable to the tendencies Bürger labels "avant-garde" and to those he relegates to aestheticist modernism.[14] As we will see in chapter 1, even signal texts of the fin de siècle in France and Britain see their aestheticist stance as unavoidably embedded in "the praxis of life." Bürger's stark idea of avant-garde praxis as the only possible mode of embeddedness forces him to attempt to isolate "modernist" autonomy as an ideological malformation. By contrast, I propose that the practices of autonomy, found throughout the varieties of modernism (in the most inclusive sense), are so many attempts to construct real relations between the institutions of art and other fields of social life.

Thus, I avoid the term *ideology* in favor of what I call *fictions of autonomy*—a phrase meant to cover the inventions of narrative, poetry, and criticism. While granting the problematic status of ideas of autonomy, my term steers clear of treating those ideas as mere deceptions or delusions. One of my central claims is that autonomy fictions are not always deceptions; they are equally capable of taking account of modernism's changing social situation. Even on a more neutral understanding of ideology as an imaginary relation to real conditions, to label aesthetic autonomy an ideology is to reduce it to a reflection of other, usually political and economic, facts—without analyzing how such a reflection could take place. Fiction, by contrast, has a wider range of possible relationships to reality: though it may distort or deceive, it can also reveal or even remake the world. Fictions circulate and act in the social world in diverse ways, some as grand as those implied by "ideology" but others more local, more fine-grained. To see aesthetic autonomy as a fiction is to invite a further analysis instead of a brusque dismissal. Though

12. Bürger, *Theory of the Avant-Garde*, 46. "Ideological," for Bürger, it should be emphasized, describes an imaginary relation to real conditions rather than an out-and-out deception.

13. Ibid., 22.

14. For a related argument, grounded in a revision of Bürger, that addresses modernism across the arts, see Walter L. Adamson, *Embattled Avant-Gardes: Modernism's Resistance to Commodity Culture in Europe* (Berkeley: University of California Press, 2007).

we should not confuse fictions with objective descriptions of reality, we know that fictions have many ways of telling truths.

I mean to take "fictions of autonomy" as, like Stephen Dedalus's *amor matris*, both objective and subjective genitive: modernist works depict or fictionalize aesthetic autonomy in many self-referential ways, and they are the products of the real-world practices and ideals of autonomy. Indeed, the process of interweaving images and themes of autonomy into novels and poems is one example—a central example—of those real-world practices: the modernists attempt to conjure autonomy into reality, to make fiction into fact. The most compelling theory of this modernist practice is Pierre Bourdieu's in *The Rules of Art*. My invocation of Bourdieu may seem puzzling to those who think of Bourdieu as a debunker of aesthetic illusions. Indeed, he, like Bürger, has sometimes seemed to want to reduce aesthetics to an ideology of the dominant class, especially in the text for which American literary scholars know him best, *Distinction*.[15] *The Rules of Art* offers a more complex and more convincing model. The aesthetic autonomy of literature, Bourdieu argues, is a "position to be made," something to be "conquered" through the work of particular writers in setting out—and institutionalizing—their own, independent standards for literary practice, self-consciously opposing themselves to less autonomous alternatives.[16]

Bourdieu proposes that the effort to secure relative autonomy for literary practice requires writers to discover and analyze, by means of the work of writing, the relations constituting their social-cultural world. Far from being deluded in their pursuit of autonomy, Bourdieu's modernists afford an understanding of their circumstances that even programmatically social realists lack. These circumstances include the very real but inexplicit rules of literary practice and the relations among artistic practitioners. In Bourdieu's terms, writers work in a *field* structured by hierarchical relations among *positions* endowed with different amounts of specifically cultural or literary power and renown (*symbolic capital*). The

---

15. Pierre Bourdieu, *Distinction: A Social Critique of the Judgement of Taste*, trans. Richard Nice (Cambridge, MA: Harvard University Press, 1984). For a recent example of this mischaracterization pervading even an extended discussion of Bourdieu by a literary scholar, see Jonathan Loesberg's otherwise suggestive "Bourdieu's Aesthetics," chap. 4 in *A Return to Aesthetics: Autonomy, Indifference, and Postmodernism* (Stanford, CA: Stanford University Press, 2005). Loesberg focuses on *Distinction*, but Bourdieu's later work in *The Rules of Art* furnishes a compelling reply to Loesberg's deconstructive charge that Bourdieu "represses the aesthetic basis of his analysis of culture and finally of aesthetics" (201). John Guillory comments lucidly on Bourdieu's reception in American literary studies and assesses Bourdieu's positions on the aesthetic in "Bourdieu's Refusal," *MLQ* 58, no. 4 (December 1997): 367–98.

16. Bourdieu, *Rules of Art*, 76, 47.

structure of the literary field then affects the way other domains of social life—other fields—relate to the literary. Some modes of relation are more autonomous than others. Modernist fictions of autonomy are distinguished by their awareness of their field; when I argue that the modernists do not deny their social embeddedness but instead confront it, it is this sense of fields and positions that I attempt to bring to light. Thus I often invoke the Bourdieuean terms as I describe the stakes and consequences of aspirations to literary autonomy, but I do not take on Bourdieu's model without some reservations. I expand his France-based ideas to a broader international modernism; the particular hierarchies Bourdieu identifies in French culture do not necessarily translate neatly outside France, though related symbolic and class hierarchies are important in all the contexts discussed in this book.[17] I also diverge at the level of method. Bourdieu's accounts of particular literary texts, from Flaubert to Mallarmé, fail to exploit the full potential of his theory, keeping instead to a basically thematic reading. This book argues that the practices of autonomy can be found, in all their complexity, at many levels of the individual work, from thematic motifs to rhetorical figures, from sentence style to plot mechanisms.[18] In spite of Bourdieu's sometimes schematic reading method, his Francocentrism, and his work's other limitations, however, his model of modernism is immensely useful to a historical account of autonomy fictions in all their variety. His conceptual vocabulary offers crucial building blocks for any attempt to explain modernist literary practices that does justice to their social and technical complexity.

Aesthetic Autonomy in Practice and Philosophy

Because of my sense of autonomy as a family of practices best understood in the framework of evolving social formations of writers, artists, readers, and critics, I do

17. Peter D. McDonald, *British Literary Culture and Publishing Practice, 1880–1914* (Cambridge: Cambridge University Press, 1997), makes a comprehensive case for a Bourdieuean approach to the British literary field in the 1890s, but the space of positions identified by McDonald is by no means identical to those found by Bourdieu in nineteenth-century France. Pascale Casanova's *The World Republic of Letters* aspires to be a fully global Bourdieuean sociology of literature; I return to her treatment of modernism's internationalism in chapter 3.

18. Bourdieu gestures in this direction in his scattered remarks on the importance of the writer's attention to literary form, as when he claims about Flaubert that "it is through this work on form that the work comes to contain those structures that the writer, like any social agent, carries within him in a practical way." *Rules of Art*, 108.

not pursue a philosophically rigorous account of what aesthetic autonomy could mean for literature or the arts in general, and I avoid categorical statements of my own about the nature of the aesthetic or the literary. Nor do I trace a full intellectual genealogy of modernist autonomy ideals. *Fictions of Autonomy* is about the meanings of modernist practices in their contemporary contexts, not the place of modernist aesthetics in a philosophical lineage. I study a looser collection of tendencies among literary writers, who found many ways to assert or suggest that their art was a law unto itself. Though these multiple versions of autonomy may not be precise logical equivalents, they represent real writerly affinities and literary historical tendencies. I group under the heading "aesthetic autonomy of literature" a set of assumptions, doctrines, and themes that have in common an idea of literature as *independent* of some circumstance with which it might otherwise seem to be entangled or as *free* from some obligation or purpose it might otherwise seem to have. These two overlapping versions of artistic liberty—independent production and freedom from purpose—are both included under the term *autonomy*. I speak of *aesthetic* autonomy because I need a more capacious rubric than the question of the *artist's* personal freedom from constraints or determinations; though that question is indeed central to my inquiry, one of modernism's distinctive positions was that the artistic *work* could enjoy a freedom which the artist, trammeled by circumstance, did not possess. Chapters 2 and 3, on impersonality and artistic exile, respectively, constitute an extended consideration of this distinction between the work's autonomy and the artist's.

The modernist versions of autonomy bear only an oblique relation to the best-known accounts of aesthetic autonomy in philosophy, which emerged in earlier periods. Intellectual history is not my primary concern here, but it will be helpful to contrast modernist autonomy briefly with two prominent predecessors in the Enlightenment and in Romanticism. The *locus classicus* for the theory of aesthetic autonomy is Kant's *Critique of the Power of Judgment*, which argues that the faculty of judgment, including the aesthetic judgment of taste, is distinct from other faculties of the mind; autonomous in the literal sense, it sets its own rules, paying no heed to the subject's interests or to the demands of morality.[19] From this thesis Kant derives his account of the disinterestedness of aesthetic judgment and his formulation of the grounds of the judgment of beauty as "purposiveness without an end."[20] Though the Kantian effort to distinguish aesthetic judgments from moral

19. Immanuel Kant, *Critique of the Power of Judgment*, ed. Paul Guyer, trans. Paul Guyer and Eric Matthews (Cambridge: Cambridge University Press, 2000).

20. Ibid., 95, 111. The more traditional translation is "purposiveness without purpose."

and self-interested ones is an important intellectual ancestor to modernist attempts to make literature an autonomous practice, the Enlightenment philosopher is far more concerned with the judgment of beauty. Kant makes scattered remarks on the freedoms of the artist (especially in his discussion of genius in the sections following the Analytic of the Sublime), but Kantian aesthetic autonomy is primarily grounded in the nature of the faculty of taste. The emphasis on judgment goes hand in hand with the centrality of natural beauty in Kant's theory; artistic productions are distinctly secondary, as in his dictum that "art can only be called beautiful if we are aware that it is art and yet it looks to us like Nature."[21] It is a long way from the Kantian theory of taste and its Enlightenment contexts to the modernist concentration on the autonomy of human artistic production among the very different institutions of late-nineteenth and twentieth-century society.[22]

Romantic versions of autonomy make a more definitive turn to the artist's activity. Nonetheless, even though there are, as we will see in chapter 4's discussion of Stevens and de Man, important continuities between Romantic and modernist ideas, these ideas remain quite distinct, when it comes to autonomy. In Friedrich Schiller's *Aesthetic Education*, we find a concentrated Romantic articulation of the idea that "Art is the daughter of Freedom."[23] But Schiller is less concerned with the worldly autonomy of artistic practice than he is with an ideal freedom of the spirit; he links aesthetics with freedom mainly to make art the means of transforming the human spirit and human society into an "aesthetic state." Romantic versions of aesthetic autonomy are often grounded in such philosophically idealist, metaphysical, quasi-apocalyptic ideas of artistic consciousness as a force that transcends ordinary existence. Though these ideas certainly persist into the twentieth century, *Fictions of Autonomy* emphasizes instead the more secular autonomy claims of late-nineteenth- and early twentieth-century literature. Those claims tend to be self-consciously modest or limiting in their scope, rarely reaching for Schillerian politico-spiritual revolutions.

Despite these differences between modernist autonomy and its Enlightenment or Romantic incarnations, those who know the aesthetic theories of earlier centuries will frequently notice affinities to the modernist versions of autonomy

21. Ibid., 185.

22. On Kantian aesthetic theory in relation to eighteenth-century contexts, see Martha Woodmansee, *The Author, Art, and the Market: Rereading the History of Aesthetics* (New York: Columbia University Press, 1994).

23. Friedrich Schiller, *On the Aesthetic Education of Man: In a Series of Letters*, ed. and trans. Elizabeth M. Wilkinson and L. A. Willoughby (London: Oxford University Press, 1967), 7.

analyzed in the pages that follow. I do not claim that any of those versions represent an absolute novelty or a break with the past. But modernist fictions of autonomy make shifts in emphasis among alternatives that had long been available—from artist to work, from the freedom of judgment to the freedom of making, from spiritualized beauties to worldly techniques. These emphases emerge in response to the particular constraints with which modernist literature comes to grips. As I already said, the major late-nineteenth- and early twentieth-century innovations happen less at the level of ideas than at the level of the social, where new institutions and practices, organized around the principles of literary and aesthetic autonomy, are coming into being in relation to new and ever-changing circumstances.

With this emphasis on the social, my treatment of aesthetic concepts is most nearly in accord not with classical aesthetics but with the "institutional" approach to the philosophy of art. This tradition of aesthetics holds that aesthetic categories, including that of autonomy, vary historically both in their explicit formulations and in their implicit, practical versions. This view is particularly associated with Arthur Danto's theory of the "artworld" and the work of George Dickie.[24] Dickie in particular argues against essentialist ideas of the nature of art and the aesthetic, claiming instead that ideals of artistic form or aesthetic disinterestedness depend on cultural conventions—that form and the aesthetic need the conventions of an artworld to be perceptible as such. But as Bourdieu argues, this strand of philosophical aesthetics needs to be complemented by a "historical and sociological analysis of the genesis and structure of the institution (the artistic field) which is capable . . . of imposing the *recognition* of the work of art as such."[25] Indeed, modernist practices and concepts of autonomy were probably necessary preconditions for the development of the institutional philosophy of art; Danto's work famously turns on Duchamp's sculpture, and Dickie's responds to the late modernist, New Critical aesthetics of Monroe Beardsley. Both philosophers acknowledge the ways in which their own theories emerge from the self-reflexive, self-problematizing aspect of early twentieth-century experimental works.

The institutional, contextualizing approach to aesthetics and the artwork has important implications for the questions of literary form that recur in this book. In the twentieth century, as in earlier periods, putatively formal categories have

---

24. Arthur Danto, "The Artworld," *Journal of Philosophy* 61, no. 19 (October 1964): 571 84; George Dickie, *Art and the Aesthetic: An Institutional Analysis* (Ithaca: Cornell University Press, 1974).

25. *Rules of Art*, 287 (emphasis in original).

frequently been central to claims for the autonomy of the literary artwork; the distinctive qualities of aesthetic form are supposed to lift the work away from its nonaesthetic purposes or determinations. These arguments draw strength from a notion of form as inherent in the perceptual or immediate features of the artwork. However, in this book, in the spirit of the institutional approach, I assume instead that the definition of literary form, like other aesthetic conventions, develops in relation to social and historical contexts. The form-content distinction is a cipher for historically shifting practices of reading and classifying writing; different conceptions of literature or art promote different features of writing to "formal" status.

Though this historicized understanding of form is natural to the Bourdieu-influenced framework I adopt in this book, a similar approach to form also emerges in two theories closely tied to modernism itself: Russian Formalism and Adorno's aesthetics. Formalists like Tynjanov and Èjxenbaum saw form as an expansive, historically changing category; Adorno repeatedly speaks of form as "sedimented content."[26] Accordingly, though the appearance of formal closure or formal distinction may undergird powerful claims to aesthetic autonomy, that appearance itself depends on the conventions of the literary field and its relation to other fields. The shifting senses of form will be especially important in the next chapter, where I offer one way of historicizing novelistic form through its relation to domestic labor, on one hand, and social "good form" or decorum on the other. More generally, the very looseness of formal categories makes it possible for modernist fictions of autonomy to comprehend their social relations even as they focus their energies on formal or aesthetic aims.[27]

26. Indeed, Èjxenbaum sees the culmination of Formalism as doing away with the notion of content altogether; see Boris M. Èjxenbaum, "The Theory of the Formal Method," in *Readings in Russian Poetics: Formalist and Structuralist Views*, ed. Ladislav Matejka and Krystyna Pomorska (Cambridge, MA: MIT Press, 1971), 3–37. Tynjanov's theory of literary history is outlined in Jurij Tynjanov, "On Literary Evolution," in Matejka and Pomorska, *Readings in Russian Poetics*, 66–78. Adorno writes, "What is specific to artworks—their form—can never, as the sedimentation of content [*Inhalt*] fully disown its origin." Theodor W. Adorno, *Aesthetic Theory*, ed. Gretel Adorno, Rolf Tiedemann, and Robert Hullot-Kentor, trans. Robert Hullot-Kentor (Minneapolis: University of Minnesota Press, 1997), 139; see also 5, 17.

27. For an extended study of the uses of the word *form* itself in British literature, especially British aestheticism and modernism, see Angela Leighton, *On Form: Poetry, Aestheticism, and the Legacy of a Word* (Oxford: Oxford University Press, 2007). Leighton's work is more oriented to intellectual history and to assessing the achievements of individual authors than is the present study, but her main finding about the polyvalence and slipperiness of "form" complements my argument.

The Fictions of Autonomy and Their Themes

This book concentrates on the relationships between autonomy practices and their contexts; I show how fictions of autonomy change according to what they seek to be autonomous from. Though my organization is loosely chronological, with the earliest texts studied in chapter 1 and the most recent texts in chapter 4, I provide a comparative historical analysis of themes rather than the history of an idea. I compare attempts to secure, in fiction and in reality, aesthetic autonomy from four kinds of constraint: labor, personality, political community, and linguistic reference. These form the themes of the chapters, a sequence of case studies, each of them comparative, in successively more comprehensive autonomy fictions. Within each chapter, I analyze particular authors, not to offer comprehensive interpretations of individual œuvres—though I frequently address scholarly debates about individual writers and works—but to show major figures participating in a shared aesthetic-social project. Indeed, most of the figures I discuss might well have appeared in more than one of the case studies. The ideals and practices of autonomy, as I remarked, slip easily from one shape to another—from, for example, the aesthete's leisured avoidance of labor to the negation of all real-world reference; though I discuss Wilde under the former head in chapter 1 and Stevens under the latter in chapter 4, another possible analysis could do the reverse. Though Adorno is central to my reflection on aesthetic impersonality and Barnes is key to the analysis of the expatriate's physical and social distance, each could be read in the frame I elaborate for the other. These overlaps bind together the project of conjuring autonomy for literature across multiple genres and languages, making it meaningful to speak, as I do, of modernism from Wilde to de Man. Nonetheless, for the sake of clear exposition, I isolate each of the autonomy themes in turn, testing my mode of analysis on four very different versions of autonomy. Only the accumulation of these examples can ultimately give weight to my general claim about the varieties of autonomy in modernism as a whole: modernism represents autonomy as a distinctive, relatively independent mode of relation with the very domains that seem to constrain it.

My argument for this general claim begins, in chapter 1, by showing that even a theme and a context that seem very remote from aesthetic questions can become central to fictions of autonomy. The theme of chapter 1 is domestic service, and the context is that of late-nineteenth- and early twentieth-century labor and class relations in Britain and France. I show that aestheticist fiction—from Wilde to Proust—uses servant characters to stage a subtle reflection on the connection between the practice of artistic autonomy and domestic labor. When

Henry James shows us Lambert Strether musing in a circle of lamplight in *The Ambassadors*, he also notes an incidental valet hovering at the edge of the circle: literary domestics, in their very stylization and marginality, form a connection between the closed circle of aesthetic form and the exploitation of labor. Moving among novels, social history, and writings by servants, I argue that the aestheticist novel uses servants to keep the social world at bay even as it recognizes servants as representatives of that same world. The realities of domestic service in the period enable this dual function, for the menial work of keeping up the appearances, the good form, of the middle- or upper-class household always has an aesthetic dimension. Aestheticist writing, far from excluding the world of labor, avows its dependence on it, dialectically incorporating that avowal into its formal effects. I show the persistence of this dialectical pattern in novels from aestheticism and decadence—Wilde's *The Picture of Dorian Gray*, Villiers de l'Isle-Adam's *Axël*, Huysmans's *À rebours*—to James's protomodernist *The Ambassadors*. Then I exhibit a similar but more elaborate incorporation of service into aesthetic form in one of modernism's great autonomy fictions, Proust's *À la recherche du temps perdu*. For all these writers, the aesthetes' very quest to make art for art's sake produces a self-reflexive awareness of their relation to—their need for, their use of—servants' labor.

Even the devoted aesthetes of early modernism indicate that the artist's autonomy depends on the hierarchies of labor, but we might wonder whether stronger, less qualified versions of autonomy are to be found among those modernist writers who sought to discover aesthetic autonomy in the artwork itself rather than in the situation of the artist. Indeed, the defense of the freestanding work may be the most notoriously absolute—and most philosophically suspect—of modernist autonomy doctrines. In chapter 2, I bring together two of the chief advocates of this version of autonomy, T. S. Eliot and Theodor W. Adorno, and I turn from the novel to two art forms more strongly associated with the idea of the self-contained work: poetry and instrumental music. In an extended comparison, I show how Eliot and Adorno elaborated the thesis that the artwork is not bound to reflect the subjectivity and personality of its creator. Adorno's important conception of "late style," above all in the music of Beethoven, is, I argue, a modernist theory of impersonality akin to the one Eliot made famous in his essays and thematized in his poems. Yet this version of autonomy is inextricable from the artwork's circumstances of production, circumstances made manifest in Adorno's and Eliot's shared emphasis on lateness. Lateness is a stance available to modernists at any age, as the preternatural aging of Eliot's early "impersonal" personae—from the marionettes of his undergraduate poems through Prufrock,

Gerontion, and Tiresias—shows, but it is also the record of the tie between the supposedly nonpersonal, autonomous artwork and the physical and emotional history
of the artist. Eliot's and Adorno's strikingly similar versions of impersonal lateness also give new significance to the Beethoven allusions of Eliot's *Four Quartets*.
Drawing on Beethoven's reception history, I show how the émigré German and
the émigré American converge on the composer's final period as a touchstone for
their paradoxical insistence upon aged and belated subjectivity as the foundation
for the autonomy of impersonality.

When pressures against the artwork's self-sufficiency seem to come not from
the particulars of social hierarchy or the weight of individual life but from a whole
surrounding society, a more flamboyant strategy for establishing artistic autonomy presents itself: simply leaving. In chapter 3, I reconsider artistic expatriation,
which has usually been treated either as the manifestation of the spirit of artistic autonomy in modernism or as the social foundation for newly autonomous
experiments in literature by modernism's exiles and émigrés. Yet the life and style
of the expatriate do not lead automatically to autonomous literary production.
In an extended reading of the work of the American expatriate Djuna Barnes, I
explore Barnes's techniques for claiming autonomy from her home nation and even
from the Parisian expatriate community. These techniques are, as Barnes shows
with particular acuity, a matter of both literary style and communal life. In her
novel *Nightwood*, Barnes refracts herself through each of her Parisian expatriate
characters, yet keeps her distance with an elusive point of view. Her depiction
of aesthetes abroad emphasizes the alienation from other people experienced by
the transnational writer trying to use expatriate displacement as the basis for a
literary position. My analysis of literary expatriation contributes to the ongoing
scholarly debates over modernist cosmopolitanism, which have usually assumed
that style can effect political and ethical commitments, either national or transnational. Though she is a cosmopolitan modernist, Barnes depicts her cosmopolitan
style as inimical to political community. I generalize my argument by reflecting on
James Joyce's status as an iconic modernist exile and "semicolonial" writer. Barnes's
writing, including her writing on Joyce, makes visible the ways in which he, too,
challenges the notion that techniques for aesthetic distance could be good models
for political commitment. As in Barnes's works, in *Ulysses* it is when autonomous
aesthetic practice becomes a lifestyle that artists must withdraw from communal
solidarity.

As comprehensive as the expatriate's displacement might appear, modernism
imagined an even more radical separation as a route to autonomy: severing all the
work's referential ties to reality. Chapter 4 analyzes claims to a semiotic freedom

by which the artwork refuses to refer to the real. I consider the extended twentieth-century career of this version of autonomy in the works of a long-lived modernist poet, Wallace Stevens, and an essayist whom I regard as a late exponent of modernism, Paul de Man. In Stevens's work, the figure of tautology enacts this hermetic refusal to relate poetry to anything other than itself: "My intention in poetry," Stevens once wrote, "is to write poetry." And yet, as I show in readings of short lyrics and long poems from across his career, Stevens's poetry never deploys tautology without invoking the shared social and linguistic context in which those tautologies acquire their difficult sense. The figure of tautology likewise takes on an unexpected significance in de Man's signal theory of literary nonreferentiality: for de Man, too, tautology leads to a version of autonomy that connects litera-ture to its historical setting *through* the refusal of reference. I analyze de Man's tautology-theory in terms of both his modernist literary-historical roots and his academic-institutional context; I show that his resemblance to Stevens becomes intelligible as a shared *modernist* pursuit of an autonomous literary language that nonetheless generates correspondences between itself and its contemporary social circumstances.

The consideration of de Man carries the overall argument into the last part of the previous century; in a brief epilogue, I indicate several important ways mod-ernist autonomy fictions remain productive and significant today. As I have been insisting, autonomy continues to be a central dilemma for academics working on literature, and I argue that my reanalysis of modernist autonomy can serve as the basis for new literary-historical work, not only within the study of modernism and the twentieth century, but across a newly capacious, sociologically and his-torically sophisticated field of literary scholarship. In gaining a new perspective on autonomy, we will also be better able to understand contemporary world litera-ture itself, for modernist autonomy's purview extends beyond the academe—and beyond Europe and the United States—as well.

Modernist Studies and the Expanded Field

With this expanded sense of the reach of modernism and the question of auton-omy in mind, some remarks on the scope of this book are in order. The aestheticist modernism I discuss embraces a wide chronological span, a certain geographi-cal breadth—England, the United States, Ireland, France, Germany, even, briefly, Belgium—and a range of literary genres: poetry, narrative, criticism, theory. I argue for the intimate relationship between some versions of aesthetic autonomy and modernist transnationalism in chapter 3; I show some of the ways autonomy doctrines have been important to the survival of the modernist enterprise even after World War II in chapter 4 and in the epilogue; and I emphasize the self-reflexivity that creates continuities between the fictions of autonomy in modernism's imaginative genres and the theories of autonomy in its critical ones throughout the book. Yet considering that recent work on modernism has, as Douglas Mao and Rebecca Walkowitz observe in their summary of "The New Modernist Studies," expanded the term to cover a wide variety of modernisms from across the globe, the authors considered here as emblematic of modernism hardly press the boundaries of an established American international-modernist canon.[28] Indeed, where I include figures who fit uneasily into that canon, I do so to demonstrate that they elaborated their own versions of canonical modernist practice. I argue that Barnes, for instance, followed Joyce's expatriate example by the means through which she distanced herself from him; I emphasize continuities rather than differences between aesthetes like Wilde or Huysmans and twentieth-century modernists like Proust; and I assimilate the critical theories of the later writers Adorno and de Man back to the modernist aesthetic practices on which they were founded. This choice stems from my desire to clarify the problems of aesthetic autonomy at their source, in the core of the modernist canon. I also want to emphasize the centrality of autonomy problems within the works that dictate the principal meanings of the term *modernist*; though the meaning of *modernism* may stretch and change, it continues to be tied up with canonical figures and their pursuit of one or another mode of autonomy. If modernist literature fascinates us, it does so partly because the questions, problems, and possibilities of autonomy remain important—though literary studies does not always acknowledge this source of fascination.

The expansion of the range of modernist studies nonetheless represents an absolutely necessary advance in knowledge, overcoming at least some of the prejudices which stand in the way of the study of literary production in its full breadth. *Fictions of Autonomy* seeks to enable this expansion, not resist it, but this book does argue for the specificity of high modernist practice in ways that complicate attempts to expand the modernist rubric. One kind of expansionist modernist studies works by transferring the various qualities associated with

28. Douglas Mao and Rebecca L. Walkowitz, "The New Modernist Studies," *PMLA* 123, no. 3 (May 2008): 737–48. Mao and Walkowitz describe a spatial expansion outside of North America and Western Europe and a "vertical" expansion from "high art" into "popular forms of culture" (737–38). See also Laura Doyle and Laura Winkiel, eds., *Geomodernisms: Race, Modernism, Modernity* (Bloomington: Indiana University Press, 2005).

canonical modernism—its cultural prestige, its adversarial character, its rupture with tradition, its formal breakthroughs—onto some alternative contemporary body of work.[29] But in the modernist period, adversarial stances and formal innovations are typically intertwined with the aspiration to autonomy; for that matter, the very canonicity of canonical modernism also has much to do with its creation of relatively autonomous institutions. But this aspiration to autonomy was not necessarily shared throughout the literary field. Though, as Michael North argues in his important study *Reading 1922*, there are many analogies between modernist and other contemporary cultural products, modernism's attempts at autonomy nonetheless give its worldly relations a particular character.[30] Indeed, the choice to pursue a relative autonomy for literature becomes meaningful precisely in relation to the existence of other possibilities. Those possibilities are not less interesting or worthwhile for not being identical to modernism, but the study of works beyond the range of the established canon must situate those works sociologically within a literary field of which autonomy-seeking high modernism is only one part. Otherwise the new modernist studies risks flattening a highly differentiated and hierarchical international literary field into so many responses to modernity in general.

The reader who grants my restricted focus may nonetheless question the absence of other canonical modernist figures and other themes related to aesthetic autonomy. I might have addressed Virginia Woolf within my discussion of servants, but for the timely work of Alison Light in her 2007 book *Mrs Woolf and the Servants*; though Light has little to say about aesthetics, her biographical study offers much suggestive detail that accords with my argument about the dependence of aestheticist form on domestic labor.[31] I glance at Gertrude Stein in chapters 3 and 4, but more remains to be said on her fictions of autonomy. Another "high" modernist, Ezra Pound, is absent from my discussions; his mature literary program had far more to do with social transformation than with autonomy, though I might nonetheless have taken up both his late style and his expatriate personae. Equally importantly, as the heterogeneity of the four autonomy themes treated here suggests, I have not exhausted all the modernist themes with a significant connection

29. Jennifer Wicke discusses the way the "rebranding" of modernism relies on the persistence of the high modernist brand in her essay "Appreciation, Depreciation: Modernism's Speculative Bubble," *Modernism/Modernity* 8, no. 3 (September 2001): 389–403.

30. Michael North, *Reading 1922: A Return to the Scene of the Modern* (Oxford: Oxford University Press, 1999).

31. Alison Light, *Mrs Woolf and the Servants* (London: Fig Tree, 2007). I discuss Light's work briefly in chapter 1.

to autonomy. As with my choice of authors to discuss, I have chosen the four areas of labor, personality, political community, and referentiality for their variety and their exemplary value, trusting that the analysis could be productively extended by others.

One further autonomy theme, however, stands out above the rest: literature's role in the marketplace. The market is the primary domain from which, in many accounts—not least Adorno's aesthetic theory—modernism's effort to create an autonomous aesthetic seeks to escape, freeing art from the demands of popularity and commercial success in the realm of mass culture. All versions of autonomy may be part of an attempt to distinguish the artwork's value from its price, and aesthetic criteria from market forces.[32] Indeed, the Bourdieuean theory of the field that I have invoked often seems to treat aesthetic autonomy as a fiction of what Bourdieu calls the "subfield of small-scale production" of the market in symbolic goods—a fiction generated precisely by specialized producers' opposition to the ways of the "subfield of large-scale production," organized to maximize short-term profits.[33]

At one time accounts like these tended to be used to indict modernism: in influential books by Andreas Huyssen and John Carey, a hostility to encroaching mass markets was seen as a symptom of modernism's elitism and its commitment to a high-cultural vision of autonomy that was either politically reactionary or impossible in practice.[34] In the past two decades, however, a more nuanced view has emerged in scholarship: many modernists had affinities for popular and mass culture; modernism devoted considerable attention, not always negative, to consumption and to the kinship between artwork and commodity; and many modernists, forgoing Olympian detachment, adopted aggressive marketing strategies for their work.[35] This last point has seemed to strike a devastating blow against

32. This idea is powerfully supported by the accounts of the gradual differentiation of literary from economic value since the eighteenth century in Poovey, *Genres of the Credit Economy*, and John Guillory, "The Discourse of Value: From Adam Smith to Barbara Herrnstein Smith," chap. 5 in *Cultural Capital*.

33. Bourdieu, *Rules of Art*, 124, figure 3.

34. Andreas Huyssen, *After the Great Divide: Modernism, Mass Culture, Postmodernism* (Bloomington: Indiana University Press, 1986); John Carey, *The Intellectuals and the Masses: Pride and Prejudice among the Literary Intelligentsia, 1880–1939* (London: Faber and Faber, 1992).

35. North, *Reading 1922*, and David E. Chinitz, *T. S. Eliot and the Cultural Divide* (Chicago: University of Chicago Press, 2003) are signal works on modernism and popular culture; on modernist consumption and commodification see especially Freedman, *Professions of Taste*; Elizabeth Outka, *Consuming Traditions: Modernity, Modernism, and the Commodified Authentic* (Oxford: Oxford University Press, 2009); Adamson, *Embattled*

pretensions to autonomy: autonomy claims can themselves be a particularly canny marketing strategy, as Rainey's *Institutions of Modernism* shows in startling detail for Joyce and Eliot. Even the sociological version of literary autonomy articulated by Bourdieu seems to rely on seeing high culture as an "anti-'economic' economy," in which marketplace failure is a mark of cultural legitimacy. From the perspective of recent work on literature and the market, that theory is, as James English argues in his Bourdieu-influenced study of literary prizes, an oversimplification that understimates the economic value of denying economic value.[36]

Yet the understanding of autonomy I advocate in this book leads to a different interpretation of this important body of revisionist work. If autonomy is understood as the absolute isolation, self-enclosure, and denial of all contexts of the artwork, then modernist literary works were clearly not autonomous from the marketplace. Modernism's embrace of practices analogous to commercial self-promotion and its complex fascination with mass culture falsify the most rigid interpretation of the Great Divide theory—an interpretation which even Huyssen distances himself from.[37] But I propose that we understand modernist autonomy as a specific *relation* between one kind of literary practice and other aspects of social life, one which seeks to cultivate a certain aesthetic distinction and a level of relative independence by means of its engagements. This mode of *relative* autonomy is precisely what research on the modernists and the marketplace has really shown modernism to have pursued. For example, Mark Morrisson has shown how modernist little magazines made use of contemporary advertising tactics pioneered in large-circulation periodicals. This does not show that all magazines, little and big, capitulated completely to marketplace demands; rather, it shows that modernists understood that their institutions of publication would uphold their relative autonomy (or the status of what Morrisson calls a "counter-public sphere") only in and through specific relations to the market.

Avant-Gardes; and Rita Felski, "Imagined Pleasures: The Erotics and Aesthetics of Consumption," chap. 3 in *The Gender of Modernity*. On self-promotion see, for example, Kevin J. H. Dettmar and Stephen Watt, eds., *Marketing Modernisms: Self-Promotion, Canonization, Rereading* (Ann Arbor: University of Michigan Press, 1996); Mark S. Morrisson, *The Public Face of Modernism: Little Magazines, Audiences, and Reception, 1905–1920* (Madison: University of Wisconsin Press, 2001); and Rod Rosenquist, *Modernism, the Market, and the Institution of the New* (Cambridge: Cambridge University Press, 2009).

36. Bourdieu, *Rules of Art*, 142; James F. English, *The Economy of Prestige: Prizes, Awards, and the Circulation of Cultural Value* (Cambridge, MA: Harvard University Press, 2005).

37. Andreas Huyssen, "High/Low in an Expanded Field," *Modernism/Modernity* 9, no. 3 (September 2002): 363–74.

Similarly, to understand, with Rainey and English—and, in fact, with Bourdieu too, because he regards the opposition between the "pure" and "commercial" poles of the cultural field not as absolute but as a continuum—that fictions of autonomy have a definite worth on the market is not necessarily to rule out the possibility of a genuine but relative autonomy in production and evaluation. If the argument I offer in this book is correct, a fuller understanding of the results of the often contentious scholarship on modernism, mass culture, and commerce is possible. We can recognize modernism's distinctive mode of relations to commodity culture, to self-promotion, to publicity, and to economic capital—relations that exist within modernist representations and in the practices detailed by book and material history—as produced by and reproduced in fictions of autonomy. On this interpretation, modernist studies has already made an extensive study of modernism's relation to the economic field with due attention to the complex issue of autonomy, an attention only partly disguised by widespread scholarly avoidance or denigration of the term *autonomy* itself. I have drawn on this body of work extensively in what follows, particularly in chapter 1's consideration of the consumerist leisure world of aestheticism and chapter 3's examination of expatriate cosmopolitanism as a lifestyle intimately wrapped up in fashion and self-promoting display. It is my hope that further work on twentieth-century literature and the marketplace can profit from using the more complex, ramified analysis of autonomy I am proposing. But for the purposes of this book, it has seemed to me more urgent to demonstrate the way the pursuit of autonomy leads modernism into domains other than the market, domains whose relation to autonomy has been more obscure to scholarship.

The value of modernist autonomy fictions consists in the surprising fact that, intricately self-reflexive as they are, they nonetheless also lead outward, joining the modernist artwork—and the relatively autonomous modernist literary field—to many other realms of imaginative and social life. High modernism attempted to uphold both meaningful social relations and meaningful literary independence at the same time; in this double aspiration contemporary literary scholars (and contemporary readers in general) may find much that is appealing. Modernist autonomy is due for a reconsideration as a necessary part of the ongoing reconsideration of modernism itself. As I show in the pages that follow, far from being an idea whose time has passed, autonomy is a practice whose ramifications in literature and scholarship we have only begun to explore.

1. Autonomy from Labor

In Service to Art for Art's Sake from Wilde to Proust

"He represents the dominance of form": one can imagine applying this sentence to any number of prominent literary modernists; according to a widespread though problematic account, the modernist dream of aesthetic autonomy leads to the elevation of aesthetic form above all other things.[1] Oscar Wilde stands near the origin of this aestheticist strain of modernist writing—but he uses that same sentence to describe a dandy's butler:

> PHIPPS, the butler, is arranging some newspapers on the writing-table. The distinction of PHIPPS is his impassivity. He has been termed by enthusiasts the Ideal Butler. The Sphinx is not so incommunicable. He is a mask with a manner. Of his intellectual or emotional life history knows nothing. He represents the dominance of form.[2]

1. The phrase "the dominance of form" does in fact crop up in a seminal theory of modernism. A key passage in the English translation of Peter Bürger's *Theory of the Avant-Garde* reads: "Since the middle of the nineteenth century ... the form-content dialectic has increasingly shifted in favor of form. The content of the work of art, its 'statement,' recedes ever more as compared with its formal aspect, which defines itself as the aesthetic in the narrower sense. From the point of view of production aesthetics, this dominance of form in art since about the middle of the nineteenth century can be understood as command over means; from the point of view of reception aesthetics, as a tendency toward the sensitizing of the recipient." Peter Bürger, *Theory of the Avant-Garde*, trans. Michael Shaw (Minneapolis: University of Minnesota Press, 1984), 19–20.

2. Oscar Wilde, *An Ideal Husband*, in *Plays of Oscar Wilde* (New York: Vintage, 1988), 291. Henceforth I cite this edition by page number parenthetically in the text.

Elsewhere, Wilde placed form at the center of his aestheticist theory of art; in "The Critic as Artist," his spokesperson says that "the real artist is he who proceeds, not from feeling to form, but from form to thought and passion," and that "Form is everything. It is the secret of life."[3] But the stage direction troubles the dogma of form. It suggests two competing explanations for the form-upholding inaccessibility of the butler's "intellectual or emotional life": "impassivity" is a requirement of the butler's job as human furniture, but Wilde also registers the deliberate artifice that has made the butler into a comic type—"the Ideal Butler." The thrust of Wilde's joke is that the exigencies of aestheticist dramatic composition coincide with the demands imposed by class structure in domestic life. In this conjunction, the witty artifice starts to seem less like innocent play and more like the suppression of human individuality by the realities of labor. Even within the Wildean celebration of stylized "masks with manners" and drawing room leisure, the figure of the domestic worker makes apparent a relationship between aestheticist form and social inequality.

Wilde's depiction of Phipps the butler is a prototypical fiction of autonomy, self-reflexively representing the primacy of aesthetic form even as it underscores form's social embeddedness. It is also an exemplary treatment of domestic service within the context of protomodernist aestheticism. In this chapter, I show that servants are deeply involved with the problem of aesthetic autonomy in an extended modernist lineage, from late-nineteenth-century aesthetes to the late James to Proust. Over and over again, such characters work to reveal the inextricable connection between a "dominant" aesthetic form and social domination. The pursuit of autonomy might be supposed to require a disavowal of any such reliance on the labor of subordinates. One of the most serious critiques of aesthetic autonomy is that it denies the artist's entanglement in the system of class, imagining that the leisured cult of pure forms banishes the world of ordinary work and its hierarchies. But I will show that because of the aesthetic character of domestic service, in fiction and in the real world, service sheds a particularly clear light on the relation between aesthetes and workers, between art for art's sake and work for a wage. That relation shows us that the aestheticist and modernist version of autonomy from labor is not what we might expect: it is relative and contextual, sensitive to the ways autonomous form carries troubling social entanglements along with it.

In my analysis of this first of this book's four major autonomy themes, I dwell on the late nineteenth century in England and France before turning to two key

---

3. Oscar Wilde, "The Critic as Artist," 2 pts., in *Intentions*, in *The Soul of Man under Socialism and Selected Critical Prose*, ed. Linda Dowling (London: Penguin, 2001), 269–70.

early modernist figures: Henry James and Marcel Proust. Because I take autonomy to be a central modernist preoccupation, I am emphasizing a basic continuity
between modernism and late-nineteenth-century aestheticism. My principal argument for this continuity emerges across the chapters of this book, as I show how
later modernist fictions of autonomy in other domains share a common structure
with those devised by aesthetes and early modernists around domestic service. For
the moment, we can note a more specific continuity between early and subsequent
phases of the pursuit of literary autonomy: aestheticist attitudes and domestic
service echo together in two key high modernist texts. On the first page of *Mrs. Dalloway*, it is to her maid, Lucy, that Woolf's protagonist says she will buy the flowers
herself, initiating her "plunge" into London sensations.[4] And Stephen Dedalus
proclaims, in the opening chapter of *Ulysses*, that his "symbol of Irish art" is "the
cracked lookingglass of a servant": domestic service is associated both with the
artist's form-making work and with the cracking of the artwork's mimetic means.[5]
But I turn now to earlier authors, whose probing of art for art's sake set the pattern
for the high modernist engagement with the problem of autonomy. The task of the
rest of this book will be to show how the model of literary autonomy emerging
from aestheticist works ramifies over the next half-century of modernist writing,
redefining modernism's relationships to many aspects of personal and social life.
The hierarchies of class and labor make up only one such aspect, but they are a
crucial starting point for my theory. As we will see, class is central to the social
meaning of aesthetic autonomy, and domestic labor is of particular relevance to
the aestheticist celebration of form.

The emergence of autonomy's social meaning can be seen by considering
Phipps's role in *An Ideal Husband* a little further. Phipps arrives at the beginning
of the third act of Wilde's comedy of manners, just after the curtain has fallen on a
scene in which Sir Robert Chiltern accuses his wife of ruining his life. The melodramatic climax of that scene threatens to undermine the comedic lightness of the
play; by changing the scene to the home of the dandyish Lord Goring, "the first
well-dressed philosopher in the history of thought" (291), the third act restores
the good-humored, superficial tone. The butler ensures this stylistic triumph by
playing the perfect straight man to Goring's witticisms: "To love oneself is the
beginning of a life-long romance," says Goring; "Yes, my lord," replies Phipps (292).
Indeed, the straight face was a prescribed characteristic of a good manservant.

---

4. Virginia Woolf, *Mrs. Dalloway* (San Diego: Harcourt, 1925), 3.

5. James Joyce, *Ulysses*, ed. Hans Walter Gabler (New York: Vintage, 1986), 1.146.
I return to this moment in my discussion of Joyce in chapter 3.

Mrs. Beeton's popular *Book of Household Management* (first published in 1861) ordains that "the footman should tread lightly in moving round, and, if possible, should bear in mind, if there is a wit or humorist of the party, whose good things keep the table in a roar, they are not expected to reach his ears."[6]

The sober acquiescence of the butler in his master's joke is, however, a kind of insubordination; far from offering a free appreciation of paradoxical wit, the servant slyly indicates that he has no choice but to play along.[7] This response, of course, only heightens Lord Goring's ironic narcissism, but it does so by depriving that narcissism of its charming innocence. Even as the joke evokes laughter, it invites speculation about the potentially insubordinate humanity lying behind the "mask with a manner." The signal of Phipps's unknowable depths is also the signal of his condition of servitude, his labor: "Yes, *my lord*." For the butler, his formal function of upholding the comic machinery and his job of upholding the decorum of aristocratic life are identical. Because the privileging of form and the privileging of the master coincide, the former is revealed to be not merely an aesthetic choice but a social one as well.

Alex Woloch has drawn a similar link between formal function and social position in *The One vs. the Many*, his comparative study of minor characters in the nineteenth-century realist novel. There he advances the provocative thesis that "in terms of their essential formal position (the subordinate beings who are delimited in themselves while performing a function for someone else), *minor characters are the proletariat of the novel*."[8] Woloch compares the dehumanizing effects of the specialization of labor in bourgeois society to the flattening effects of characterization on minor characters; their identity is reduced to their function. But whereas Woloch is concerned with the complications in the aesthetic of realism created by the nonrealism of the flat character, I am emphasizing the challenge to aestheticism of the potential realism of minor characters like servants.[9] Stylized and conventional, characters like Phipps fit neatly into the world of art for art's sake, just as a

6. Isabella Beeton, *The Book of Household Management*, new ed. (London: Ward, Lock, 1880), 1007, §2317.

7. This insubordinate potential of the perfect performance of a role has also been important in queer theory's understanding of what it means to cite a gender norm. See Judith Butler, *Bodies That Matter: On the Discursive Limits of "Sex"* (New York: Routledge, 1993), esp. 232. Butler's discussion also usefully recalls the limits to the subversive potential of this kind of performance, for butlers as for queer subjects.

8. Alex Woloch, *The One vs. the Many: Minor Characters and the Space of the Protagonist in the Novel* (Princeton, NJ: Princeton University Press, 2004), 27 (emphasis in orginal).

9. Despite this contrast in emphasis, I do mean to extend to the fin de siècle and modernism Woloch's basic theoretical argument that "narratives themselves allow and solicit us

perfectly impassive butler fits in among the other elegant furnishings of an aristocratic drawing room. If, however, the character makes us aware of truths of class intruding into the magic circle of art, he comes to stand for the unpleasant material and human social reality—the unwanted content—that he is meant to exclude.

Wilde forces us to realize that Phipps represents the dominance of form *for a living*. In adverting us to this truth, Wilde's description of the butler points toward a *dialectical* conception of form as synthesized from the very elements of social life that exceed the purely formal—and it suggests that even a frippery like Wilde's play is not merely a fantasy of inconsequential, mannered, narcissistic playfulness with no acknowledgment of the aristocratic privilege and social inequality on which the realization of the fantasy rests. It is not quite the case that, as Jeff Nunokawa claims in *Tame Passions of Wilde*, "the compulsion to labor could hardly be further removed from the society of conspicuous leisure that is the only one to show up on Wilde's map"; the occluded labor of the servant, because of its *aesthetic* significance, surreptitiously steals a central place on Wilde's map.[10] In *An Ideal Husband*, the confessedly elitist preoccupation with manner comprehends a knowledge of what it tries to exclude, even as it continues to attempt to maintain its formal hold over that troubling social content.

Aesthetic Autonomy? Our Servants Will Do That for Us

I return to Wilde later, but first I want to expand more broadly on the connections, in fiction and in history, between these unlikely partners, aesthetes and servants. Consider one founding text of French aestheticism, Villiers de l'Isle-Adam's long drama *Axël* (published in part in 1872, in full 1885–86; partially revised at the author's death in 1889). Villiers's play culminates in the hero's rejection of religion, worldly wealth, and love in favor of a suicide that celebrates imagination above all other things. Axël d'Auërsperg's speech imploring his lover, Sara de Maupers, to die with him rather than live out their dreams of travel, power, and romantic ecstasy includes a notorious reference to his domestics:

> Why realize them [our dreams]? ... they are so beautiful! ...

to construct a story—a distributed pattern of attention—that is at odds with, or divergent from, the formed pattern of attention in the discourse" (41).

10. Jeff Nunokawa, *Tame Passions of Wilde: The Styles of Manageable Desire* (Princeton, NJ: Princeton University Press, 2003), 95. Though I dissent from Nunokawa's description of Wilde's social vision here, I share his interpretation of Wilde's works as socially pointed in their partly critical, partly acquiescent relation to the norms of capitalist society.

All the realities, what would they be tomorrow, compared with the mirages we have just lived? …

To agree to live after that would be but a sacrilege against ourselves. Live? Our servants will do that for us.[11]

The climax of *Axël* forms the cornerstone of Edmund Wilson's classic account of modernism, *Axel's Castle*. For Wilson, Axël's rejection of the world is typical of aestheticism and its descendant in modernism (which Wilson called "Symbolism"); he regards the preference for fantasy over reality with suspicion, describing it as dangerously "indifferen[t]" to and "detached" from society.[12] Arraigning Axël for his lack of social conscience, Wilson says: "It will easily be seen that this super-dreamer of Villiers's is the type of all the heroes of the Symbolists, of our day as well as of his."[13]

Wilson is not wholly unfair in choosing Villiers's rather absurd late Romantic performance as representative; in the 1890s, after his death, Villiers became an icon for the French Symbolists. Speaking for the Symbolists in 1896, Remy de Gourmont said of Villiers: "He is always among us and in us, by his work and the influence of his work, which the best writers and artists of the present moment undergo, and with joy."[14] Axël is, in his aristocratic disdain for worldly goods and his preference for fantasy over reality, the ideal practitioner of aestheticism. His stance resembles the Wildean pose. In Wilde's dialogue "The Critic as Artist," Gilbert rhapsodizes over the superiority of literary art to life: "Nothing that one can imagine is worth doing, and … one can imagine everything."[15] For Wilson, such

---

11. Philippe Auguste Villiers de l'Isle-Adam, *Axel*, trans. June Guicharnaud (Englewood Cliffs, NJ: Prentice-Hall, 1970), 182–83; the first ellipsis is in the original, and the rest mark my abridgements. "À quoi bon les réaliser [les rêves]? … ils sont si beaux! … Toutes les réalités, demain, que seraient-elles, en comparaison des mirages que nous venons de vivre? … Accepter, désormais, de vivre, ne serait plus qu'un sacrilège envers nous-mêmes. Vivre? les serviteurs feront cela pour nous." Villiers de l'Isle-Adam, *Axël*, in *Œuvres complètes*, ed. Alan Raitt and Pierre-Georges Castex with Jean-Marie Bellefroid (Paris: Gallimard, 1986), 2:671–72. I retain Villiers's decadent and wholly superfluous *tréma* on his hero's name.

12. Edmund Wilson, *Axel's Castle: A Study of the Imaginative Literature of 1870–1930* (1931; New York: Farrar, Straus and Giroux, 2004), 211.

13. Ibid., 210.

14. "Il est toujours parmi nous et il est en nous, par son œuvre et par l'influence de son œuvre, que subissent et avec joie les meilleurs d'entre les écrivains et les artistes de l'heure actuelle." Remy de Gourmont, *Le livre des masques* (Paris: Mercure de France, 1963), 58 (translation mine).

15. Wilde, "Critic as Artist," 252.

a stance makes Axël a harbinger of the solipsism of post-Symbolist modernism's "experimentation in the field of literature alone."[16] Thus, in Wilson's tremendously influential account, Villiers's hero's dichotomy of aesthetic fantasy, on one hand, and the mere "life" of servants, on the other, stands as the inauguration of modernist autonomy doctrine.

Yet Villiers's play makes Axël's dismissal of life as for the servants more than reflexive snobbery; it indicates just how essential servants are to the formation of the aesthetic dream. The earlier acts of the play idealize Axël's life in the middle of the Black Forest, infinitely removed from venal bourgeois modernity, sustained by his familial ties to his servants, an operatic cast of loyal armsmen and pages depicted at great length. One of the signs of Axël's nobility is the blessing he gives to his page Ukko's wedding on the day of his own death. Indeed, that wedding takes place in the last pages of the play, forming the backdrop to the protagonists' *Liebestod*. Villiers's staging of his conclusion makes clear that Axël's triumphant withdrawal from life only acquires meaning in the context of the people he pays to continue to live it. The aestheticism of *Axël* still requires servants for both support and contradiction: support, by their labor, of its aristocratic disdain for the material realities of life; contradiction, by their living that life, of their master's denial of terrestrial existence. Their appearances represent the ground of ordinariness, what the final sentence of *Axël* calls "the hum of Life,"[17] against which their masters' actions stand out. The paradox of their service to the work, therefore, is that as much as they function to exclude the everyday, they are the trace of that exclusion. Servants literally keep the doors of their masters' houses, but they contain within their own small roles the ways of the pressing, laboring, nonaristocratic world.

The liminal status of literary servants in the works I am discussing stems in part from the realities of domestic service in the period. Paradoxically, those realities make servant characters particularly well suited to the representation of "the dominance of form" over any realism about the life of labor. It might seem that the more flattened and stylized the servant characters are, the less realistic the depiction of contemporary service must be. Nonetheless, such resistance to current reality *is* related to the historical status of domestic service. In a society marked by industrialization and economic rationalization, service has a residual, archaic aspect; the paternalistic relationship imagined between the master or mistress and the servant contrasts with the contractual situation of the industrial proletariat and its

16. Wilson, *Axel's Castle*, 211.
17. Villiers, *Axel*, 190. "Le bourdonnement de la Vie." *Axël*, 2:677.

managers.[18] Isolated in individual middle- or upper-class homes, servants were unlike other members of the working class in their working conditions, their compensation (lower cash wages being to some degree balanced by room and board as well as livery in some cases), and the fact that their labor neither produced nor sold any tangible good. In addition, though domestic service was still a very widespread occupation in England, France, and America in the 1890s and 1900s, the servant workforce had already slowed its rate of growth or begun to contract, and it shrank rapidly from World War I onward.[19] The increasingly anachronistic position of servants, therefore, can even augment a Wildean atmosphere of aristocratic disdain for the scrabbling materialism of modern life.

Similarly, the realities of a servant's subordination to the master—the all-consuming hours of work, the confinement to the domestic world of the house, and the dependence, in the absence of board-wages, on the house's kitchen for food—makes a suggestive parallel to a typical servant character's subordination to the formal structure of fiction, and a suggestive contrast to the comparative independence and self-assertion of other groups of laborers.[20] John Robinson, giving "A Butler's View of Men-Service" in 1892, wrote that "when a man enters service he sacrifices all freedom. Any preconceived notions he may have of living his life in

18. This contrast was perhaps more marked in employers' ideas about servants than in actual fact. Beeton's *Book of Household Management* asserts of personal servants that "deference to a master and mistress, and to their friends and visitors, is one of the implied terms of their engagement; and this deference must apply even to what may be considered their whims." Beeton, *Book of Household Management*, 1025, §2416. But Theresa McBride argues that in reality "the paternalistic tradition was weaker in England than in France. The English middle classes by the middle of the nineteenth century were much closer than the French to accepting a contractual relationship between masters and servants like that of employers and employees. English mistresses had been introduced through women's magazines and the increasing activity of women's organisations to the idea that servants should be treated like other workers." Theresa M. McBride, *The Domestic Revolution: The Modernisation of Household Service in England and France, 1820–1920* (London: Croom Helm, 1976), 32.

19. See McBride, *Domestic Revolution*, 111. The parallel decline in live-in service in America occurred somewhat later, in the 1920s, and was complicated by the demographics of race and immigration; see David M. Katzman, *Seven Days a Week: Women and Domestic Service in Industrializing America* (New York: Oxford University Press, 1978), 44–94. Alison Light's *Mrs Woolf and the Servants* (London: Fig Tree, 2007) constitutes a case study of service in one English social milieu at this transitional moment.

20. See McBride, *Domestic Revolution*, 9. In an earlier phase of the institution of service, servants came from and returned to (lower-)middle-class backgrounds, but by the late nineteenth century, service was an unambiguously working-class, low-status occupation. For an account of the changing status of service, see Ellen Jordan, *The Women's Movement and Women's Employment in Nineteenth Century Britain* (London: Routledge, 1999), 64–67.

a particular way must be thrown to the winds."[21] Earlier in the century, a footman named William Tayler wrote in his diary that "the life of a gentleman's servant is something like that of a bird shut up in a cage. The bird is well housed and well fed but is deprived of liberty."[22]

Like the bird in the cage, servants have an ornamental, semiotic function as much as a practical one. Servants are signs of the wealth and elevated social position of their masters. This holds true particularly for the menservants, members of the upper levels of the complex, gendered internal hierarchy of service, who appear in most of my nineteenth-century examples. Male domestics like butlers, valets, and footmen were considered a luxury for nineteenth-century middle-class families, to be hired only in addition to housemaids, nursemaids, and cooks. Reading domestic economy manuals from the second half of the nineteenth century, John Burnett writes: "It seems certain that menservants were increasingly regarded as status symbols confined to clearly 'successful' business and professional men. A manservant was now almost invariably associated with ownership of a coach and horses, and 'carriage folk' constituted a clearly-defined stratum of the middle or upper classes."[23] Indeed, Veblen remarks in *The Theory of the Leisure Class* that "it is this aptitude and acquired skill in the formal manifestation of the servile relation that constitutes the chief element of utility in our highly paid servants."[24] It is true that the highly paid butler is not a typical servant; above all, service was predominantly a women's occupation by this period.[25] Though this "formal" function may not have been the only "utility" of typical servants, servant-ownership of any kind is in itself a status marker—as the attention lavished on the codes of service by the quintessentially middle-class Isabella Beeton testifies. Real servants can belong to the order of signs for the servant-owning classes, which makes the association of service with aesthetic concerns of form and style yet stronger.

21. John Robinson, "A Butler's View of Men-Service," *Nineteenth Century* 31, no. 184 (June 1892): 927.

22. William Tayler, *The Diary of William Tayler, Footman, 1837*, ed. Dorothy Wise (London: St. Marylebone Society, 1962), 62.

23. John Burnett, introduction to pt. 2, "Domestic Servants," in *Annals of Labour: Autobiographies of British Working-class People, 1820–1920*, ed. John Burnett (Bloomington: Indiana University Press, 1974), 144.

24. Thorstein Veblen, *The Theory of the Leisure Class* (1899; Boston: Houghton Mifflin, 1973), 56.

25. For a summary of historians' views on the increasing "feminization" of service over time, see Bridget Hill, *Servants: English Domestics in the Eighteenth Century* (Oxford: Clarendon, 1996), 36–43.

This interplay between the semiotics of service and the semiotics of artistic style is redoubled for fictional servants, no matter how conventionalized those servants are. Indeed, as Bruce Robbins observes in *The Servant's Hand*, his study of service in the Victorian novel, literary servants' aesthetic qualities are only heightened when writers draw on the long history of literary conventions in the representation of domestics. As Robbins says, the stylized servant becomes "a sort of permanent residue, always already anachronistic … inseparable from precedent, convention, self-conscious literariness."[26] What makes aestheticist and modernist servants distinctive, however, is that this "self-conscious literariness" suits the pursuit of art for art's sake particularly well. Aestheticism laid great stress on the transformation of material reality into literary form; as Oscar Wilde writes in "The Decay of Lying":

> "Life and Nature may sometimes be used as part of Art's rough material, but before they are of any real service to art they must be translated into artistic conventions …. As a method Realism is a complete failure."[27]

Servants serve art best, according to Wilde, when that art poses itself against realism—or, to put it another way, when it adopts a modernist commitment to aesthetic autonomy over documentation of social conditions. Robbins makes the same point, asserting that servant figures represent a "continuity" between realism and modernism.[28] But in the end of the Victorian period and the beginning of the twentieth century, the formal-social signification of servants has implications for a self-consciously form-dominated art. The integration of servants *into aesthetic form* means that autonomous form, in subordinating "Life and Nature," points up its own relationship to the subordination of labor.

Wilde: The Truth of Masks with Manners

Wilde's novel *The Picture of Dorian Gray* uses the ambiguous nature of servant characters to complicate its already ambivalent treatment of the aestheticist celebration of the beauties of form. Like *Axël*, though without Villiers's unvarying solemnity, *Dorian Gray* directs our attention and our sympathy toward characters who reject the ordinary world of work in favor of the pursuit of pleasure and artistic beauty. "They are the elect," says Wilde's preface, "to whom beautiful things mean only

26. Bruce Robbins, *The Servant's Hand: English Fiction from Below* (New York: Columbia University Press, 1986), 34.

27. Oscar Wilde, "The Decay of Lying: An Observation," in *Intentions*, in *Soul of Man*, 191.

28. Robbins, *Servant's Hand*, 160.

Beauty," and the novel's long catalogs of elegant objects seem to invite the readers to join the elect.[29] Of course, the novel's Gothic dénouement seems to overturn such theories by killing off its artist, Basil Hallward, as well as its amoral pleasure-seeker, Dorian Gray. Yet despite its horror story conclusion, Wilde's novel treats the theme of the dominance of form with something other than ethical revulsion; Wilde disclaims "ethical sympathies" in the preface as "an unpardonable mannerism of style" (167). Most importantly, the quasi-aristocratic tone of Wilde's text itself implicates him as a proponent, against bourgeois norms, of art for art's sake. Regenia Gagnier has made the crucial observation that *Dorian Gray* excludes the middle class from representation; she writes, "In exclusively representing the part of society that he did—idle aristocrats and romantic artists—Wilde offended an ethic of industry and productivity. He seemed to expose himself as a presumptuous social climber who penetrated aristocratic circles with offensive ease."[30] Yet servants are not excluded from the novel, and attending to the work of servants in *Dorian Gray* can illuminate the aesthete's social position through his concern for the beauties of form.

Wilde's novel is strangely full of incidental appearances by minor servant characters, from the butler who announces Dorian Gray in the first chapter to the servants who discover his body in the last. In a transition quite analogous to the one which introduces Phipps in *An Ideal Husband*, the beginning of the book's eighth chapter shows Dorian waking up the day after he has had his quarrel with Sibyl Vane and seen the first change in his portrait:

> It was long past noon when he awoke. His valet had crept several times on tiptoe into the room to see if he was stirring, and had wondered what made his young master sleep so late. Finally his bell sounded, and Victor came softly in with a cup of tea, and a pile of letters, on a small tray of old Sèvres

29. Oscar Wilde, *The Picture of Dorian Gray: The 1890 and 1891 Texts*, vol. 3 of *The Complete Works of Oscar Wilde*, ed. Joseph Bristow (Oxford: Oxford University Press, 2005), 167. Henceforth I cite the 1891 (book publication) version given in this edition parenthetically in the text.

30. Regenia Gagnier, *Idylls of the Marketplace: Oscar Wilde and the Victorian Public* (Stanford, CA: Stanford University Press, 1986), 65. Gagnier goes on to claim that "*Dorian Gray*'s decadence lay in its distance from and rejection of middle-class life. This, not stylistics, is how decadence in British literature should be understood" (65). I suggest, however, that stylistics is an integral part of Wilde's social stance or position in the cultural field, and, conversely, that decadent style gives us unexpectedly nuanced hints about its practitioner's class situation. Jeff Nunokawa's *Tame Passions of Wilde* makes an argument along parallel lines.

china, and drew back the olive-satin curtains, with their shimmering blue lining, that hung in front of the three tall windows. (248)

Carrying the aesthete's collection of delicate things, Victor the valet introduces an interlude of lightly superficial relief from the melodrama of Dorian's confrontation with his conscience. Victor's own flat characterization contributes to that lightness; he is no more than the caricatural—or Ideal—French valet when he says to his master, "Monsieur has well slept this morning" (248). Simply by occupying the scene-setting position at the start of the chapter, Victor negotiates for the book its characteristic alternation between a picture of high-society aesthetes chatting wittily among their exquisite possessions and a Gothic narrative of moral corruption.

Victor's contribution to the book's tonal doubleness corresponds to the feelings he evokes in his master. Even for Dorian, he holds the threat of the picture at bay: "He almost dreaded his valet leaving the room. He knew that when he was alone he would have to examine the portrait" (249). Yet the valet's allegiance to the gleefully superficial aspect of the book is not as unambiguous as it may seem. The narrative gives us more reason to suppose that Dorian's valet is not just a "mask with a manner" than An Ideal Husband did about Phipps. When the narrative shows us Dorian sleeping, it slips briefly, via indirect discourse, into the servant's own perspective: "His valet ... had wondered what made his young master sleep so late." That glimpse of the valet's inner life suddenly becomes all too real to Dorian when the guilty man worries that Victor has discovered the secret of the portrait. The tenth chapter begins with Dorian's fearful contemplation of what the servant's servility may conceal:

> When his servant entered, he looked at him steadfastly, and wondered if he had thought of peering behind the screen. The man was quite impassive, and waited for his orders. Dorian lit a cigarette, and walked over to the glass and glanced into it. He could see the reflection of Victor's face perfectly. It was like a placid mask of servility. There was nothing to be afraid of, there. Yet he thought it best to be on his guard. (268)

The valet's perfect fulfillment of his role—he is the very "mask with a manner," a "placid mask of servility"—no longer reassures his master. In his tortured conscience, Dorian realizes that a mask is a surface that may hide anything underneath. As Wilde says in his preface, "Those who go beneath the surface do so at their peril" (168).

It is as though the idea of Victor "peering behind the screen" gives rise to Dorian's own wish to peer behind Victor's screen, to see more than "the reflection of Victor's face" in the mirror. Dorian thinks, "It was a horrible thing to have a spy in one's house. He had heard of rich men who had been blackmailed all their lives by some servant who had read a letter" (273).[31] The servant still represents the dominance of form for Dorian, but that dominance is no longer a reassuring sign of the varied pleasures of beautiful things and sparkling wit; instead, the mirror, in showing Dorian not his own lovely reflection but the potentially deceptive surface of his servant's face, reveals to him that the mask of form signifies a world of terrifying, unknown content.[32]

Except that it does not. Of course, no reader of *Dorian Gray* ever takes Dorian's paranoia about his valet seriously; we know that the butler didn't do it. Indeed, Victor soon disappears from the novel, displaced by Dorian's fear of Basil Hallward and James Vane, which, along with Dorian's aesthetic pastimes, occupies much of the rest of the book. We find out in the course of Basil's fateful visit with Dorian that Victor "married Lady Radley's maid, and has established her in Paris as an English dressmaker" (292). Dorian realizes that the valet's menace was illusory; Victor lives out a parodic version of a conventional marriage plot, achieving a comforting, upwardly mobile social outcome. Yet even this happy outcome is a reminder that there *was* a drama of class alongside the drama of conscience, one urgent enough to call for this narratively superfluous resolution.

Wilde's interest in such a class drama is not merely hypothetical. His essay "The Soul of Man under Socialism" explicitly links the problem of social hierarchy and class to that of art for art's sake. "All authority," he writes, "is quite degrading."[33] Indeed, his utopian vision in that essay adumbrates a world in which aesthetic pursuits might be set free from the taint of exercising or being the victim of coercive

---

31. That "no man is a hero to his valet" is of course a commonplace of the culture of domestic service; Beeton, discussing "Attendants on the Person," quotes that proverb and goes on to stress the importance for such servants of "polite manners, modest demeanour, and a respectful reserve" at such length that one feels the anxiety caused by the proximity of personal servants to their masters. Beeton, *Book of Household Management*, 1016, §2360.

32. Victoria Rosner has made a parallel observation about the frame-maker, Mr. Hubbard, upon whom Dorian calls to carry his portrait up to his attic: like a servant, Hubbard is someone "whose job it is to mediate between the two realms [of art and life]." For this very reason, as Rosner says, he poses a threat to the autonomy of art from life, even as his work is devoted to the literal, material support of that autonomy. *Modernism and the Architecture of Private Life* (New York: Columbia University Press, 2005), 55.

33. Oscar Wilde, "The Soul of Man under Socialism," in *Intentions*, in *Soul of Man*, 138. Henceforth I cite this edition parenthetically in the text.

social power. Service in particular, under the more damning name of "slavery," appears at the essay's conclusion as both essential and in contradiction to Wilde's "Individualism," of which art is "the most intense mode" (142):

> The new Individualism, for whose service Socialism, whether it wills it or not, is working, will be perfect harmony. It will be what the Greeks sought for, but could not, except in Thought, realize completely, because they had slaves, and fed them; it will be what the Renaissance sought for, but could not realize completely, except in Art, because they had slaves, and starved them. It will be complete, and through it each man will attain to his perfection.[34] (160)

Wilde's idea of the modern slave includes all the poor, of course, and his socialism, like that of so many others, makes much more of the industrial proletariat than of domestic servants. Yet Wilde's essay, like Dorian's strange aside to Basil about his old valet, still implies that the fate of aesthetic pursuits and the fate of people like Victor are fundamentally entangled.

Just how threatening that entanglement might be is, inevitably, illustrated by the story of Wilde's disgrace. The class anxieties summoned up by Wilde's glances at servants in his works are the same anxieties exploited by his adversaries at the time of his libel trial, when they made heavy weather of Wilde's liaisons with various young lower-class men.[35] The Marquess of Queensberry's lawyer emphasized the contrast between the aristocratic pretensions of Wilde's art with the class of his lovers:

> His books were written by an artist for artists; his words were not for Philistines or illiterates. Contrast that with the way in which Mr. Wilde chose his companions! He took up with Charles Parker, a gentleman's servant, whose brother was a gentleman's servant; with young Alphonse Conway, who sold papers on the pier at Worthing; and with Scarfe, also a gentleman's servant. Then his excuse was no longer that he was dwelling

---

34. Wilde in his socialist-aestheticist individualism anticipates by a hundred years the concluding utopian vision of John Guillory's *Cultural Capital*: "Socializing the means of production and consumption would be the condition of an aestheticism unbound, not its overcoming." *Cultural Capital: The Problem of Literary Canon Formation* (Chicago: University of Chicago Press, 1993), 340. The convergence of Wilde's and Guillory's critiques of the nexus of aesthetics and social status indicates how much of such a critique is immanent in aestheticist practice itself.

35. Gagnier treats this aspect of the trial in *Idylls of the Marketplace*, 146–47.

in regions of art but that he had such a noble, such a democratic soul (Laughter.), that he drew no social distinctions.[36]

This attack forms the reverse image of Wilde's attempt in "The Soul of Man under Socialism" to reconcile "dwelling in regions of art" and his "democratic soul"; like the essay, Wilde's trial shows how volatile the linkage between aestheticism and the serving class could be, how uncomfortably they sit together in bourgeois society—even as Wilde's own erotic life illustrates how those working-class people in the living room could draw the aesthete's gaze.[37]

The linkage between service and aestheticism draws even the most incidental serving persons in *Dorian Gray* into the knot of interrelated formal function and social allegory. Most striking is the nameless servant of Lord Henry's Aunt Agatha who draws to an end one of the novel's society scenes. Lord Henry has been telling his aunt's guests that "the only things one never regrets are one's mistakes":

> He played with the idea, and grew wilful; tossed it into the air and trans-
> formed it; let it escape and recaptured it; made it iridescent with fancy,
> and winged it with paradox .... He was brilliant, fantastic, irresponsible.
> He charmed his listeners out of themselves, and they followed his pipe
> laughing .... At last, liveried in the costume of the age, Reality entered the
> room in the shape of a servant to tell the Duchess that her carriage was
> waiting.[38] (*Dorian Gray*, 204–5)

It might seem that the quip "Reality entered the room in the shape of a servant" means exactly the opposite of "He represents the dominance of form." The servant

36. H. Montgomery Hyde, ed., *The Trials of Oscar Wilde* (London: William Hodge, 1948), 166.

37. As Gagnier points out, Wilde's class transgression is all the more offensive in that his aristocratic mannerisms were mostly pretension. Wilde's own background and upbringing was, according to Richard Ellmann, "resolutely middle-class," even if his father, a physician, was knighted. No matter what his seeming pretensions and aspirations, then, Wilde should by no means be regarded as unproblematically an ally of the upper classes or a residual social order. Richard Ellmann, *Oscar Wilde* (New York: Vintage, 1988), 10.

38. The chapter in which this passage appears was added by Wilde for the 1891 book publication of *Dorian Gray*. Like many of Wilde's substantial additions to the 1890 magazine version, this episode is superfluous to the advancement of the main plot; its contribution is atmospheric, a display of Lord Henry's—and Wilde's—style for its own sake. The appearance of a servant figure is not incidental to the significance of such decorative moments and the literary dominance of form they strive for. On the differences between Wilde's two texts of his novel, see Joseph Bristow's introduction and editorial introduction to the Oxford critical edition (*Dorian Gray*, xi–lxviii).

cuts off Lord Henry's treatment of a foolish, paradoxical idea to remind the duchess of everyday business, undercutting the dominance of the conversation by the aesthete's verbal style. Yet just as the duchess's business turns out to be trivial, a meeting with her husband at his club, so the idea of "Reality" as a liveried servant reduces it to parody. The satirically inflated expression implies that the supposedly real life to which the servant calls the duchess is hardly less fantastic and irresponsible than Lord Henry's iridescent fancies. In fact, the "Reality" may amount to nothing more than the construction of the chapter: a butler and a footman had bowed Lord Henry into the scene at Lady Agatha's (200), and now the servant representing "Reality" brings the inconclusive, wandering, paradoxical wit of Lord Henry to a coda. Still, to make a member of the working class, no matter how costumed, the representative of "Reality" glances at a reality more governed by material necessity than either the formal closure of a book chapter or the pastimes of aristocrats—the reality of the servant's confined, unfree life, perhaps even of the limitations of working-class life more generally. Even if servants' job is to conceal such a life behind masks of impassivity and servility, Wilde cannot resist off-hand, semi-serious hints that the mask is constructed by hard work.

Huysmans: The Decadent Master–Servant Dialectic

Domestic labor is almost inescapable in the world of the aesthetes. That inescapability is in fact a central theme of one of the bibles of aestheticism, Joris-Karl Huysmans's À rebours (Against Nature, 1884). This would perhaps surprise Dorian Gray, who is so corrupted by the "yellow book," which Wilde described as derived from Huysmans's novel during his 1895 prosecution of the Marquess of Queensberry for libel.[39] It would also suggest that the legacy of the novel's aestheticist techniques and styles involves more than a wholesale rejection of the social world.[40]

39. Wilde, *Dorian Gray*, 274; Hyde, *The Trials of Oscar Wilde*, 130; . In his biography of Wilde, Richard Ellmann describes Wilde's reaction to Huysmans's novel, published at the same time as Wilde's own marriage: "He said to the *Morning News*, 'This book of Huysmans is one of the best I have ever seen.' ... Wilde drank of it as a chaser after the love potions of matrimony." Ellmann, *Oscar Wilde*, 252–53.

40. Rita Felski, in an essay treating *À rebours* and *Dorian Gray* together as prototypical of modernist style and ideology, offers a powerful reading of these works as unrepentantly elitist. Felski argues that "the primary division" in aestheticist works is "between the refined and the vulgar, a division that separates the self-conscious aesthete from the common and sentimental herd," and that such a distinction is "simultaneously aesthetic and political." "The Counterdiscourse of the Feminine in Three Texts by Wilde, Huysmans, and Sacher-Masoch," *PMLA* 106, no. 5 (October 1991): 1100. I concur in Felski's description of class

Still, most of *À rebours* is apparently a manual of how to live without any other people; Huysmans's hero Jean des Esseintes, seeming to anticipate Lord Goring's dictum "Other people are quite dreadful," adopts a willed exile where he holds intercourse only with objects of beauty suited to his taste.[41] For plot the novel substitutes the cataloging of various domains of taste—books, paintings, perfumes, flowers; thus the hero's relationships with things substitute for what would be in a more conventional nineteenth-century novel his relationships with people. Yet the novel does specify how des Esseintes sustains his day-to-day life—with the employment of "the two old servants who had looked after his mother and who between them had acted as steward and concierge at the Château de Lourps."[42]

Still, the aristocrat does his utmost to make his old servants purely functional elements of his household, as little noticeable as human beings as possible:

> He took with him to Fontenay this faithful pair who had been accustomed to a methodical sickroom routine, trained to administer spoonfuls of physic and medicinal brews at regular intervals, and inured to the absolute silence of cloistered monks, barred from all communication with the outside world and confined to rooms where the doors and windows were always shut . . . .
>
> Des Esseintes gave up the first floor of the house to them; but he made them wear thick felt slippers, had the doors fitted with tambours and their hinges well oiled, and covered the floors with long-pile carpeting, to make sure that he never heard the sound of their footsteps overhead.[43] (32)

---

distinction as a central "aesthetic and political" quality of premodernist aestheticism; but I argue that for Huysmans as for others, such a distinction becomes unstable when the aesthete has to depend on the herd for domestic service.

41. Wilde, *An Ideal Husband*, 292.

42. Joris-Karl Huysmans, *Against Nature*, trans. Robert Baldick (Harmondsworth, UK: Penguin, 1959), 32. "Après la vente de ses biens, des Esseintes garda les deux vieux domestiques qui avaient soigné sa mère et rempli tout à la fois l'office de régisseurs et de concierges du château de Lourps." Joris-Karl Huysmans, *À rebours*, 2nd ed., ed. Marc Fumaroli (Paris: Gallimard, 1977), 97. Henceforth I cite the translation parenthetically in the text, with the French original in the notes.

43. "Il fit venir à Fontenay ce ménage habitué à un emploi de garde-malade, à une régularité d'infirmiers distribuant, d'heure en heure, des cuillerées de potion et de tisane, à un rigide silence de moines claustrés, sans communication avec le dehors, dans des pièces aux fenêtres et aux portes closes . . . . Il leur céda le premier étage de la maison, les obligea à porter d'épais chaussons de feutre, fit placer des tambours le long des portes bien huilées et matelasser leur plancher de profonds tapis de manière à ne jamais entendre le bruit de leurs pas, au-dessus de sa tête." *À rebours*, 97.

The perversely dispassionate tone of this passage is emblematic of the novel as a whole; it duplicates the ruthless logic and ingenuity with which des Esseintes sets out to accommodate his own sensibilities. He does not want to hear the servants; therefore he outfits them with appropriately padded footwear and makes the necessary changes to their floor. (Wilde took similar measures with his "scout" at Oxford.[44]) He also arranges a nonverbal language of ringings of their bell so as not to have to speak to them. Nonetheless, the passage makes evident the dependence of des Esseintes on other people despite his antisociality: his servants are "accustomed to a sickroom routine." He may be able to treat them like so much furniture, to come close to obliterating their humanity, but ultimately his needs make him an invalid, dependent on helpers to supply his regular dose of sensation like so many "spoonfuls of physic and medicinal brews." Indeed, the action of the narrative, insofar as it has one apart from the enumeration of subjects of taste, consists in the decline of des Esseintes's health.

Like a chronic invalid, des Esseintes uses his domestics to sustain his pathological state; their nursing is not a cure but the means by which the narrative can unfold. Just as he insulates their floor from the noise of their steps, so they insulate him from the outside world by doing the chores, facilitating his aesthetic hermitage by their habituation to "the absolute silence of cloistered monks, barred from all communication with the outside world." Nonetheless, they maintain for him a link to the world outside the house at Fontenay, and not only because they do the shopping. When des Esseintes develops sensory hallucinations, it is a servant who verifies that they are hallucinatory:

> Noticing a strong scent of frangipane in the room ... he rang for his servant.
>
> "Can't you smell something?" he asked.
>
> The man sniffed and said that he smelt nothing unusual. There was no doubt about it: his nervous trouble had returned in the form of a new sort of sensual illusion.[45] (118)

---

44. See G. T. Atkinson, "Oscar Wilde at Oxford," *Cornhill Magazine*, n.s. 66 (May 1929): 560; cited in Ellmann, *Oscar Wilde*, 46. But such attitudes were not the exclusive province of budding aesthetes; Beeton tells her middle-class audience that the creaking of servants' shoes in the drawing room is "an abomination." *Book of Household Management*, 1009, §2328.

45. "Sa chambre embauma la frangipane .... Il sonna son domestique:—Vous ne sentez rien, dit-il? L'autre renifla une prise d'air et déclara ne respirer aucune fleur: le doute ne pouvait exister; la névrose revenait, une fois de plus, sous l'apparence d'une nouvelle illusion des sens." *À rebours*, 214.

Whereas a Wilde character like Lord Henry might argue for the equivalence or even superiority of hallucination to reality—Dorian visits opium dens—Huysmans's hero turns to the servant on whom he so much relies and immediately concludes that he is afflicted with "nervous trouble." The servant's declaration leads to the abolition of any doubt that the "sensual illusion," which in other circumstances might be the very sensation des Esseintes seeks, is only a disguise for mental disease. In their external perspective on their master, the servants share the point of view of the narrative itself: incidental though they may seem, they are woven into Huysmans's novelistic fabric.

The role of des Esseintes's servants as unavoidable verifiers of their master's sickness is essential to the construction of the last part of the novel, in which des Esseintes's decline begins to interrupt his aesthetic pursuits and occupy more of the narrative's attention. The narrator seems to draw away from des Esseintes, to invest less fully in his obsessive ministering to his own tastes. The moment of greatest narrative distance comes when, in a brief respite from his illness, des Esseintes formulates a plan to travel to London. Instead of telling us this directly, the narrative briefly assumes the perspective of the servants: "One afternoon, the bell rang with brief calls, and Des Esseintes ordered that his bags were to be packed for a long journey" (130).[46] It is the servants, not the master, who hear the bell ring for them. Only after a near-slapstick scene of hurried packing do we return to the perspective of des Esseintes and learn, retrospectively, that the idea of traveling to London was precipitated by a reading of Dickens.

Erich Auerbach seems to have passed over this detail when he dismissed *À rebours* as taking a "strictly unipersonal approach to reality" in the last chapter of *Mimesis*.[47] As with *Dorian Gray* showing Victor looking at his sleeping master, Huysmans's narrative, in making use of the servants' perspective, shows that they *have* a perspective, that the book is not wholly absorbed in the master's aesthetic solipsism. In Auerbach's influential literary history, "multipersonal" modernism in the manner of Woolf "evolved" from aestheticist unipersonal subjectivism. But this account stands in need of correction: already in Huysmans, aestheticism or protomodernism is not limited to what Auerbach calls—conflating des Esseintes's point of view with that of the narrative—"an extremely subjective, individualistic,

46. Translation modified to reflect the grammar of the original. "Une après-midi, les timbres sonnèrent des appels brefs, et des Esseintes prescrivit qu'on lui apprêtât ses malles, pour un long voyage." *À rebours*, 213.

47. Erich Auerbach, *Mimesis: The Representation of Reality in Western Literature*, trans. Willard R. Trask (Princeton, NJ: Princeton University Press, 1953), 542.

and often eccentrically aberrant impression of reality."[48] Indeed, Auerbach's own terms become indistinct when he turns to Huysmans's most direct modernist successor, for in Proust, says Auerbach, the unipersonal and multipersonal methods "overlap."[49] In Huysmans—and, as I argue shortly, in Proust—servants expand the "unipersonal" into a socially wider-ranging form of representation. Though aestheticism is not the "objective" realism toward which Auerbach's argument tends, its apparent solipsism is overcome in those moments when it registers the aesthete's dependence on his domestic employees.[50]

Eventually, des Esseintes finds that he has exhausted the interest of his former aesthetic delectations. The novel's earlier catalogs of taste showed des Esseintes alone; now, as he wearily goes through his library of French literature, he has the help of his servant. The servant acts like an icon of the hero's exhaustion:

> "Lord! how few books there are that are worth reading again," sighed Des
> Esseintes, watching his man as he climbed down the step-ladder he had been
> perched on and stood to one side [s'effaçait] to let his master have a clear
> view of all the bookshelves.[51] (194–95)

The servant tries to efface himself so that des Esseintes can contemplate all his shelves, but he still protrudes into the middle of his employer's version of Mallarmé's "*La chair est triste, hélas! et j'ai lu tous les livres.*" The servant is a reminder that Des Esseintes is no longer able to plunge himself wholly into the world of books—or, rather, that the world of books included this figure of the laboring, unaesthetic other all along.

This lesson receives one more iteration at the end of the novel. When Des Esseintes has abandoned his experiment in exile and is returning to Paris, the final sign of his defeat is the door closing, in the penultimate paragraph, "behind the manservant, who disappeared carrying a bundle of books" (219).[52] This self-referential symbol—des Esseintes's books are carried away as Huysmans's book

48. Ibid., 536.

49. Ibid.

50. These moments of expansion show why modernism need not be wholly limited in its scope to a privileged, subjective world. The classic argument that it is so limited is Georg Lukács's "The Ideology of Modernism," in *The Meaning of Contemporary Realism*, trans. John Mander and Necke Mander (London: Merlin, 1962), 17–46.

51. "—Mon Dieu! Mon Dieu! qu'il existe donc peu de livres qu'on puisse relire, soupira des Esseintes, regardant le domestique qui descendait de l'escabelle où il était juché et s'effaçait pour lui permettre d'embrasser d'un coup d'œil tous les rayons." *À rebours*, 315.

52. "Sur le domestique qui emportait des paquets de livres." *À rebours*, 349.

ends—catches up the servant once more. Just as previously the servants had been necessary to des Esseintes's aesthetic enterprise, now they are instrumental to its closure. Servants become the means by which the novel contemplates itself. Huysmans constructs a miniature allegory of this fact in the scene that sets off the final crisis of des Esseintes's illness, at the moment he thinks he is recovering: "He felt in fuller possession of his faculties and asked his man to hand him a mirror. After a single glance it slipped from his hands. He scarcely knew himself." (206).[53] The most isolated of heroes requires his servant so that he can look at himself in the mirror, and the result is disaster, the very disaster feared by Dorian Gray when he thinks of his valet: the servant's presence intensifies the master's consciousness that the two images of himself disagree horribly.[54] The impassivity of the servants, the silence he has required of them, suddenly turns out to be a trap; instead of protecting des Esseintes's wholeness from the incursions of others, it has allowed him to become alienated from himself without ever noticing.

The servant appears at the cracks in des Esseintes's literal and figurative mirrors—that is, in his reading of books that model À rebours itself and in his attempts to recognize his own face in the mirror. The servant bears that critical symbolic weight because he represents his master's reliance on a dependent other even at the heart of his apparent aestheticist escape from the materialistic world of contemporary Paris. Huysmans's use of mirrors thus brings him as close as anyone to a literary working out of Hegel's dialectic of master and servant in the Phenomenology.[55] The master's apparent position of autonomous self-consciousness is overturned by his dependence on another, whose consciousness acquires an authority of its own. Hegel writes, "The truth of the independent consciousness is accordingly the servile consciousness of the bondsman .... Just as lordship showed that its essential nature is the reverse of what it wants to be, so too servitude in its consummation will really turn into the opposite of what it immediately is."[56] Yet what in Hegel is seemingly only allegory becomes an explicit reflection on

53. "Il se posséda mieux et demanda au domestique de lui présenter une glace; elle lui glissa aussitôt des mains; il se reconnaissait à peine." À rebours, 330.

54. It seems to me likely that this scene in Huysmans's novel lies behind Wilde's attribution of a "somewhat grotesque dread of mirrors" to the hero of Dorian's yellow book (276), even though this detail is sometimes cited as a difference between Wilde's and Huysmans's novels (Ellmann, Oscar Wilde, 317; Bristow, ed., Dorian Gray, 395 n105.13–14). The theme of the troubled specularity of the master–servant relation is common to both.

55. See G. W. F. Hegel, Phenomenology of Spirit, trans. A. V. Miller (Oxford: Clarendon Press, 1977), 111–19.

56. Ibid., 117.

the artist's social dependency in Huysmans.[57] The service des Esseintes's nameless domestics finally perform is, like that of servants in Wilde, one of unstable demarcation. They separate des Esseintes from society so that he may seek isolation; they hold society out, but—though des Esseintes attempts to disguise it—they themselves *are* society let in. Long before the hero's climactic, grotesque disintegration, they function to indicate how he—and his narrative—are inextricably tied to the menial labors of others. Huysmans's showpiece of decadence is also an early demonstration of the complex dependencies built into the aesthete's life.

Henry James: The Subtlety of Service

Like *À rebours*, Henry James's late novel *The Ambassadors* (published in 1903) shapes itself around the pursuits and fantasies of a solitary man. Taking as its subject the transforming effect of French aesthetic delights and perils, *The Ambassadors* is in fact James's most aestheticist creation.[58] More than his other works, even more than the other monuments of his late style, *The Ambassadors* occupies a crucial juncture in the history of aesthetic autonomy. Combining the theme of aesthetic experience with conspicuously heightened structural and stylistic effects, the novel sets a modernist pattern, inaugurating what Mark McGurl calls "the Jamesian modernist tradition"; Jonathan Freedman describes *The Ambassadors* as "perhaps the greatest single example of the new aestheticism James built on the ruins of the old."[59] Already in the period of modernism itself, E. M. Forster asserted the centrality of formal concerns in James's novel, discussing *The Ambassadors* under the heading of "Pattern" in *Aspects of the Novel*:

57. For an exposition and critique of Hegel's model within a study of Victorian writing, see Jonathan Taylor, "Introduction: Master-Slave Relations, Master-Slave Pacts," in *Mastery and Slavery in Victorian Writing* (Houndmills, UK: Palgrave Macmillan, 2003), 1–20.

58. In his important essay on "The Jamesian Lie," Leo Bersani argues that James's is a "richly superficial art" in which a concern with social surfaces and forms merges with the elevation of the value of surface beauty and aesthetic forms. "The Jamesian Lie," chap. 5 in *A Future for Astyanax: Character and Desire in Literature* (Boston: Little, Brown, 1976), 132. For a recent exposition of the alternate view that James's principal concerns are ethical, see Robert B. Pippin, *Henry James and Modern Moral Life* (Cambridge: Cambridge University Press, 2000); Pippin discusses *The Ambassadors* in chap. 6.

59. Mark McGurl, *The Novel Art: Elevations of American Fiction after Henry James* (Princeton, NJ: Princeton University Press, 2001), 7; Jonathan Freedman, *Professions of Taste: Henry James, British Aestheticism, and Commodity Culture* (Stanford, CA: Stanford University Press, 1990), 192.

> We shall see in it pattern triumphant, and we shall also be able to see the sacrifices an author must make if he wants his pattern and nothing else to triumph .... Everything is planned, everything fits: none of the minor characters are just decorative ... they elaborate on the main theme, they work. The final effect is pre-arranged, dawns gradually on the reader, and is completely successful when it comes. Details of the intrigue may be forgotten, but the symmetry created is enduring.[60]

He goes on to condemn James for slighting "most of human life,"[61] but Forster's own connection between the dominance of form ("pattern triumphant") and the subservient labor of minor characters ("they work") suggests inadvertently that the triumph of pattern may include an awareness of the work of subordinates. Indeed, James's aestheticism has its servants, as Wilde's has its butlers and Huysmans's its domestics; as with those earlier authors, James's technique exhibits the importance *for that technique itself* of these household laborers. Despite all the differences from Villiers, Wilde, and Huysmans implied by his idiosyncratic manner, his American origins, his long prior career as a novelist, and his concern in *The Ambassadors* with the business-like, buttoned-up world of Woollett, Massachusetts, James's treatment of servants in his late novel resembles those other writers closely. This resemblance implies that he shares in their elevation of form *and* their understanding of form's situatedness in a structure of class distinction, including the distinction between masters and servants.[62]

Precisely because surface appearances and transient impressions are so important to Strether's Parisian experience, servants can open up an avenue for inferences about social structure. In other works by James, servants do not necessarily have such an unexpected function; they may contribute to plot devices—like *The American*'s Mrs. Bread, the retired housekeeper who knows the Bellegardes' compromising secret—or they may be part of the decor, as when Milly Theale, at Maud Lowder's for the first time, categorizes "the attitude of the servants" alongside "the shape of the forks, the arrangement of the flowers" in her excited vision of London

60. E. M. Forster, *Aspects of the Novel*, ed. Oliver Stallybrass (London: Edward Arnold, 1974), 104–5.

61. Ibid., 109.

62. Freedman's important account of James in relation to aestheticism, professionalization, and the marketplace complements the argument I am pursuing here. But unlike Freedman, I emphasize continuities among the fictions of autonomy produced by aestheticism, by James, and by later modernists, rather than the differences between what he calls "the volatile and unstable example of aestheticism" and "that more austere form of aestheticism we call modernism." Freedman, *Professions of Taste*, xvii.

society.[63] In *The Ambassadors*, though, as in Wilde and Huysmans, even the incidental servants matter to aestheticism. One such appears at the end of the scene between Strether and Madame de Vionnet in which they confront the problems raised by the arrival of the Pococks. Strether is trying to take his leave:

> Her face, with what he had by this time grasped, told him more than her words; whether something had come into it, or whether he only read clearer, her whole story—what at least he then took for such—reached out to him from it. With the initiative she now attributed to Chad it all made a sense, and this sense—a light, a lead, was what had abruptly risen before him. He wanted, once more, to get off with these things; which was at last made easy, a servant having, for his assistance, on hearing voices in the hall, just come forward. All that Strether had made out was, while the man opened the door and impersonally waited, summed up in his last word. "I don't think, you know, Chad will tell me anything."[64]

The narrative self-consciously brings in a servant to "make easy" Strether's escape. The servant waits "impersonally" because his sole purpose is to fulfill a narrative function; by ending the scene, "the man" instigates one of those delays in the explanation of meanings which are so characteristic of the novel, what Ian Watt calls the "delayed specification of referents."[65] This delay forms part of the novel's aestheticism; it permits the narrative to linger over impressions rather than conclusions,

63. Henry James, *The Wings of the Dove*, ed. John Bayley (London: Penguin, 1986), 149. Of course, not all ordinary workers are flattened in James's fiction. His 1898 novella *In the Cage* develops a more intricate consciousness of the relations between the upper and lower classes—and it does so through its service-employee protagonist, a telegraphist. Observing high-society life from her cage, she develops a preoccupation with impressions and surfaces that anticipates Strether's. Thus Jamesian consciousness is not limited to the bourgeoisie, but its intensities, here as in the *The Ambassadors*, seem to draw attention to class inequality: the richness of the heroine's speculations depends on the social division between her and her customer Captain Everard and on the limits this division places on her knowledge. When she finally learns more—by means of a butler's gossip—the story ends: "It was better surely not to learn things at all than to learn them by the butler." Henry James, *In the Cage*, in *Complete Stories, 1892–1898*, ed. John Hollander and David Bromwich (New York: Library of America, 1996), 916. See also the account of the telegraphist's cage-like socioeconomic situation in Jill Galvan, "Sympathy and the Spiriting of Information *In the Cage*," chap. 1 in *Sympathetic Medium: Feminine Channeling, the Occult, and Communication Technologies, 1859–1919* (Ithaca, NY: Cornell University Press).

64. Henry James, *The Ambassadors*, ed. Harry Levin (London: Penguin, 2003), 365–66. Henceforth I cite this edition parenthetically in the text.

65. Ian Watt, "The First Paragraph of *The Ambassadors*: An Explication," *Essays in Criticism* 10, no. 3 (July 1960): 255.

vagueness rather than sharp specificity.[66] But the servant also brings to the surface the aristocracy of Madame de Vionnet's manner—the good form that is so essential to her evasions, the riches and the social hierarchy which justify the mysteriousness in which Strether revels. The chapter-ending moment therefore creates an analogy—quite reminiscent of Wilde's description of the Ideal Butler—between the way the aristocrat uses an "impersonal" servant as one more enchanting decoration in her beautiful apartments and the way the novel makes use of that same "impersonal," flatly minor character of the servant to round off its forms.

This appearance of the servant evokes the chill Strether feels a little earlier, when Madame de Vionnet reveals that she has arranged a marriage for her daughter: "It was—through something ancient and cold in it—what he would have called the real thing" (364). Like the arranged upper-class marriage, domestic service belongs to an older order of institutions, one to which American bourgeois individualism and belief in the freedom of choice are quite alien. Jeanne de Vionnet's lack of self-determination is, like that of the servant, marked by class. Unlike Jeanne, however, the servant has a special relationship to Jamesian *form*, in the closing of the chapter. That relationship in turn suggests that novelistic construction may be as involved in social coercion as Madame de Vionnet's aristocratic aesthetic.

This Wildean use of domestics becomes even more marked in the treatment of the novel's only named servant character. Chad Newsome's valet is called Baptiste. He makes his first appearance when Strether, visiting Chad after his confrontation with Mrs. Pocock, finds the young man absent:

> Chad's servant had by this time answered for his reappearance .... Strether spent an hour in waiting for him—an hour full of strange suggestions, persuasions, recognitions; one of those that he was to recall, at the end of his adventure, as the particular handful that most had counted. The mellowest lamplight and the easiest chair had been placed at his disposal by Baptiste, subtlest of servants; the novel half-uncut, the novel lemon-coloured and tender, with the ivory knife athwart it like the dagger in a *contadina*'s hair, had been pushed within the soft circle—a circle which, for some reason, affected Strether as softer still after the same Baptiste had remarked that in the absence of a further need of anything by Monsieur he would betake himself to bed. (425)

66. According to Richard Ellmann, "deferral was for James what instant satisfaction was for Pater." I refuse this contrast; deferral in James *is* instant aesthetic satisfaction. Richard Ellmann, "James Amongst the Aesthetes," in *Henry James and Homo-Erotic Desire*, ed. John R. Bradley (Basingstoke, UK: Macmillan, 1999), 28.

Baptiste is Phippsian in his duties to good form, and, as Phipps is the "Ideal Butler," Baptiste is the "subtlest of servants." But he is more than a minor comic touch; he is the presiding spirit of one of the hours "that most had counted" for Strether—and, implicitly, for the novel itself. That hour consists predominantly of fleeting impressions ("strange suggestions") and the pleasures of a novel whose sensuousness ("lemon-coloured and tender") even des Esseintes or Dorian Gray would relish. Baptiste adds the coup de grâce by effacing himself, allowing Strether the illusion of a solitary encounter with beautiful things and charming thoughts, just as the passive construction of "had been pushed" occludes the agency of the valet. The "soft circle" of lamplight becomes a kind of geometric image for the completeness and closure of aesthetic reverie; in fact, James uses the image of the circle of light for that of the autonomous literary work in his preface to *The Wings of the Dove*.[67] Nonetheless, the narrative makes us aware that the satisfactions of closure are the product of the valet's work, his maintenance of the boundary of Strether's space.

This scene may seem, then, to resemble the novel's prominent moments of ruptured aestheticism, in which Strether, mesmerized by an aesthetic impression, is suddenly interrupted by his interests in other people: the encounter with Madame de Vionnet in Notre Dame, the appearance of the lovers on the river at the book's climax. Like those crucial turns in the "pattern triumphant" of the novel's plot, this description of Strether's hour in Chad's apartment poses a threat to an aestheticism of impressions; but precisely because Chad's valet is *not* important to the plot or significant to Strether's social life, that threat is not one of rupture. Instead, the aesthetic episode only becomes lovelier, "softer still," for Baptiste's service—forcing us to include that servile relation *within* the realm of the aesthetic, with a discomfort that the style of the passage makes us feel.

The Dorian Gray–like unease Baptiste can provoke in this moment of reading recalls nothing so much as the corruption of Dorian by the "yellow book."[68] Even in celebrating the ethereal pleasures of Jamesian consciousness, the narrative ironically registers with Baptiste's stylish exit just how much "Monsieur" continues to have many "further needs"—needs that will not be satisfied in the subsequent meeting with Chad or anywhere else in the book. Pricking the "soft circle" with the paper-knife, Baptiste disrupts Strether's self-enclosure and adds a trace of

67. "The circle of the work itself." James, *The Wings of the Dove*, 41.

68. The note of danger added by the dagger-like ivory knife echoes, faintly, the "poisonous[ness]" of the yellow book; the darkness of the hour of reading is the same (Dorian reads by the "wan light" of "one solitary star"); and Baptiste's exit reverses the interruption of Dorian's entrancement by his (French!) valet's reminders "of the lateness of the hour." Wilde, *Dorian Gray*, 274–75.

menace to the atmosphere, a menace ironically noted when he is later described as preparing a supper of "light cold clever French things" for Chad (497). As Strether waits for Chad, his fleeting, light, clever impressions—his "relish quite ... like a pang" (426)—cover over a cold emptiness of which Baptiste, in perfecting those impressions for Strether, only gives another reminder.[69]

The moment of aestheticist exaltation includes the troubling labor of the servant; by a striking symmetry, the disintegration of Strether's Parisian aesthetic idyll calls forth the image of a domestic servant. The day after Strether has surprised Chad and Madame de Vionnet in the countryside, she asks him to see her; he finds her "afraid for her life," and she bursts into tears. He can hardly comfort her when she says her despair is "no matter":

> He could n't say it was *not* no matter; for he was serving her to the end, he now knew, anyway—quite as if what he thought of her had nothing to do with it. It was actually moreover as if ... he could think of nothing but the passion, mature, abysmal, pitiful, she represented, and the possibilities she betrayed. She was older for him to-night, visibly less exempt from the touch of time; but she was as much as ever the finest and subtlest creature, the happiest apparition, it had been given him, in all his years, to meet; and yet he could see her there as vulgarly troubled, in very truth, as a maidservant crying for her young man. The only thing was that she judged herself as the maidservant would n't; the weakness of which wisdom too, the dishonour of which judgement, seemed but to sink her lower. (483)

Now that Strether is fully aware that Madame de Vionnet's relationship with Chad is sexual, she is no longer a spirit of aesthetic purity for him; he sees her "giving up all attempt at a manner" (483), her passion disrupting the personal style Strether so admires. He imagines this stylistic rupture in terms of the loss of class position, the revelation that the Countess is "vulgarly troubled." Yet Strether's thought processes hold a contradiction: even as he inwardly regrets her likeness to a "maidservant," he finds himself "serving her to the end." In the imagery of Strether's meditation, then, service stands both for the breakdown of manner by vulgar human entanglements and for his continued devotion to the perfect manner of this "finest and subtlest" aristocrat. The phrase "serving her to the end" looks ominously to the end of her

---

69. For a consideration of this menacing aspect of domestic servants in James's "The Jolly Corner," see Brian McCuskey, "Not at Home: Servants, Scholars, and the Uncanny," *PMLA* 121, no. 2 (March 2006): 421–36. McCuskey's discussion of the importance of the repression of class distinctions to the psychoanalytic notion of the uncanny complements my own consideration of the use of class hierarchies for the elevation of aesthetic form.

liaison with Chad, the end of Strether's journey, and the end of the novel—one final, melancholy association between service and aesthetic closure.

"The only thing was that she judged herself as the maidservant would n't": Strether's last revelation is that Madame de Vionnet, bears, like him, the burden of self-consciousness. Crude as the class prejudice of Strether's formulation may appear, it is an essential component of aesthetic self-reflection: only by both treating servants as part of the domestic decoration and regarding them as manifestations of vulgar reality can the narrative reveal the social impurities inherent in form. This insight into the mixed character of the fiction of autonomy's relation to labor, discomfiting though it might be, does not translate into a full-blown critique of service. Neither, however, does it fall into a wholehearted celebration of the beauties of the social order. Mark Seltzer has argued, in an important Foucauldian reading of James's work, that there is a "criminal continuity" between Jamesian technique and the techniques of political power.[70] But Jamesian style, in bringing to light the class domination within the "dominance of form," does not work to render the existing social order appealing. Instead, though with some ambivalence, James makes available a potentially subversive understanding of the workings of class in tandem with the workings of aesthetics.

The significance of this possible subversion constitutes one important dimension of difference between James and decadents like Wilde and Huysmans. Like their prototype Villiers, Wilde and Huysmans make the aesthete a grotesque figure, subject to bodily and psychological corruption and decay, too exaggerated to be taken for the artist himself. This obvious and quasi-moralizing technique, ostentatiously placing the pursuit of aesthetic autonomy in quotation marks, masks the subtler—and more thoroughgoing—probing of aesthetic form in the labor of servants. Strether's renunciation of the Parisian life, on the other hand, is no such theatrical disavowal of aestheticism: insofar as he leaves the scene in order to have gained nothing more for himself than "wonderful impressions," as Maria Gostrey says (512), he affirms the autonomy of the aesthetic. The asceticism of this "new" aestheticism (as Freedman calls it) redirects the search for the privileged artistic realm from the decadent lifestyle to the Jamesian late style itself, the wonderful impressions and the pleasurable cognitive puzzles created by James's intense pressure on the English-language systems of prononimal reference, verbal mood, and syntactic subordination. The local linguistic challenges of *The Ambassadors*, in bewildering us, transform us into so many Strethers sitting alone in the lamplight

---

70. Mark Seltzer, *Henry James and the Art of Power* (Ithaca, NY: Cornell University Press, 1984), 24.

turning over our perceptions—and waited on by James himself, intruding narratively only in the most self-effacing ways, writing preface after preface assuring us that the objects before us are creations of pure technique. Despite the flamboyance of the fin-de-siècle writers, James has more at stake in the status of aesthetic form than they do: his literary form is identified with "the process of vision" that, James says in the preface to his novel, "is the business of my tale and the march of my action, not to say the precious moral of everything" (34). The elevation of this process as an autonomous value is the very principle of the late James's practice. With James, then, the dialectical role of service reaches further than it did in Villiers or even Wilde. It is not just the aesthete's day-to-day life or the logic of plot that includes servants when ordinary work is supposedly excluded. In *The Ambassadors*, aesthetic form, the very thing that would seem to be necessarily purified of any connection to the world of labor, is most intensely itself when it includes the kindred work of servants.

Proust: Service in the Magic Circle

We may wonder whether the intricacies of the fictions of autonomy studied here are less an anticipation of modernism than the result of a lingering allegiance to nineteenth-century realism. Protomodernist though the late James may be, he is also a survival from the Victorian age. The question remains, then, whether more full-throated modernist defenders of the autonomy of art pursue any comparable exploration of the role of laborers in aesthetic pursuits. When Bruce Robbins remarks in *The Servant's Hand* that servants in the nineteenth-century novel represent "a modernist element that jars the complacency of realism's unself-conscious focus on the here-and-now of a limited circle of social destinies," he hints at the connections among service, modernism, and form that I wish to explore now.[71] It is not necessary, however, to make an exhaustive catalogue or typology of modernist servants. The results of such an exercise would, I believe, largely mirror those of Robbins's compelling work on the narrative functions of servants in Victorian literature.[72] It would be more telling, for the purposes of this study of autonomy, if there

71. Robbins, *Servant's Hand*, 160–61.

72. In *Mrs Woolf and the Servants*, Alison Light has made an extensive exhaustive biographical study of Woolf's servants and their mistress. As far as literary scholarship goes, Light's study, despite its value as biography and social history, does not add much to Robbins's treatment of servants and literary convention. Light concentrates on individual psychology, on one hand, and large-scale changes in the lives of women on the other; she

were a central modernist novel, one that was widely understood as a standard-bearer for the autonomy of art, that was also preoccupied with domestic service. Then it would be possible to ask whether that fiction of autonomy understood its relation to labor as James's and the aesthetes' fictions did. In fact, there is such an exemplary novel: Marcel Proust's *À la recherche du temps perdu*.

Without undertaking a comprehensive interpretation of Proust's immense work, I argue that domestic service is indeed implicated in Proust's particular vision of the autonomy of art in the *Recherche*. The presence of Françoise, the narrator's cook, housekeeper, and lifelong nurse, runs through Proust's novel from start to finish. Françoise offers a particular challenge to the sorts of readings I have been giving, because she is far from being an incidental or flat character. Her personal relationships, as well as her role in the novel's representation of aesthetic experience and artistic creation, are far more complex. And although the *Recherche* mostly confines its attention to bourgeois and aristocratic society, the narrator's and the author's attitudes about servants and the working classes are generally far more nuanced than the mixture of decadent complacency and vague worry depicted in Huysmans, Wilde, or even James.[73] Yet setting Françoise alongside some of the *Recherche*'s minor servants reveals the roles all of them play in the work's frustrated and paradoxical attempt to secure an art autonomous not only from labor but from historical time itself; domestics have a surprisingly deep connection to Proust's characteristic ambition of waking from the nightmare of history. And the persistent theme of Françoise's own artistry will allow me to elaborate on the specular aspect of the master–servant relationship hinted at in Wilde, Huysmans, and James: in Proust, we will see the unease with which the modernist recognizes a kindred form-maker in his servant. The fictional Marcel and the real Proust both welcome domestics and their labor into the timeless aesthetic realm with a profound ambivalence, an ambivalence best exemplified by the mixture of love, condescension, and fear displayed toward Françoise herself.

One moment from *La Prisonnière* may serve to exemplify the omnipresence of Françoise in the life and art of the *Recherche*'s narrator:

---

does not construct links between service and form of the kind I am describing. She does, however, usefully indicate the formal ambivalence of servants, who "were part of the so-called real-life" both repelled and encompassed by Woolf's writerly project of "try[ing] to combine, as she put it, the two worlds, 'outer' and 'inner.'" *Mrs Woolf and the Servants*, 225.

73. For Jean-Yves Tadié, "One of the virtues of *À la recherche du temps perdu* is the interest shown in ordinary people, in rural society and in the working classes." Jean-Yves Tadié, *Marcel Proust: A Life*, trans. Euan Cameron (New York: Penguin, 2000), 609.

> Françoise would come in to light the fire, and in order to make it draw,
> would throw upon it a handful of twigs, the scent of which, forgotten for a
> year past, traced round the fireplace a magic circle within which, glimpsing
> myself poring over a book, now at Combray, now at Doncières, I was as
> joyful, while remaining in my bedroom in Paris, as if I had been on the
> point of setting out for a walk along the Méséglise way, or of going to join
> Saint-Loup and his friends on manoeuvres.[74]

Françoise lights the fire, generating by her labor the "magic circle" in which memory and the present moment coalesce for the narrator; the twigs she throws into
the hearth carry the sensory stimulus, that "scent ... forgotten for a year past," that
breaks through the narrator's forgetfulness. Like Shakespeare's lonely mage Pros-
pero, the narrator needs solitude to practice his art, but he seems to need his servant
even more. If Françoise's labor is required to produce the joyous transtemporal
epiphany, aesthetic autonomy involves at least one social relationship from the
outset. And Françoise is present for the narrator's development from the opening
pages of Du côté de chez Swann to the final section of Le Temps retrouvé.

In fact, this very omnipresence of Françoise constitutes the clue to the explanation of the paradox of servants in the Recherche. Françoise's endless service
is a thoroughly unrealistic circumstance; already in the novel's opening, she has
assumed the role of senior servant and matron, which she continues to fulfill to the
end and beyond, her virtues and foibles recurring in scene after scene. The narrator insistently reminds us that Françoise represents a throwback to the peasantry of
the ancien régime, that she is, as her name indicates, a type of eternal Frenchness.
In short, Françoise may enter—she may even create—the narrator's "magic circle"
because she already exists, for the purposes of the novel, outside time. Despite her
status as a domestic laborer and lower-class woman, she is a paradoxical icon of all

74. Marcel Proust, In Search of Lost Time, trans. C. K. Scott Moncrieff, Terence Kilmartin,
and D. J. Enright (London: Chatto and Windus, 1992), 5:21. "Françoise venait allumer le feu
et pour le faire prendre y jetait quelques brindilles dont l'odeur, oubliée pendant tout l'été,
décrivait autour de la cheminée un cercle magique dans lequel, m'apercevant moi-même
en train de lire tantôt à Combray, tantôt à Doncières, j'étais aussi joyeux, restant dans ma
chambre à Paris, que si j'avais été sur le point de partir en promenade du côté de Méséglise
ou de retrouver Saint-Loup et ses amis faisant du service en campagne." Marcel Proust, À
la recherche du temps perdu, ed. Jean-Yves Tadié et al. (Paris: Gallimard, 1987–89), 3:536.
Henceforth I cite the Moncrieff-Kilmartin-Enright translation parenthetically in the text,
with the original in the four-volume Pléiade edition in the notes; or I simply give the page
numbers for both the translation and the original, in that order, parenthetically in the text.
Occasionally—where noted—I have modified the translation to reflect the French more
literally.

that Proust's art and his artist aspire to be. Even Proust's other servant characters, in their conventionality and anachronism, reproduce this dynamic of Françoise in little; what I said above about the aesthetic and anachronistic quality of domestic service at the end of the nineteenth century applies a fortiori to Proust, writing in the first decades of the twentieth.

Service in this period, as I argued with respect to England, is a meeting place of aesthetic concerns and class-bound labor relations. Céleste Albaret's memoir *Monsieur Proust* testifies to this meeting in real life: Albaret, Proust's live-in housekeeper for the last eight years of his life, describes herself as having been totally absorbed into an existence whose sole function was the production of the *Recherche*. Proust's gossipy talks with her were really, she says, dry runs for the novel.[75] Albaret, perhaps influenced by her knowledge of Proust's novel, recurs to the metaphor of the "magic circle" to describe her experience of sharing Proust's life (117, 324).[76] "I not only lived in the same rhythm as he did," she says, "but ... I lived entirely for him" (45).[77] And, she insists, Proust lived only for his book. "To find material for his book," she writes, "he would have done anything. That was what kept him going" (66); elsewhere she asserts that "what interested him in people ... was the material they might provide for his book" (239).[78] In fact, Albaret is as staunch a defender of art's autonomy, the separation between fiction and life, as anyone: "To think M. Proust's books are a factual account of his life is to give little credit to his imagination" (86).[79] Yet she testifies, hyperbolically, to the incorporation of her life into Proust's art; even as her memoir gives poignant

75. Céleste Albaret, *Monsieur Proust*, as told to Georges Belmont, trans. Barbara Bray (New York: New York Review Books, 2003), 118. Céleste Albaret, *Monsieur Proust*, souvenirs recueillis par Georges Belmont (Paris: Robert Laffont, 1973), 150. Henceforth I cite the translation parenthetically in the text, with the French original in the notes.

76. "Le cercle enchanté." *Monsieur Proust*, 149, 389.

77. "Et non seulement je vivais à son rythme, mais on peut dire que ... je ne vivais que pour lui." *Monsieur Proust*, 64.

78. "Pour aller chercher la provende de son livre, il aurait fait n'importe quoi. Cela le portait"; "Ce qui l'intéressait chez les gens ... c'est l'analyse de ce qu'ils pouvaient représenter pour son livre." *Monsieur Proust*, 89, 285.

79. "Mais aller croire que ses livres sont le récit réel de la vie de M. Proust, c'est vraiment faire peu de cas de son imagination." *Monsieur Proust*, 112. A similar protest appears in the 1965 memoirs of Ernest A. Fossgren, a Swede who was briefly in Proust's service. Reacting in hostility to the second volume of George Painter's biography of Proust, Fossgren wrote that Painter had no facts but merely "changed, rehashed and rephrased" Proust's novel into a biography. *The Memoirs of Ernest A. Fossgren: Proust's Swedish Valet*, ed. William C. Carter (New Haven, CT: Yale University Press, 2006), 140. On the other hand, the editor of Fossgren's memoir doubts its own reliability.

evidence of her reverent love for him, it also makes clear the total submission to his rule and his life under which she lived.

The dynamic by which service both supports the aesthetic endeavor and undermines its purity and isolation plays a prominent part in the most intense recollective sequence of the novel. When Marcel enters the matinée of the Princesse de Guermantes in *Le Temps retrouvé*, he is thinking regretfully that he must give up his hopes of being a writer. In the courtyard of the Hôtel de Guermantes, the shout of a chauffeur causes him to leap out of the way of a car—and, regaining his balance, he suddenly recalls the uneven paving stones of Venice with the same joy as he has had in the book's most iconically epiphanic moments (6:216; 4:445). Then another servant, meeting Marcel as he enters the hôtel, sends him into the library to prevent him from interrupting a musical performance, displacing the future writer from the social scene, where he would find distraction in idle pleasure (6:218; 4:446). Yet again, in the "second intimation [*second avertissement*]" of involuntary memory in the library, a domestic, attempting but failing to efface himself completely, knocks a spoon against a plate, causing Marcel to recall vividly the sound of a workman adjusting a train wheel and the sight of trees with which it was associated (6:218–19; 4:446–47). The servants, producing all the contingencies of Marcel's revelations, act as time's messengers: they operate as part of the mechanism of the artwork.

It becomes clear that a logic of form governs the servants' presence as Marcel has the crucial third vision in the series:

> And then one would have said that the signs which were, on that day, to pull me out of my discouragement and restore to me my faith in literature intended to multiply, for, a butler who had been for a long time in the service of the Prince de Guermantes having recognised me and brought to me in the library where I was waiting, so that I might not have to go to the buffet, a selection of petits fours and a glass of orangeade, I wiped my mouth with the napkin which he had given me; and instantly, as though I had been the character in the *Arabian Nights* who unwittingly accomplishes the very rite which can cause to appear, visible to him alone, a docile genie ready to convey him to a great distance, a new vision of azure passed before my eyes, but an azure that this time was pure and saline and swelled into blue and bosomy undulations, and so strong was this impression that the moment to which I was transported seemed to me to be the present moment: more bemused than on the day when I had wondered whether I was really going to be received by the Princesse de Guermantes or whether everything round me

would not collapse, I thought that the servant had just opened the window on to the beach and that all things invited me to go down and stroll along the promenade while the tide was high, for the napkin which I had used to wipe my mouth had precisely the same degree of stiffness and starchedness as the towel with which I had found it so awkward to dry my face as I stood in front of the window on the first day of my arrival at Balbec.[80] (6:219; translation modified)

Although the narrator locates agency in the whim of what "the signs … intended," it is clear enough that the long-serving butler, whose recognition of him anticipates Marcel's own memorial recognition, presides over this climactic revelation of the redemptive promise of literature. In the fanciful analogy to the *Arabian Nights*, the "docile genie" is hard to place: if the napkin is the magic lamp, what really "transports" Marcel? His senses? His mind? Fate? Of course, the docile genie has an all too obvious analogue in the servant, a connection further reinforced by the pun on *servir*, "serve," lying hidden in the derivation of the word *serviette*, "napkin." For the butler, agent of the fortuitous appearance of the magical napkin, serves the requirements of plot and of the "faith in literature"—as the narrator makes clear with his coy "one would have said [*on eût dit*]." So, too, the chauffeur in the courtyard and the servant with the spoon, as agents of contingent yet crucial events, act on behalf of narrative itself, upholding Proust's literary-aesthetic order.

Proust's use of servants therefore renders them integral to the aesthetics of the novel's theory of time. Proustian involuntary memory is, at the very least, a plot device, a special subset of recurrent motifs; every revelation Marcel has linking two instants in the novel validates the perception that it possesses structure, that its

---

80. "Alors on eût dit que les signes qui devaient, ce jour-là, me tirer de mon décourage-ment et me rendre la foi dans les lettres, avaient à cœur de se multiplier, car, un maître d'hôtel depuis longtemps au service du prince de Guermantes m'ayant reconnu et m'ayant apporté dans la bibliothèque où j'étais, pour m'éviter d'aller au buffet, un choix de petits fours, un verre d'orangeade, je m'essuyai la bouche avec la serviette qu'il m'avait donnée; mais aussitôt, comme le personnage des *Mille et une Nuits* qui sans le savoir accomplissait précisément le rite qui faisait apparaître, visible pour lui seul, un docile génie prêt à le transporter au loin, une nouvelle vision d'azur passa devant mes yeux; mais il était pur et salin, il se gonfla en mamelles bleuâtres; l'impression fut si forte que le moment que je vivais me sembla être le moment actuel; plus hébété que le jour où je me demandais si j'allais vraiment être accueilli par la princesse de Guermantes ou si tout n'allait pas s'effondrer, je croyais que le domes-tique venait d'ouvrir la fenêtre sur la plage et que tout m'invitait à descendre me promener le long de la digue à marée haute; la serviette que j'avais prise pour m'essuyer la bouche avait précisément le genre de raideur et d'empesé de celle avec laquelle j'avais eu tant de peine à me sécher devant la fenêtre, le premier jour de mon arrivée à Balbec." *Recherche*, 4:447.

episodes are arranged according to a formal law that transcends the mere recording of personal impressions or a contingent historical moment. The servant's function as a nexus of plot and time can be seen in miniature in the description of the butler as "for a long time in the service [*depuis longtemps au service*] of the Prince de Guermantes": *longtemps* simultaneously gives an incidental explanation (why this servant remembers the long-reclusive Marcel) and echoes back to the opening word of the *Recherche* ("*Longtemps, je me suis couché de bonne heure*"), reduplicating the circular form created by Marcel's memories. Just when they are needed, servants appear to shore up the architecture of the narrative; they already stand halfway outside of time, leading the artwork's way to transcendence. The ready availability of servants stems from their lack of social mobility; the Prince de Guermantes's butler has been in the same job, and the same class position, for decades. He does not participate in one of the novel's principal signs of the progression of time, the social ascents and descents experienced by the bourgeois and aristocratic characters. This fixity—however plausible or implausible in terms of real social life—makes the servant available as a link across time and across narrative.[81]

A sense of unease often accompanies the service that domestics perform for the novel's aesthetic construction. At the very end of *Le Temps retrouvé*, Marcel plans to write his novel with the help of Françoise. Thinking of his old nurse's skill at patching, he imagines that she can help him put together what she calls his "paperoles":

> These "paperies [*paperoles*]," as Françoise called the pages of my writing, it was my habit to stick together with paste, and sometimes in this process they became torn. If necessary, couldn't Françoise help me to consolidate them just as she stitched patches on to the worn parts of her dresses or as, on the kitchen window, while waiting for the glazier as I was waiting for the printer, she used to paste a piece of newspaper where a pane of glass had been broken?[82] (6:433; translation modified)

---

81. Not coincidentally, the novel's one example of a link between the servant classes and social ascent breaks the fictional frame. Françoise's heroic cousins, the Larivières, who, though they are millionaires, go back to work to save their nephew's widow, receive the tribute of being named as the only nonfictional people in the book, "real people, who exist [*des gens réels, qui existent*]" (6:191; 4:424).

82. "À force de coller les uns aux autres de ces papiers que Françoise appelait mes paperoles, ils se déchiraient çà et là. Au besoin Françoise ne pourrait-elle pas m'aider à les consolider, de la même façon qu'elle mettait des pièces aux parties usées de ses robes, ou

A tone of pleading doubt invades the rhetorical question in which the speaker here imagines Françoise repairing the unity of his work. Despite the power of the analogy of her work to his, which functions on two levels—the papers are literally to be glued together, but the work of the Proustian writer also requires interconnection and superposition, "stick[ing] together" the fragments of experience—the disturbing fact is that Françoise is uneducated as well as debilitated by age and therefore unsuitable for the job of literary amanuensis. The narrator attempts to convert a metaphor in which Françoise's work is shown to resemble Marcel's into a vision in which Françoise can actually render material aid to the latter's task. He wants to work "in a way almost as she worked herself," but he must regretfully qualify the wish in a parenthesis: "(or at least as she had worked in the past, for now, with the onset of old age, she had almost lost her sight)" (6:432–33).[83] He has a powerful need for the fantasy of his old servant's help.

Céleste Albaret says that she invented the system of gluing in extra patches to Proust's real-life notebooks. Unlike Françoise, Albaret was a young woman at the time, more than twenty years Proust's junior.[84] This difference between the biography and the novel throws into relief the importance, and the complicating effect, of Françoise's capacity to transcend time. It is not a question of a minor logical inconsistency; Proust could not have introduced a new, youthful, secretarial housekeeper here without spoiling the powerful closural effect of having the same woman who acted as the nurse of the boy of "Combray" help the narrator of *Le Temps retrouvé* give final form to the work which has emerged from the narration of those very childhood experiences. Yet the fear of making writing depend on the servant has been present from the start, as well: in the drama of the mother's bedtime kiss in *Du côté de chez Swann*, the child Marcel wants to send a note to his mother, but "My fear was that Françoise ... might refuse to take my note [*porter mon mot*]" (1:31; 1:28). This terror, that the servant will somehow not be there to *porter le mot* or "bear the word" of the writer, emerges once more to haunt even the narrator's last peroration. The integrity and the unity of the novel are made to depend on the servant performing a task of which she is well nigh incapable.

---

qu'à la fenêtre de la cuisine, en attendant le vitrier comme moi l'imprimeur, elle collait un morceau de journal à la place d'un carreau cassé?" *Recherche*, 4:611.

83. "Comme elle (du moins comme elle faisait autrefois: si vieille maintenant, elle n'y voyait plus goutte)." *Recherche*, 4:610–11.

84. Albaret herself narrates the invention of what she calls "paste-ons [*béquets*]," which she distinguishes from the pasted-together loose pages called *paperoles*: see *Monsieur Proust*, 273–77 (translation); *Monsieur Proust*, 325–28 (original). On the "*paperoles*," see Tadié, *Marcel Proust*, 534.

Françoise's unsuitability—or rather, the impropriety of the task the narrator devises for her—threatens to put the novel's formal procedures in jeopardy. This becomes apparent in the narrator's next theoretical statement:

> And yet as in a book individual characters, whether human or of some other kind, are made up of numerous impressions derived from many girls, many churches, many sonatas, and combined to form a single sonata, a single church, a single girl, should I not make my book in the same way that Françoise made that *bœuf à la mode* which M. de Norpois had found so delicious, just because she had enriched its jelly with so many carefully chosen pieces of meat?[85] (6:434; translation modified)

Not only the device of the rhetorical question but also the snobbish validation of Françoise's culinary artistry by recalling the appreciation of the Marquis de Norpois index the class-based worries that underlie this apparently climactic, celebratory passage. Those worries are all the more troublesome because the metaphor of the jelly describes the interaction between the artist's craft and his social existence, the way he brings the material of experience under aesthetic control: is that mode of control really analogous to the work of a household cook, whose talents serve her bourgeois masters in their attempts to impress an aristocratic guest? Is the work really comparable to the food, which is eaten once, digested, and then gone forever? Françoise's kitchen labors furnish an image of dependence and transience, not of the autonomy and the transcendence of time toward which the narrator's theories seem to point.[86]

The reference to Françoise's *bœuf à la gelée* is also another example of the servant's strange kinship to recollection, however, and to this extent Françoise *does* stand for permanence as well as ephemerality. The reference to the specific aspic

---

85. "D'ailleurs, comme les individualités (humaines ou non) sont dans un livre faites d'impressions nombreuses qui, prises de bien des jeunes filles, de bien des églises, de bien des sonates, servent à faire une seule sonate, une seule église, une seule jeune fille, ne ferais-je pas mon livre de la façon que Françoise faisait ce bœuf mode, apprécié par M. de Norpois, et dont tant de morceaux de viande ajoutés et choisis enrichissaient la gelée?" *Recherche*, 4:612.

86. Leo Bersani comments on a further troubling aspect of the passage, which threatens to destabilize the artwork as a whole: "This statement has peculiar consequences for our retrospective sense of Marcel's relationship to the other characters: his very uncertainties about some of them seem somewhat unconvincing, since, it turns out, they are his novelistic creations . . . . The novel we have been reading is a novel written by a character whose 'real' life . . . exists only by implication." *Marcel Proust: The Fictions of Life and Art* (New York: Oxford University Press, 1965), 195.

enjoyed by M. de Norpois sends readers all the way back to *À l'ombre des jeunes filles en fleurs* and Marcel's childhood in Paris. That episode emphasizes not the endurance of the artwork once it has been created but the joy of the artist in her work:

> And ever since the day before, Françoise, rejoicing in the opportunity to devote herself to that art of cooking at which she was so gifted, stimulated, moreover, by the prospect of a new guest, and knowing that she would have to compose, by methods known to her alone, a dish of *bœuf à la gelée*, had been living in the effervescence of creation; since she attached the utmost importance to the intrinsic quality of the materials which were to enter into the fabric of her work, she had gone herself to the Halles to procure the best cuts of rump-steak, shin of beef, calves'-feet, just as Michelangelo spent eight months in the mountains of Carrara choosing the most perfect blocks of marble for the monument of Julius II. Françoise expended on these comings and goings so much ardour that Mamma, at the sight of her flaming cheeks, was alarmed lest our old servant should fall ill from overwork, like the sculptor of the Tombs of the Medici in the quarries of Pietrasanta.[87] (2:18)

Certainly the comparison of a cook picking out rumpsteak to a sculptor selecting marble belongs to the mock-epic, yet in the expansiveness of Proustian syntax, Françoise's artistic elation takes on reality, acquiring sufficient complexity and scale to compare to the exuberance of Michelangelo. It is perhaps the artist's patrons who come off worst in the analogy—for modern readers, Michelangelo's greatness far outshines that of Pope Julius II or even the Medicis, despite the fact that they were rulers of their society. The passage implies that gifted artists may work on commission without betraying their greatness, provided that they, like Françoise and Michelangelo, "devote themselves to their art." The

---

87. "Et depuis la veille, Françoise, heureuse de s'adonner à cet art de la cuisine pour lequel elle avait certainement un don, stimulée, d'ailleurs, par l'annonce d'un convive nouveau, et sachant qu'elle aurait à composer, selon des méthodes sues d'elle seule, du bœuf à la gelée, vivait dans l'effervescence de la création; comme elle attachait une importance extrême à la qualité intrinsèque des matériaux qui devaient entrer dans la fabrication de son œuvre, elle allait elle-même aux Halles se faire donner les plus beaux carrés de romsteck, de jarret de bœuf, de pied de veau, comme Michel-Ange passant huit mois dans les montagnes de Carrare à choisir les blocs de marbre les plus parfaits pour le monument de Jules II. Françoise dépensait dans ces allées et venues une telle ardeur que maman voyant sa figure enflammée craignait que notre vieille servante ne tombât malade de surmenage comme l'auteur du Tombeau des Médicis dans les carrières de Pietrasanta." *Recherche*, 1:437.

description of Françoise as "our old servant" demonstrates that she has a kind of immortality within the work—already old and provoking worries about her health, she nonetheless survives to be the object of the narrator's writing fantasies in *Le Temps retrouvé*. Her perfection in her servant's art renders her necessary to the entire narrative.

Françoise's art of cooking, however, draws a particular strain of suffering and violence into the magic circle of narrative form. For the same cook who—as we discover in the second section of "Combray"—infuses for Marcel's invalid great-aunt Léonie the tea in which the time-transcending madeleine is dipped (1:59; 1:50) is also the persecutor of kitchen maids. In the midst of the suffering of the maid called "Giotto's Charity," a digressive paragraph throws the cruelty of Françoise's art into further relief. Marcel watches in horror as Françoise slaughters a chicken with complete brutality, but he is by no means inclined to deprive himself of her artistic labor: "But who would have baked me such hot rolls, made me such fragrant coffee, and even ... roasted me such chickens?" (1:145).[88] The exquisite scent of the "fragrant coffee"—like the scent of the roast flesh of the chicken described just before (1:144; 1:120)—immediately recalls the Proustian magic of asparagus: Marcel imagines that the vegetable's "celestial hues" betray the presence of "exquisite creatures who ... played (lyrical and coarse in their jesting like one of Shakespeare's fairies) at transforming my chamber pot into a vase of aromatic perfume."[89] Yet the spell of art, by which even a chamber pot can become a perfumed vase, depends on a cruelty even greater than the slaughter of chickens:

> Many years later, we discovered that if we had been fed on asparagus day after day throughout that summer, it was because their smell gave the poor kitchen-maid who had to prepare them such violent attacks of asthma that she was finally obliged to leave my aunt's service.[90] (1:147–48).

Of course, the benighted "poor kitchen-maid" is not the only character in the *Recherche* to suffer from crippling respiratory problems. Yet if he resembles the

88. "Mais qui m'eût fait des boules aussi chaudes, du café aussi parfumé, et même ... ces poulets? ..." *Recherche*, 1:120; ellipses in original.

89. "Il me semblait que ces nuances célestes trahissaient les délicieuses créatures ... [qui] jouaient, dans leurs farces poétiques et grossières comme une féerie de Shakespeare, à changer mon pot de chambre en un vase de parfum." *Recherche*, 1:119.

90. "Bien des années plus tard, nous apprîmes que si cet été-là nous avions mangé presque tous les jours des asperges, c'était parce que leur odeur donnait à la pauvre fille de cuisine chargée de les éplucher des crises d'asthme d'une telle violence qu'elle fut obligée de finir par s'en aller." *Recherche*, 1:122.

abused subordinate in his illness, Marcel also, as the narrator will insist, resembles Françoise in his artistry. And just as Marcel reflects both the suffering kitchen maid and the cruel artist of her agonies, so Françoise is both the quintessence of the novel's art, including its defiance of ordinary time, and the opposite of that art, an unsophisticated, unimaginatively toiling avatar of the real. She is therefore doubly, dialectically indispensable to the artist's, and the novel's, existence; she may age, go blind, her "neck bent with fatigue and obedience" (4:155),[91] but unlike the kitchen maid, she must never be driven away, despite the suffering she causes and the resistance she offers. The tortured analogy between Marcel and the servants shows that if the novel's aesthetic forms can incorporate the social truths of service, the ills of servitude will fall on the artistic master.

Those ills surface at one of the novel's affective climaxes, the section about Marcel's grief for his grandmother called "The Intermittencies of the Heart [*Les intermittences du cœur*]." Marcel does not really begin to grieve for his grandmother until Françoise tells him the story of the photograph he has of her. Marcel had mocked his grandmother for her coquetry when the photograph was taken, but, as Françoise reveals, she was in fact in terrible pain at the time and trying to conceal it from her grandson. In a poignant parallel between Marcel and his grandmother, the young man also struggles to hide his pain as recognition and sorrow dawn—to hide it, that is, from the servant. At the same time, Marcel pities Françoise, thinking of "those poor maidservants who cannot bear to see us cry" (4:204).[92] No sooner does the narrator begin to pity such compassionate servants, however, then he reverses direction:

> It is true that those same servants who cannot bear our tears will have no hesitation in letting us catch pneumonia because the maid downstairs likes draughts and it would not be polite to her to shut the windows. For it is necessary that even those who are right, like Françoise, should be wrong also, so that Justice may be made an impossible thing.[93] (4:204)

---

91. "Cou courbé par la fatigue et l'obéissance." *Recherche*, 3:132.

92. "Ces pauvres femmes de chambre qui ne peuvent pas nous voir pleurer." *Recherche*, 3:174.

93. "Certes ces mêmes domestiques qui ne peuvent supporter nos larmes, nous feront prendre sans scrupule une fluxion de poitrine parce que la femme de chambre d'au-dessous aime les courants d'air et que ce ne serait pas poli de les supprimer. Car il faut que ceux-là mêmes qui ont raison, comme Françoise, aient tort aussi, pour faire de la Justice une chose impossible." *Recherche*, 3:174.

Once again, respiratory ailment, the personal demon of Marcel and the biographical Proust alike, appears in conjunction with servitude, rendering the imagined threat posed by those stubborn servants less trivial and more personal to the narrator than it might appear. It is consequential enough, in fact, to make Françoise into an icon of the pure contradiction that renders justice impossible.

As Marcel recognizes, Françoise never stops being his menacing subordinate, even when she becomes his admired or beloved artistic double. The novel's many comic scenes of Françoise's old-fashionedness, stubbornness, and ignorance—and, in a darker tone, the condescending and resentful remarks she endures from Marcel at his worst—indicate that her subordination renders her quite unsuitable as a model for the sort of artist the narrator wishes to become. In reflecting her master, the servant shows the impurity and transience of the artist's work. In disdaining to mystify the conditions of his artistic production, Proust takes stock of the imperfect social relations literature must maintain, even as he celebrates it. As Leo Bersani says in another context, "The very point of Proust's novel would seem to be to destroy the illusions novelists usually seek to cultivate."[94]

This pessimism appears in one of the novel's absurdly humorous versions of the servant's uneasy and intimate connection to Proustian time and Proustian writing:

> But Françoise suffered from one of those peculiar, permanent, incurable defects which we call pathological: she was never able either to read or to express the time correctly .... I was never able to understand whether the phenomenon that occurred was situated in her vision or in her mind or in her speech; the one thing certain is that the phenomenon never failed to occur. Humanity is very old. Heredity and cross-breeding have given insuperable strength to bad habits, faulty reflexes.[95] (5:171; translation modified)

The servant's "pathological [*maladif*]" freedom from time may, says the narrator, be situated in vision, or thought, or language—we could well say the same for the

94. Bersani, *Marcel Proust*, 247. Michael Sprinker, in his Marxian analysis, puts it even more severely: "Proust understood perfectly well [that] someone must ultimately pay the price for the privilege exercised by the ruling classes not to engage in productive labor." *History and Ideology in Proust* (Cambridge: Cambridge University Press, 1994), 185.

95. "C'était chez Françoise un de ces défauts particuliers, permanents, inguérissables, que nous appelons maladifs, de ne pouvoir jamais regarder ni dire l'heure exactement .... Je n'ai jamais pu comprendre si le phénomène qui avait lieu alors avait pour siège la vue de Françoise, ou sa pensée, ou son langage; ce qui est certain, c'est que ce phénomène avait toujours lieu. L'humanité est très vieille. L'hérédité, les croisements ont donné une force insurmontable à de mauvaises habitudes, à des réflexes vicieux." *Recherche*, 3:662.

kind of art described by the narrator of the *Recherche*. But in contemplating this version of an extratemporal artistic sensibility, the narrator feels not triumph and immortality but the terrible weariness of painful human existence, arriving only at the stark realization that "Humanity is very old." The great expanse of time is not only a realm in which the aesthetic can acquire its autonomy, outliving any single human life; it is also a theater for the "insuperable" persistence of bad habits. Proust makes the moving admission that the aesthetic and formal principles that seek to overcome the passage of time are indissolubly linked to human labor and human suffering—his own and that of others. Françoise herself believes that masters and servants will exist "as long as the world goes round" (3:22)[96]; in constructing his monument with her help and on the model of her labor and that of other servants, Proust does not suggest otherwise.

Aestheticist Self-Consciousness

Dorian Gray's opinion is that "the canons of good society, are, or should be, the same as the canons of art. Form is absolutely essential to it" (287). Conversely, aestheticism from Wilde to Proust finds that the forms of art depend on those of social organization. But this is not to say that the pursuit of autonomy is simply Dorian Gray–like hypocrisy, a surface beauty concealing only ugliness and egotistical malice. In the aestheticist and modernist examples I have examined in this chapter, aesthetic form retains its primacy, but it sacrifices abstract, geometric purity, becoming instead the signifier of relations between artists and other people, including the people who work for them. Fictions of autonomy from Villiers onward use domestics to avow this relation rather than hide it.

Simultaneously needed within and excluded from the aesthete's self-enclosure, servants become a crucial element of form. Aestheticizing narratives repeatedly use them at moments of self-reflection, just because they help establish the dominance of form or even, most markedly in the case of Proust, because they offer a counterpart to the writer's own formally creative labors. Certainly, the narratives discussed in this chapter—like almost all the other works discussed in this book—do not forswear class attitudes. They tend to regard servants as vulgar, ignorant workers and to relegate them to minor status or flat characterization to use them as part of an alluring literary construction. Despite the critical and even satiric distance Wilde, Huysmans, James, and Proust establish from their protagonists and their fictions'

---

96. "Tant que le monde sera monde." *Recherche*, 2:327.

upper-crust milieux, their work undoubtedly implicates itself in social hierarchy and its injustices.[97] None of them really hid from this implication, though Wilde is, at least at the moment of his utopian fantasy in "The Soul of Man under Socialism," particularly candid:

> At present, in consequence of the existence of private property, a great many people are enabled to develop a certain very limited amount of Individualism. They are either under no necessity to work for their living, or are enabled to choose the sphere of activity that is really congenial to them and gives them pleasure. These are the poets, the philosophers, the men of science, the men of culture .... Upon the other hand, there are a great many people who, having no private property of their own, and being always on the brink of sheer starvation, are compelled to do the work of beasts of burden, to do work that is quite uncongenial to them, and to which they are forced by the peremptory, unreasonable, degrading Tyranny of want. These are the poor, and amongst them there is no grace of manner, or charm of speech, or civilization, or culture, or refinement in pleasures, or joy of life.[98]

I have been arguing, however, that by using servant characters in *Dorian Gray* and in *An Ideal Husband*, Wilde, like Huysmans in *À rebours*, James in *The Ambassadors*, and Proust in the *Recherche*, goes beyond such an explicit statement, toward the discovery that the cultivation of aesthetic form for its own sake both relies on and reveals this mechanism of subjugation.[99]

Yet Wilde makes clear that he values the individual aesthetic achievement even as he condemns the system in which it is possible for some but not all, and he is

97. William Empson, in his 1935 essay arguing for the impossibility of proletarian literature, makes a similar connection between the aesthetic distance of the writer from his or her society and the bourgeois's melancholy acceptance of social stratification as (supposedly) ineradicable. I suggest that the highly self-conscious formal procedures of writers like Wilde, James, and Proust make manifest this complicity when they confront the figure of the servant. See William Empson, "Proletarian Literature," in *Some Versions of Pastoral*, rev. ed. (New York: New Directions, 1974), 3–23.

98. Wilde, "Soul of Man," 129.

99. Amanda Anderson, in her work on Victorian detachment, has also argued for an ethical significance to Wildean aesthetics; for Anderson, however, Wilde has a "tendency to make interracial or international expansiveness, rather than interclass understanding, the site of ethical development. This allows him to speak disparagingly of philanthropy, reform, and realism, without entirely abandoning the ethical sphere." *The Powers of Distance: Cosmopolitanism and the Cultivation of Detachment* (Princeton, NJ: Princeton University Press, 2001), 151. I argue that on the contrary, the rejection of realism allows Wilde to rethink ethical problems of social class in subtle ways. I return to cosmopolitanism in chapter 3.

hardly inclined to see that system overthrown at any cost to himself. Even the fervor of "The Soul of Man" can envision systemic change only by means of the total mechanization of industrial labor. Servants themselves, of course, are not on the horizon of Wilde's social program at all—but they are, precisely, on the horizon of his fictions. Whether they are Wilde's slyly insubordinate domestics, Villiers's unromantically unsuicidal pages, Huysmans's solitude-shattering servants, James's all-too-conspicuously perfect valets, or Proust's beloved, needed, and implausible Françoise and her ilk, servants challenge the purity of the aesthetic even as they serve it. Still, this does not mean that the pursuit of autonomy is necessarily ideologically blinded or doomed in advance. My analysis rather suggests that we credit the aesthetes, fin-de-siècle and modernist, with an unexpectedly keen insight about their own practice and its social ties. When fictions of autonomy consider domestic labor, they demystify aesthetic form by relating it to a world of work and class division. These versions of autonomy begin to face the social problems formal mastery entails—starting with the problem of holding mastery over other human beings—even if those problems cannot be resolved from within the artwork itself.

2. Autonomy from the Person
Impersonality and Lateness in Eliot and Adorno

Of all the modernist versions of autonomy, none is more personal than lateness. For an artist to attain a liberated, idiosyncratic "late style" seems to require paying the price of bodily aging and psychological alienation from the social present; artists with a late style must *live* autonomy as a personal mood and a personal experience. Yet for Theodor Adorno, the preeminent modernist theorist of the late style, describing that style in terms of the arduous experience of the artist betrays aesthetic autonomy. In his essay "Beethoven's Late Style," written in 1934, Adorno dismisses references to the late Beethoven's biography as a reduction of art to the status of documentation. For Adorno, lateness inheres not in the artist's experience of aging but in aesthetic form—and, he claims, the "formal law [*Formgesetz*]" of late style brings about the *evacuation* of the personal, of biographical experience, from the late work.[1] The autonomy of lateness is not a merely subjective freedom of untrammeled personal expression. Rather, late style is an *objective* liberation, through form, from the limitations imposed by biographical contingency.

Adorno's description of lateness as a version of the dominance of form converges with an iconic modernist theory of autonomy in poetry: T. S. Eliot's "Impersonal" aesthetic. "Tradition and the Individual Talent" (1919) made that

---

1. Theodor W. Adorno, "Beethoven's Late Style," in *Beethoven: The Philosophy of Music*, ed. Rolf Tiedemann, trans. Edmund Jephcott (Stanford, CA: Stanford University Press, 1998), 123. Henceforth cited as "BLS" in the text. Theodor W. Adorno, "Spät-stil Beethovens," in *Beethoven: Philosophie der Musik*, ed. Rolf Tiedemann (Frankfurt: Suhrkamp, 1993), 180. Henceforth cited as "SB" in the notes.

aesthetic famous: "Poetry is not a turning loose of emotion, but an escape from emotion; it is not the expression of personality, but an escape from personality."[2] Poetry is free, an "escape," only insofar as it refuses to express personality. Eliot's poetic practice, however, expresses one aspect of personal existence over and over again: a fatigued sense of age. The Eliotic point of view, whether named (Prufrock, Gerontion, Tiresias) or anonymous (*Four Quartets*), strains for the freedoms of disembodiment, but always in an atmosphere of lateness, overburdened with a long past whose weight is a physical sensation. Eliot shares with Adorno not just the goal of an impersonally autonomous, nonsubjective aesthetic but the specific and paradoxically biographical election of late style as the route to objectivity.

Late style in the manner of Eliot and Adorno is, like the aestheticist use of domestic servants, powerfully shaped by a preoccupation with the autonomy of the aesthetic. This preoccupation unites the two writers as modernists; the émigré German philosopher-critic and the émigré American poet-critic both envision lateness not as a mere reflection in art of the process of aging but as an independent property of a putatively self-governing artistic work. Yet just as the most fervent aesthetes may, as we saw in the last chapter, discover that their celebrations of the "dominance of form" necessarily include the ordinary labor of their servants, so too, late style takes a dialectical turn back toward the constraints of personal existence from which it strives to be autonomous. Eliot and Adorno seek to convert facts of personal life into a position within the artistic field—the position of pure, impersonal, autonomous art. But that conversion leaves traces within Eliot's and Adorno's handling of impersonality; their fiction of autonomy from the person is not simply an abstract doctrine but a practice that gestures toward the aged artistic personality even as it endeavors to detach the work from its creator.

Though the conjunction of Eliot and Adorno may seem improbable, each illuminates the other. Eliot's criticism helps us see how Adorno's musical and aesthetic theories strive for autonomy from personality in particular; Adorno's concept of late style brings out the dialectical relationship between impersonality and aging in Eliot's poetry as it unfolds in forms and themes—a relationship that neither Eliot's New Critical advocates nor more recent scholars have fully recognized. But the comparison also advances my general claim about aesthetic autonomy in this period. Indeed, the apparent remoteness of Eliot and Adorno from one another suggests the hypothesis that where they find common ground,

2. T. S. Eliot, "Tradition and the Individual Talent," in *The Sacred Wood: Essays on Poetry and Criticism*, 7th ed. (London: Methuen, 1950), 58. Henceforth cited as "Tradition" in the text.

shared large-scale cultural forces are at work.[3] I propose aesthetic autonomization itself, considered as a social process operating across the field of international literature in the modernist period, as an explanation for the resonances between these two writers. But I argue that impersonality, like the Proustian magic circle, was something more complex, and less dishonest, than a comprehensive denial of the artwork's conditions of production. The late stylist's relation to personality models autonomy as a way of incompletely transforming constraints into freedoms, while signaling those freedoms' relative, partial quality. Advocates for and observers of art's relative autonomy, Adorno and Eliot both use lateness as a key figure for this flexible, contradictory, contextually sensitive understanding of the aesthetic.

Adorno's Theory of Impersonality

It may seem far-fetched to link Adorno's musical writings with Eliot's poetics. Even given that the two shared certain modernist premises, why not turn to Adorno's own writings on poetry and literature in general? One reason, which I develop in the last section of this chapter, is that Adorno's ideas on music can shed light on Eliot's treatment of music, including Beethoven's music, in his criticism and poetry. But musical themes furnish only a particular example of a more general pattern: the recurrent pairing of lateness and impersonal aesthetics. Adorno works out his theory of lateness most fully for Beethoven, but he extends it to all the arts, including literature. By pursuing the affinities between Eliot's impersonality theory and Adorno's late style, we can see them developing an aesthetics quite unlike the theories conventionally attributed to either. Adorno's late stylistics, like Eliot's, turn on a contradictory fascination with and rejection of personality and subjective expression.

Adorno's essays on poetry have been most valued in literary studies for their connections between lyric and society and their emphatic defense of the politics implicit in lyric aesthetics, but we can see Adorno's commitment to an impersonal aesthetic even in his radio address "On Lyric Poetry and Society." In this text, Adorno declares that the substance of a poem "is not merely an expression of individual impulses and experiences. Those become a matter of art only when

---

they come to participate in something universal by virtue of the specificity they acquire in being given aesthetic form."[4] The heart of his theory is that in lyric "language itself acquires a voice," and language is inescapably social.[5] But this ventriloquism is possible only because the poet's personality has etherialized itself. It leaves "no remaining trace of mere matter"[6] ; Adorno's phrase recalls Eliot's image of the poet's mind as a platinum catalyst in "Tradition and the Individual Talent," which leaves no trace in the reaction product. Despite Adorno's apparent emphasis on lyric's relation to society, depersonalization is logically prior to the social and critical aspects of aesthetic autonomy in his theory.

Indeed, Adorno had already worked out a theory of depersonalization in "Beethoven's Late Style." For him, the particular form of autonomy made possible by the end of life is autonomy from the person. Despite the manifest reference to the personal mortality of the artist, late style does not simply represent the dying man's experience. In his essay, Adorno denounces such a biographical interpretation:

> The accepted explanation is that they [late works] are products of a subjectivity or, still better, of a "personality" ruthlessly proclaiming itself, which breaks through the roundedness of form for the sake of expression, exchanging harmony for the dissonance of its sorrow and spurning sensuous charm under the dictates of the imperiously emancipated mind. The late work is thereby relegated to the margins of art and brought closer to documentation. Accordingly, references to Beethoven's biography and fate are seldom absent from discussions of his last works.[7] ("BLS," 123)

---

4. Theodor W. Adorno, "On Lyric Poetry and Society," in *Notes to Literature*, ed. Rolf Tiedemann, trans. Shierry Weber Nicholsen (New York: Columbia University Press, 1991), 1:38. Henceforth cited as "Lyric Poetry." "Denn der Gehalt eines Gedichts ist nicht bloß der Ausdruck individueller Regungen und Erfahrungen. Sondern diese werden überhaupt erst dann künstlerisch, wenn sie, gerade vermöge der Spezifikation ihres ästhetischen Geformtseins, Anteil am Allgemeinen gewinnen." Theodor W. Adorno, "Rede über Lyrik und Gesellschaft," in *Noten zur Literatur*, ed. Rolf Tiedemann (Frankfurt: Suhrkamp, 1974), 50. Henceforth cited as "Lyrik und Gesellschaft."

5. "Lyric Poetry," 1:43. "Die Sprache selber [wird] laut." "Lyrik und Gesellschaft," 56.

6. "Lyric Poetry," 1:43. "Ohne Rest von bloßem Stoff." "Lyrik und Gesellschaft," 56.

7. "Die übliche Ansicht pflegt das damit zu erklären, daß sie Produkte der rücksichtslos sich bekundenden Subjektivität oder lieber noch 'Persönlichkeit' seien, die da um des Ausdrucks ihrer selbst willen das Rund der Form durchbreche, die Harmonie wende zur Dissonanz ihres Leidens, den sinnlichen Reiz verschmähe kraft der Selbstherrlichkeit freigesetzten Geistes. Damit wird das Spätwerk an den Rand von Kunst verwiesen und dem

Adorno treats biographical explanation, with its underlying idea of art as the expression of personality, as a threat to the late work's status as art. In "the field of documentation," Adorno continues scornfully, "any recorded conversation of Beethoven carries more weight than the C♯ minor String Quartet" ("BLS," 123–24). [8] For Adorno, to dwell on the artist's emotion and his aging is to slight the aesthetic qualities of art in favor of the trivialities of "documentation." He prefers to emphasize what he calls the "formal law" of Beethoven's late works, which is such that it "cannot be subsumed under the heading of 'expression'" (123). [9] Lateness inheres, paradoxically, not in its relation to the end of life but in the very absence of any direct expression of the artist's mortality.

In this treatment of personality in art, Adorno could almost be echoing the Eliot of "Tradition and the Individual Talent." In that essay, Eliot, too, had disdained the expression of personality: "The bad poet is usually unconscious where he ought to be conscious, and conscious where he ought to be unconscious. Both errors tend to make him 'personal'" ("Tradition," 58). More surprisingly, Eliot makes the connection to aging: "The mind of the mature poet differs from that of the immature one not precisely in any valuation of 'personality,' not being necessarily more interesting, or having 'more to say,' but rather by being a more finely perfected medium in which special, or very varied, feelings are at liberty to enter into new combinations" (53–54). Indeed, the "most individual parts" of a poet's work in "the period of full maturity" are those in which that poet has given himself fully over to the tradition, that "ideal order" of artistic monuments looming over every artistic work (48, 50). The hubris of the thirty-year-old Eliot, with two slim volumes of poetry to his name, setting out to define "full maturity" makes his own sense of advanced age—and his sense of belatedness with respect to the history of poetry—integral to his rejection of personality. His defense of art as an "ideal order" shows that Eliot, too, advocates art's autonomy by defending it from personality. [10]

Dokument angenähert; tatsächlich pflegt denn auch bei Erörterungen über den letzten Beethoven der Hinweis auf Biographie und Schicksal selten zu fehlen." "SB," 180.

8. "Die Grenzlinie zum Dokument," within which "jedes Konversationsheft Beethovens mehr zu bedeuten hätte als das cis-moll-Quartett." "SB," 180.

9. "Das Formgesetz der Spätwerke ist aber jedenfalls von der Art, daß sie nicht im Begriff des Ausdrucks aufgehen." "SB," 180.

10. "Tradition and the Individual Talent" is not Eliot's most explicit defense of art's autonomy. In a 1923 essay in the Criterion he wrote, simply: "I have assumed as axiomatic that a creation, a work of art, is autonomous." T. S. Eliot, "The Function of Criticism," Criterion 2, no. 5 (October 1923): 38. Reprinting the essay nine years later, he changed "autonomous" to "autotelic." "The Function of Criticism," in Selected Essays, 1917–1932

Using the ripeness of age to repudiate personality leaves an opening, however, through which personality can return. Eliot attributes affect to the work even though the poet's personality has supposedly been driven out:

> There are many people who appreciate the expression of sincere emotion in verse, and there is a smaller number of people who can appreciate technical excellence. But very few people know when there is expression of *significant* emotion, emotion which has its life in the poem and not in the history of the poet. The emotion of art is impersonal. And the poet cannot reach this impersonality without surrendering himself wholly to the work to be done. ("Tradition," 59)

This peroration to "Tradition and the Individual Talent" draws attention back to the poet's disciplined "surrender" even as it claims that emotion is not personal. A parallel rhetoric governs the near juxtaposition of the ideal of the professional poet, "surrendering himself wholly to the work to be done," and the idea of an elite "very few" who, synthesizing an awareness of "emotional" content and "technical" form, apprehend the impersonal significance of poetry. Impersonality, like tradition itself, can only be obtained "by great labour" in Eliot (49): poetry is a "*métier*" (52), demanding a "process of depersonalization" in which "art may be said to approach the condition of science" (53). Eliot's poetic professional imbues his works with his own self-effacement. As his famous rider says: "Of course, only those who have personality and emotions know what it means to want to escape from these things" (58). The author is not so easily killed off: both the production and the reading of the poem remain subjective, personal experiences—experiences precisely of the withering of personality. This remainder of experience points back to the self-discipline of the would-be professional, "scientific" poet and to his intensely personal efforts to produce an impersonally autonomous work.[11] Or, in

---

(New York: Harcourt, Brace, 1932), 19. For my purposes, it is enough to recall that in his early career as a critic Eliot acted, in general, as an advocate of aesthetic autonomy.

11. The paradoxically personal quality of Eliot's ideal of impersonality has been noticed by many scholars of Eliotic professionalism. See in particular Louis Menand, "Literature and Professionalism," pt. 2, chap. 5 in *Discovering Modernism: T. S. Eliot and His Context*, 2nd ed. (Oxford: Oxford University Press, 2007); Langdon Hammer, "Towards the Institute of Literary Autonomy and Tradition," chap. 1 in *Hart Crane and Allen Tate: Janus-Faced Modernism* (Princeton, NJ: Princeton University Press, 1993); Gail McDonald, *Learning to Be Modern: Pound, Eliot, and the American University* (Oxford: Clarendon, 1993); and, in a more negative vein, Jonathan Freedman, *Professions of Taste: Henry James, British Aestheticism, and Commodity Culture* (Stanford, CA: Stanford University Press, 1990).

a more graphic formulation from Eliot's *The Use of Poetry and the Use of Criticism*, the poet turns "blood into ink."[12]

Adorno carries out the same dialectical reversal—and uses equally physical, deathly imagery. Personality returns as the negative image of the process of impersonalization in the late artwork:

> The force of subjectivity in late works is the irascible gesture with which it leaves them. It bursts them asunder, not in order to express itself but, expressionlessly, to cast off the illusion of art. Of the works it leaves only fragments behind, communicating itself, as if in ciphers, only through the spaces it has violently vacated. Touched by death, the masterly hand sets free the matter it previously formed. The fissures and rifts within it, bearing witness to the ego's finite impotence before Being, are its last work.[13] ("BLS," 125)

Despite the denial of expression, Adorno's description of the "formal law" of late work is saturated with personal specificity: the "irascible gesture" of impersonalization does violence to the work; the forming hand is "masterly." These attitudes cohabit awkwardly with Adorno's formal rules in his norm of late style. This contradiction is the true content of Adorno's ideal of impersonality: the only personality that matters in late work is an *ascetic* personality striving to erase itself and leave an autonomous artwork behind. It is hardly an accident if this elimination of personality occurs under the sign of impending death. In his Beethoven notebooks, Adorno wrote: "The late style is the self-awareness of the insignificance of the individual, existent. Herein lies the relationship of the late style to *death*."[14] For Adorno, the "ego's finite impotence" provides an opportunity for the work to divest itself of contingent individuality, as though the work were itself the death of the author. Or, as Eliot says in a later essay, remarking on "the final handing over . . . of the poem

---

12. T. S. Eliot, *The Use of Poetry and the Use of Criticism* (London: Faber and Faber, 1933), 154.

13. "Die Gewalt der Subjektivität in den späten Kunstwerken ist die auffahrende Geste, mit welcher sie die Kunstwerke verläßt. Sie sprengt sie, nicht um sich auszudrücken, sondern um ausdruckslos den Schein der Kunst abzuwerfen. Von den Werken läßt sie Trümmer zurück und teilt sich, wie mit Chiffren, nur vermöge der Hohlstellen mit, aus welchen sie ausbricht. Vom Tode berührt, gibt die meisterliche Hand die Stoffmassen frei, die sie zuvor formte; die Risse und Sprünge darin, Zeugnis der endlichen Ohnmacht des Ichs vorm Seienden, sind ihr letztes Werk." "SB," 183.

14. *Beethoven*, 161 (emphasis in original). "Der Spätstil ist das Selbstbewußtsein von der Nichtigkeit des Individuellen, Daseienden. Darin beruht das Verhältnis des Spätstils zum Tode." *Beethoven: Philosophie der Musik*, 233.

to an unknown audience": "Let the author, at this point, rest in peace."[15] Nonetheless, the shade of the artist haunts both writers' descriptions of the emergence of an impersonal style from personal mortality.

Edward Said points to this turn back to personality in the course of his analysis of Adorno's lateness as a theoretical, critical stance.[16] Said emphasizes the resemblances between Adorno's late style and Adorno himself: "Lateness is being at the end, fully conscious, full of memory, and also very (even preternaturally) aware of the present. Adorno, like Beethoven, becomes therefore a figure of lateness itself, an untimely, scandalous, even catastrophic commentator on the present."[17] Drawing on the charismatic critical power of the figure of the late artist, Said defends the difficulty of late style as a sign of alienation and a critique of its contemporary culture. Beethoven's last works, he asserts, constitute "a form of exile."[18] To the last phase of Beethoven's work he attributes all the social and political significance of exile—exile like Adorno's, or Cavafy's (whom he discusses elsewhere in *On Late Style*), or Said's own. That significance depends, paradoxically, both on the autonomy afforded by impersonality and on the highly particular attitudes of the alienated late-style artist.[19]

The situation of "Beethoven's Late Style" within the history of Beethoven reception helps to make clear why that essay embraces the paradox of lateness as impersonality. In his book *Beethoven in German Politics*, David Dennis has shown the persistent symbolic importance of Beethoven to political debates in Germany in the nineteenth and twentieth centuries.[20] Dennis documents the ways every political tendency—conservative, centrist, and radical—sought to appropriate Beethoven for its own purposes; Adorno's own time saw a symbolic struggle in Germany to make Beethoven communist, moderate, or National Socialist. Adorno's critical emphases are at odds with all these tendencies. German political interpretations of Beethoven turned on his "heroic" or middle period; Adorno

15. T. S. Eliot, "The Three Voices of Poetry," in *On Poetry and Poets* (New York: Farrar, Straus and Cudahy, 1957), 109.

16. Edward W. Said, *On Late Style: Music and Literature Against the Grain* (New York: Pantheon, 2006). Said has been most responsible for bringing Adorno's idea of late style to the attention of scholars outside musicology, and Said's writings on late style have greatly influenced the present discussion.

17. Ibid., 13.

18. Ibid., 7–8.

19. I treat the relationship between exile and autonomy, including Said's reflections on that relationship, at length in chapter 3.

20. David B. Dennis, *Beethoven in German Politics, 1870–1989* (New Haven, CT: Yale University Press, 1996).

dwells on the late period. The popular Beethoven was the Beethoven of the symphonies; Adorno puts the last quartets and piano sonatas at the core of his late-period canon, works that Dennis sees playing a far smaller role in the politicization of Beethoven.[21]

Most significantly, Dennis observes, "Within this cacophony of voices, one generalization seems to hold true: in the minds of German politicians, the sound of Beethoven's music is inextricably entwined with his biography .... Most sources in this context refer to his works not as inspirational in and of themselves, but as triggers of thoughts about the life led by their creator."[22] The impersonality of Adorno's treatment of Beethoven evades this tradition while attempting to conserve the idea of Beethoven's extramusical significance. By the same token, Adorno diverges from the scholarly readings of Beethoven then gaining currency, which rejected the "Romantic picture of Beethoven" and often linked this reemergent "classical" Beethoven to the results of new formalist techniques of analysis (as in the pioneering work of the music theorist Heinrich Schenker).[23] Adorno appropriates the scholarly rhetoric of formalism in his celebration of the late period's "formal law," but, underscoring Beethoven's formal "fissures," he makes Beethoven an immanent critic rather than a cheerful adherent of classicism.[24] Furthermore, Adorno imagines that he can rederive Beethoven's power as a political symbol from that formal law. The derivation, however, dependent as it is on the powerful idea of lateness, surreptitiously brings back into the model the biography so important to German political culture.

Adorno's Beethoven takes on relevance in the early twentieth century for reasons beyond this significance in political culture. The theory of Beethoven's late style dovetails with the larger concerns of Adorno's work on modernist art. Late

---

21. Dennis, *Beethoven in German Politics*, 20. See also Scott Burnham, *Beethoven Hero* (Princeton, NJ: Princeton University Press, 1995).

22. Dennis, *Beethoven in German Politics*, 19. In her reception history of the late string quartets, Kristin Knittel also observes that "Beethoven's biographical circumstances played a much larger role in the critical reception of these pieces than did their musical content." Kristin M. Knittel, "From Chaos to History: The Reception of Beethoven's Late Quartets" (PhD diss., Princeton University, 1992), 8.

23. Arnold Schmitz's *Das romantische Beethovenbild* was published in 1927. In an essay surveying the history of Beethoven reception, Scott Burnham observes: "Musical thought in 1920s Germany takes a decidedly objective turn, namely, the turn to form." "The Four Ages of Beethoven: Critical Reception and the Canonic Composer," in *The Cambridge Companion to Beethoven*, ed. Glenn Stanley (Cambridge: Cambridge University Press, 2000), 283.

24. By contrast, mainstream Beethovenians like August Halm, according to Burnham, "celebrated Beethoven's music above all as a triumph of formative power." Ibid.

Beethoven becomes an anticipatory icon of modernist aesthetic autonomy. As Said says, Adorno's Beethoven is "the prototypical modern aesthetic form, and by virtue of its distance from and rejection of bourgeois society and even a quiet death, it acquires an even greater significance and defiance for that very reason."[25] Late style, then, is one more outgrowth of Adorno's preeminent aesthetic obsession, the idea of the work of art as having come into its own, in the modern period, as irreconcilably detached from "the empirical world."[26] Indeed, Adorno's evocation of the composer's last quartets and piano sonatas sounds neither classical nor Romantic: the style of those pieces is, he says, characterized by "abrupt stops," "turning its hollowness outward," using units of conventional musical material only for "the naked depiction of themselves" ("BLS," 126, 125).[27] Adorno's late Beethoven is practically a member of the Second Viennese School.

When Adorno uses Beethoven to generalize about the late works of all "significant artists," his avant-garde vocabulary becomes even more striking: "As a rule, these works are not well rounded, but wrinkled, even fissured. They are apt to lack sweetness, fending off with prickly tartness those interested merely in sampling them. They lack all that harmony which the classicist aesthetic is accustomed to demand from the work of art, showing more traces of history than of growth" (123).[28] The late artist "bursts" his works "asunder," "cast[ing] off the illusion of art" (125).[29] The association between lateness, Beethoven, and modernism persists

25. Said, *On Late Style*, 13–14.

26. Theodor W. Adorno, *Aesthetic Theory*, ed. Gretel Adorno, Rolf Tiedemann, and Robert Hullot-Kentor, trans. Robert Hullot-Kentor (Minneapolis: University of Minnesota Press, 1997), 1. Henceforth cited as *Aesthetic Theory* in the text. "Aus der empirischen Welt." Theodor W. Adorno, *Ästhetische Theorie*, ed. Gretel Adorno and Rolf Tiedemann (Frankfurt: Suhrkamp, 1970), 10. Henceforth cited as *Ästhetische Theorie* in the notes.

27. "Jähe Abbrechen"; "das Werk ... kehrt seine Höhlung nach außen"; "in der nackten Darstellung ihrer selbst." "SB," 184, 183.

28. "Sie sind gemeinhin nicht rund, sondern durchfurcht, gar zerrissen; sie pflegen der Süße zu entraten und weigern sich herb, stachlig dem bloßen Schmecken; es fehlt ihnen all jene Harmonie, welche die klassizistische Ästhetik vom Kunstwerk zu fordern gewohnt ist, und von Geschichte zeigen sie mehr die Spur als von Wachstum." "SB," 180.

29. "[Er] sprengt sie [die Kunstwerke] ... um ... den Schein der Kunst abzuwerfen." "SB," 183. Always *his* works, never *hers*, in Adorno. Essentially no women inhabit Adorno's world of art, a significant fact for the problems of late style, where the decay of a gendered body intrudes on aesthetic development. Where the masculinism of Adorno's aesthetic is important, I restrict myself to masculine pronouns, not wanting to give the false impression of a gender-neutral Adorno. It is therefore perhaps worth emphasizing that despite the influence of Adorno's aesthetic ideas on my own, I present Adorno's ideas not as valid theories of art but as cultural artifacts with an important standing in European modernism. Whichever

in Adorno's thinking to the end of his career; in 1966, in an impromptu radio talk on Beethoven's last works, he says that the presence in late Beethoven of "holes, artistically contrived fissures," allies him with the difficulty of "modern music, as exemplified by Arnold Schoenberg's statement: 'My music is not lovely.'"[30] In its fragmentation, dissonance, and rejection of artistic illusion, Adorno's transhistorical late style is another version of his favored aesthetic of modernism.

By turning to Beethoven's lateness as a protomodernist precursor, however, Adorno complicates his attempts to explain modernist style historically. Typically, Adorno accounts for modernism by pointing either to social conditions like the ever more refined division of labor, the advance of industrial capitalism, and the inhumane quality of life in capitalist society, or to an art-internal dialectic in which existing forms and themes are constantly becoming taboo. By contrast, lateness explains artistic practices not in terms of historical change but in terms of the personal condition of the artist, the confrontation between a "significant" artistic subjectivity and its mortality. The concept of "late style" seems to isolate the aspects of that confrontation which do not change from one place or epoch to another. At times Adorno seems to flaunt his anachronisms; in *Aesthetic Theory*, he cites Beckett's work as an example of art "sealed tightly against superficial rationality," but goes on to say, "This is by no means the exclusive prerogative of modern art but equally evident in the abbreviations in late Beethoven, in the renunciation of superfluous and to this extent irrational ornamentation" (*Aesthetic Theory*, 115).[31] In Adorno's theory of late style, even this principal characteristic of his modernism—its struggle with "rationality"—floats free of the twentieth century. Though Adorno's invocation of late Beethoven lends a legitimating prestige to Beckett's style, it threatens to dissolve chronological distinctions altogether.

At the same time, Adorno's lateness can be a historical feature of the modern as well as a transhistorical phenomenon. In the "Draft Introduction" to *Aesthetic Theory*, he writes of "the fatal aging of the modern" in the context of a discussion

Adornian ideas are salvageable for any contemporary theory of late style, his ideas about gender will not be among them.

30. Theodor W. Adorno, "Beethoven's Late Style," in *Beethoven*, appendix 3, 191. "Die Musik hat gleichsam Löcher, kunstvolle Brüche .... [Es gibt] eine Beziehung zu gewissen Phänomenen der modernen Musik, wie dem Satz von Arnold Schönberg 'My music is not lovely.'" "Über den Spätstil Beethovens," in Adorno, *Beethoven: Philosophie der Musik*, 270–71.

31. "Die gegen Oberflächenrationalität dicht isolierte Kunst Becketts"; "sie ist aber keineswegs eine Prärogative der Moderne sondern ebensogut, etwa an den Verkürzungen des späten Beethoven, dem Verzicht auf die überflüssige und insofern irrationale Zutat abzulesen." *Ästhetische Theorie*, 176.

of Schoenberg (342).[32] Indeed, he is preoccupied throughout *Aesthetic Theory* with the idea that art was perhaps, in his time, coming face to face with its own death. Music provides the prototypical example of the pall of mortality cast over the art of the entire modernist period: "It is thinkable, and not merely an abstract possibility, that great music—a late development—was possible only during a limited phase of humanity" (*Aesthetic Theory*, 3).[33] And Adorno and Horkheimer speak of the art of Europe before fascism as "art in its late phase" in *Dialectic of Enlightenment*.[34] Of course, the quality of lateness pervading modernist art or modernity in general bears only a relation of analogy to the lateness of a human life nearing its end. But it is a telling analogy, for it shows how, in Adorno, the aesthetic of modernism can become *personal*, intimately bound up with the feeling of mortality.[35]

With this turn back to the personal, on the far side of the impersonalizing techniques of late style, Adorno's aesthetics take on an aspect quite different from what appears in descriptions like Fredric Jameson's or Andreas Huyssen's. These writers have shaped the standard picture of Adorno's theories as staging a confrontation between modern art and the sinister, reified social totality of late capitalism.[36] This Adorno, though a partisan of modernism, has little to do with the usual way of seeing Eliot as a high-cultural formalist with a conservative social agenda. By contrast, late style shows both writers concerned not with social transformation but with remodeling the relationship between the artist's work and the artwork. Lateness keeps the emphasis on autonomy but shifts the angle of vision to a *process*

32. "Das fatale Altern der Moderne." *Ästhetische Theorie*, 509.

33. "Vorstellbar und keine bloß abstrakte Möglichkeit, daß große Musik—ein Spätes—nur in einer beschränkten Periode der Menschheit möglich war." *Ästhetische Theorie*, 13.

34. Max Horkheimer and Theodor W. Adorno, *Dialectic of Enlightenment: Philosophical Fragments*, ed. Gunzelin Schmid Noerr, trans. Edmund Jephcott (Stanford, CA: Stanford University Press, 2002), 105. "Der späten Kunst." Max Horkheimer and Theodor W. Adorno, *Dialektik der Aufklärung: Philosophische Fragmente* (Frankfurt: Suhrkamp, 1981), 154.

35. For a more recent theory of belatedness as a central feature of modernism across the arts, see T. J. Clark, *Farewell to an Idea: Episodes from a History of Modernism* (New Haven, CT: Yale University Press, 1999). Clark argues that "modernism" consists in "fixing the moment of art's last flowering at some point in the comparatively recent past, and discovering that enough remains from this finale for a work of ironic or melancholy or decadent continuation to seem possible nonetheless" (371). In effect, he generalizes the stance of *The Waste Land* to all the art of a long modernist period.

36. See Fredric Jameson, *Late Marxism: Adorno, or, The Persistence of the Dialectic* (London: Verso, 1990), especially pt. 3, and Andreas Huyssen, *After the Great Divide: Modernism, Mass Culture, Postmodernism* (Bloomington: Indiana University Press, 1986). By contrast, Shierry Weber Nicholsen's general exposition of Adorno's aesthetics in *Exact Imagination, Late Work: On Adorno's Aesthetics* (Cambridge, MA: MIT Press, 1997) dwells on his ideas about late style and subjectivity.

of autonomization. For both writers, impersonality is achieved only by adverting to the very personal marks of the late-style artist's asceticism. This is both a less rigid conception of autonomy and a thematically narrower, tightly specified way of linking modernist art to its circumstances of production and reception.

Eliot's Late Style, 1910–58

Even if elements of the biographical return in this description of late style, biological age drops out as an explanation of late work. The criterion of lateness is not the position of a work in the chronology of a writer's career but the combination of impersonalization and a self-consciously late subjectivity—a subjectivity which, for the modernist artist, is available at any age. In fact, just such a combination occupies Eliot throughout his poetry, from his earliest works to his last.[37] Rather than trace a stylistic development across all the poet's works, then, I exhibit successively more elaborate versions of the Eliotic late style, offering not comprehensive interpretations but models for thinking about the cultural work Eliot's poetry carries out through its own self-reflexivity.[38] The most straightforward case lies in the middle of Eliot's career, with his deployment of aged prophet-figures as personae in *The Waste Land*. The earlier "Gerontion" expands such a figure into an entire poem of fragmented, decrepit impersonality; but I also show how the stylistic tactics of "Gerontion" are latent in works as divergent, chronologically and temperamentally, as Eliot's undergraduate poem "Humouresque (After J. Laforgue)" and his late verse plays. Finally, I develop an extended comparison between Eliot's allusions to music in *Four Quartets* and Adorno's theory of late Beethoven, demonstrating how both writers work on their cultural contexts to develop musical lateness as a mode of depersonalization and a species of relative autonomy.

Adorno's evocations of the fractures, wrinkles, and fissures of Beethoven's late music immediately bring to mind Eliot's own imagery of the waste land. Eliot's long poem, though it certainly carries the weight of a cultural past that seems to be on the verge of a chaotic end, may not appear to have much to do with personal aging. Yet Eliot considered printing his earlier poem "Gerontion" (the "little

---

37. In her biography of Eliot, Lyndall Gordon speaks of his propensity for role-playing in daily life: "The most long-lived mask was an ageing man, tired out at twenty-one." *T. S. Eliot: An Imperfect Life* (New York: Norton, 1998), 208.

38. I dissent from critical accounts that describe a radical break in Eliot's career. For example, Marjorie Perloff's recent attempt to reclaim an "avant-garde Eliot" sees the impersonality of "Prufrock" as the key to a poetic revolution that Eliot abandoned in the aftermath of World War I. See Marjorie Perloff, "Avant-Garde Eliot," in *21st-Century Modernism: The "New" Poetics* (Malden, MA: Blackwell, 2002), 7–43.

old man") "as prelude" to *The Waste Land*. Though Pound dissuaded him from using "Gerontion" this way,[39] Eliot went on to substitute one little old person for another, placing the Cumaean Sybil at the head of the poem. This mythical figure combines a despairing vision of age ("I wish to die," she says in the dead language of ancient Greek) with prophetic power. *The Waste Land* returns to this conjunction, of course, in the figure of Tiresias, "old man with wrinkled dugs," the spectator-participant in the encounter between the typist and the "young man carbuncular."[40] Eliot's infamous, inscrutably wry note about the Greek prophet claims that "Tiresias, although a mere spectator and not indeed a 'character,' is yet the most important personage in the poem, uniting all the rest .... What Tiresias *sees*, in fact, is the substance of the poem" (*CP*, 72). Tiresias's longevity goes hand in hand with his prophetic ability to "*see*"—and, in fact, "foresuffer[ ]" (62)—beyond the partiality of personhood. Precisely because of his grotesque, hermaphroditic bodily aging, he can occupy every position in the panorama of the poem, even while maintaining the impersonal autonomy of being "a mere spectator and not indeed a 'character.'"[41]

To read Eliot in terms of the impersonality theory of "Tradition and the Individual Talent" might seem to repeat New Critical analyses that more recent scholarship has called into question.[42] But the close correspondence between Adornian late style and the "depersonalization" of "Tradition and the Individual Talent" helps us see how Eliot's essay is quite consistent with the disruptive

39. For the January 1922 exchange between Eliot and Pound, see T. S. Eliot, *The Letters of T. S. Eliot*, rev. ed., vol. 1: *1898–1922*, ed. Vivien Eliot and Hugh Haughton (London: Faber and Faber, 2009), 629–30. Eliot wrote Pound, "Do you advise printing Gerontion as prelude in book or pamphlet form?"; Pound replied, "I do *not* advise printing Gerontion as preface."

40. T. S. Eliot, *Collected Poems, 1909–1962* (New York: Harcourt Brace, 1963), 61–62. Henceforth, except where otherwise noted, I cite Eliot's poems from this edition, abbreviated *CP*, by page number.

41. Writing from a queer theoretical perspective, Tim Dean has advanced a similar reading of Tiresias as a figure of aesthetic impersonality. For Dean, impersonality is "a strategy of access, rather than a strategy of evasion"; "aesthetic impersonality in *The Waste Land*," he goes on to specify, "is pictured as a virtually intolerable discipline of self-dispossession." Dean's emphasis on the intricate gender and sexual dynamics of impersonality complements my own on lateness as an approach to the relation between bodily existence and aesthetic autonomy. Tim Dean, "T. S. Eliot, Famous Clairvoyante," in *Gender, Desire, and Sexuality in T. S. Eliot*, ed. Cassandra Laity and Nancy K. Gish (Cambridge: Cambridge University Press, 2004), 44, 62.

42. Lawrence Rainey, for example, emphasizes the divergence between the "classicism" of *The Sacred Wood* and the "histrionics" of *The Waste Land* in *Revisiting "The Waste Land"* (New Haven, CT: Yale University Press, 2005).

poetics he devised for *The Waste Land*. Despite the dry tone of the essay, its version of poetic impersonality is not an Olympian reserve but a publicly emotion-laden struggle to assemble fragments of texts and experiences together in order to purge the contingencies of personality that generated them. *The Waste Land*, with an aged prophetess at its start and an "old man" watching from its center, rhymes neatly with that account. As a fiction of autonomy, *The Waste Land* negotiates between the contingency of the "personal and wholly insignificant grouse against life" (as the older Eliot called it) and the rigidity of a universalizing mythic structure.[43]

Had "Gerontion" appeared at the head of *The Waste Land*, it would have made lateness even more central to this negotiation than it already was. For this first poem in Eliot's *Ara Vos Prec* (in England; in America *Poems*) (1920), coming on the heels of "Tradition and the Individual Talent" and the doctrine of impersonality, follows a process of depersonalization through mortality strongly recalling the one described by Adorno. Eliot's title, naming the putative speaker, means "little old man," but the poem is hardly an account of an old man's life or personality. The epigraph from *Measure for Measure*, beginning "Thou hast nor youth nor age," defuses a literal reading of the opening line, "Here I am, an old man in a dry month" (*CP*, 29). The opening stanza consists of scene-setting lines of vaguely allegorical allure and uncertain, unpleasant meaning: "I was neither at the hot gates ... My house is a decayed house, / And the jew squats on the window sill" (*CP*, 29). At its end, an indented line makes a visual caesura, and, in Adorno's phrase, "the work ... turn[s] its hollowness outwards" ("BLS," 126):

> I an old man,
> A dull head among windy spaces. (*CP*, 29)

Removing the copula from the opening line, the speaker reduces himself even further, dwarfed by the "windy space" of the blank half-line. He is at once impossibly old, with a memory reaching back to the battle of the "hot gates," Thermopylae, and dead and buried. There is a "field overhead," and in the third stanza, he is "under a windy knob" (29–30).[44] His persona dispersed across time and space, Gerontion exists to lend an atmosphere of old age to an impersonal voice.

43. Eliot's remark is quoted in T. S. Eliot, *The Waste Land: A Facsimile and Transcript of the Original Drafts Including the Annotations of Ezra Pound*, ed. Valerie Eliot (New York: Harvest, 1971), 1.

44. Michael Levenson has suggested that *The Waste Land* opens with a parallel situation, "look[ing] at spring from the point of view of a corpse." *A Genealogy of Modernism: A Study of English Literary Doctrine, 1908–1922* (Cambridge: Cambridge University Press, 1984), 172.

Unreal as Gerontion may be as a character, his voice is still the source of the poem. His aging or afterlife enables poetic speech; by contrast, when the second stanza unexpectedly conjures up the infant Jesus, he is, in phrases from Lancelot Andrewes, "The word within a word, unable to speak a word, / Swaddled with darkness" (29). Embodied youth, in this poem, necessarily lacks language. Another blank space cuts off the end of the stanza midline, forestalling any further rhetorical reliance on the mythology in which incarnated youth and the word come together:

> In the juvescence of the year
> Came Christ the tiger
>
> In depraved May, dogwood and chestnut, flowering judas,
> To be eaten, to be divided, to be drunk
> Among whispers[.] (29)

Across the stanza break, the syntax hiccups, as "Christ the tiger" is betrayed to "flowering judas" and three passive infinitivals whose subject hovers ambiguously between the tiger and "dogwood and chestnut." Eventually the stanza can only come back around to the "old man in a draughty house" (30). Against this failure of incarnation as a basis for language, Gerontion's bodiless head, a withered, hollowed-out skull, provides a windy space for poetry to continue its late existence. The final stanza reiterates this anti-incarnational poetics with a line-and-a-half pair of nominals: "Tenants of the house, / Thoughts of a dry brain in a dry season" (31). Everything that precedes these concluding lines seems to stand in apposition to them; the whole poem becomes simultaneously the shards of an aged subjectivity ("thoughts of a dry brain") and a group of autonomous "tenants of a house."

Lateness and an impersonal aesthetic seem to be integral to poetic voice in "Gerontion"; they also form the basis for Eliot's most characteristic stylistic procedure: the fragment. Eliot's startling shifts from one register of discourse to another, from apparently literal description to allegory or fantasy, from contemporary colloquialism to literary allusion, play a role similar to that of fragmentation in Adorno's theory of late Beethoven. For Adorno, "fissures," "wrinkles," and "rifts" that refuse smooth, organic wholeness constitute the "formal law" of late Beethoven. Instead of expressing the composer's personality, they mark personality's absence. At the same time, according to Adorno, Beethoven made extensive use of conventional musical idioms; but, declining to integrate them smoothly into his late pieces, he leaves them "naked," "no longer imbued and mastered by subjectivity, but left standing" ("BLS," 125).[45]

This recognizably modernist doctrine of defamiliarization and bricolage corresponds to Eliot's allusions. Pieces of inherited language jostle against one another in "Gerontion," leaving ambiguous whether they have been made the speaker's own or whether they are quoted with some level of irony or distance. They undermine a reading of the poem as a coherent personal self-expression. In cognitive terms, this late style's treatment of inherited material poses severe problems of *metarepresentation*: not only do readers searching for meaning have to determine Eliot's attitude to the statements of the speaker of "Gerontion"; they also have to guess, with few clues, that speaker's attitude to fragmentary but obviously alien phrases like "The word within a word, unable to speak a word" (*CP*, 29).[46] Eliot's impersonal aesthetic, especially his playful experimentation with the dramatic monologue, depends crucially on such metarepresentational challenges, constantly putting poetic statement at multiple levels of distance from self-expression. Adorno's figurative picture of fragmented conventions, "splinters, derelict and abandoned ... [that] themselves become expression" ("BLS," 125),[47] also evokes this cognitive problem of meaning attribution (what does each abandoned splinter express?) as a characteristic of late style. Yet Adorno's dialectic also shows how these difficulties can themselves give expression to a recalcitrant, aged consciousness.

"Gerontion" represents such difficulty through a rhetoric of recursive thinking that evokes the winding passages of cognition. In the long fourth stanza, an imperative to "think" propels the language along, its objects enjambed into the subsequent line: "After such knowledge, what forgiveness? Think now / History has many cunning passages .... Think now / She gives when our attention is distracted" (*CP*, 30). Though this dislocated thought dominates the stanza, the first-person singular has disappeared from it, suppressed by the syntax of the imperative. Adorno,

---

45. "Von Subjektivität nicht mehr durchdrungen und bewältigt, sondern stehengelassen." "SB," 183.

46. For this use of the cognitive-scientific concept of metarepresentation, I have drawn on Lisa Zunshine, *Why We Read Fiction: Theory of Mind and the Novel* (Columbus: Ohio State University Press, 2006); Dan Sperber, ed., *Metarepresentations: A Multidisciplinary Perspective* (Oxford: Oxford University Press, 2000); and Dan Sperber and Deirdre Wilson, "Relevance Theory," in *The Handbook of Pragmatics*, ed. Laurence R. Horn and Gregory Ward (Oxford: Blackwell, 2005), 607–32.

47. "Als Splitter, zerfallen und verlassen, schlagen sie endlich selber in Ausdruck um." "SB," 183.

too, describes such a disappearance: "The empty phrase is set in place as a monument to what has been—a monument in which subjectivity is petrified" ("BLS," 126).[48] Yet as Adorno's phrase suggests, late style somehow still signals the subjectivity whose end it commemorates. Eliot's late subject keeps his impersonality even when he returns to the first person:

> Think at last
> We have not reached conclusion, when I
> Stiffen in a rented house. Think at last
> I have not made this show purposelessly
> And it is not by any concitation
> Of the backward devils.
> I would meet you upon this honestly. (*CP*, 30–31)

This return of the "I" suggests less a bodily resurrection—Gerontion is too insubstantial as a person—than the persistence of dried-out cognition in the depersonalized poem itself. Though the speaker may "stiffen," the fact that the poem, this collection of "tenants of a house," continues for twenty-five-or so more lines lies manifest on the page. The extension of the poem is the survival of thought "with a thousand small deliberations" (31). The self-directed irony at this morbid aesthetic pleasure is the last trace of affect as the dessicated speaker thinks himself away. But such traces make room for personal expression in the poem even after the "draughty house" has been emptied. Eliot shares Adorno's paradoxical emphasis on the emotive force of nonsubjective lateness: "The force of subjectivity in late works is the irascible gesture with which it leaves them" ("BLS," 125).

Even the shadowy devotional strain of "Gerontion" collaborates in the process of depersonalization. The occasional hints of yearning toward a disembodied "you" only strengthen the speaker's determination to throw away the accoutrements of bodily existence: "I have lost my passion: why should I need to keep it / Since what is kept must be adulterated?" (*CP*, 31). The ideal of spiritual purity blends into Eliot's impersonal ideal of aesthetic purity; the loss of passion serves poetic ends as much as immortal longings. And when, in a second rhetorical question, Gerontion dismisses the senses—"I have lost my sight, smell, hearing, taste and touch: / How should I use them for your closer contact?" (31)—he might almost be addressing the reader of his newly nonsensual verse. As the question dismisses the senses, the very idea of a "closer contact" falls into a silent stanza break. The fourteen-line

---

48. "Die Floskel einsetzt als Denkmal des Gewesenen, worin versteint Subjektivität selber eingeht." "SB," 184.

coda following that break mentions neither "you" nor "I." Whatever the status of the yearnings in the poem, the speaker can only utter them through late style.

Eliot's late style begins earlier even than 1919. We can trace it back at least as far as the poem he published in the *Harvard Advocate* of January 1910, "Humouresque (After J. Laforgue)." In "Humouresque," Eliot introduces the first of many poetic personae who move under the shadow of mortality:

> One of my marionettes is dead
>> Though not yet tired of the game
> But weak in body as in head:
>> A jumping-jack has such a frame.[49]

The humor of the premise lies in the fact that the marionette was never alive: the poet animates him only to kill him off. Nor does the marionette receive much animation from the oxymoronic description of "The kind of face that we forget, / Locked in a comic, dull grimace"—practically a rictus of death. The marionette's individuality suffers a second way, from the poet's insistence on the puppet's subservience to fashion, with a "mouth that knew the latest tune" and an arrival in an afterlife heralded as "The snappiest fashion."[50]

With self-conscious staginess, the young Eliot displays the procedure by which the poet empties out personality to make it into art. In the opening pair of stanzas, the use of the first person—quite infrequent in his early poetry—lets Eliot avow the difference between living speaker and dead marionette explicitly, yet by the end of the poem, as the first-person forms disappear, the speaker comes close to identifying with his toy:

> Logic—a marionette's all wrong
> Of premises—but in some star
> A life!—but where would it belong?
> And after all—what masque bizarre![51]

This Dickinson-like quatrain, with its dashes and scrambled syntax, heightens the tone, replacing the nonchalance of the earlier stanzas with exclamations of the late

---

49. I quote from the text of Eliot's notebook version, in T. S. Eliot, *Inventions of the March Hare: Poems, 1909–1917*, ed. Christopher Ricks (New York: Harcourt Brace, 1996), 325. Eliot published a corrected text in *Poems Written in Early Youth* (New York: Farrar, Straus and Giroux, 1967), 24–25. The divergences between these texts (and the one published in the *Advocate*) are, with the exception discussed in the text, not relevant to my argument.

50. Eliot, *Inventions of the March Hare*, 325.

51. Ibid.

Romantic, Laforguean pathos of the alienated individual. Despite layers of ironic reversal ("but," twice in two lines, and "And after all") and the disappearance of the "I" at the overt level, these remain the poem's most emotionally charged lines. A printing error in 1910 obscured the intensity; the *Advocate* printed "But, even at that, what mark bizarre!" On the other hand, when the elder Eliot corrected the text for publication in *Poems Written in Early Youth*, he changed the *Advocate*'s "mark" to "mask."[52] "Masque," as an ironic description of the marionette's life, fits the context best, but the variant makes clear that the alternate reading, in which the poem seems to admit that the marionette is a "mask bizarre" for the poet, remains available. If so, it would make explicit the style of lateness underlying the impersonally satiric manner: "Humouresque" becomes not direct self-expression but the record, marked by premature forebodings of bodily weakness and death, of the transformation of painful emotion into the inanimate aesthetic object that is the poem.

Eliot's last works for the stage hark back to this aspect of the marionette theater of his undergraduate poetry. In the first act of *The Cocktail Party* (1949), the Unidentified Guest (later revealed to be the therapist-priest Reilly) tells the hero Edward that his shock at being left by his wife is "a loss of personality . . . . You no longer feel quite human. / You're suddenly reduced to the status of an object— / A living object, but no longer a person." Edward himself, however, describes the sensation of self-alienation in terms of lateness: "I have met myself as a middle-aged man / Beginning to know what it is to feel old."[53] He might almost have said: "I have met myself as a marionette." Even *The Elder Statesman* (1958), which treats an aging man's reconciliation with his past, carries a rider reinstating the relation between lateness and impersonality. Lord Claverton's epiphany, in which he realizes that "What I want to escape from / Is myself, is the past," seems almost a deliberate reversal of the "escape from personality" of "Tradition and the Individual Talent"; he declares, regretfully, "I've spent my life in trying to forget myself, / In trying to identify myself with the part / I had chosen to play. And the longer we pretend / The harder it becomes to drop the pretence."[54] The irony of identifying Eliot with the character he conjures up here is obvious, however. Indeed, the play is headed with dedicatory lines to his wife proclaiming, "The words mean

52. Ibid., 326, collation; see the note (by John Hayward) on "Humouresque" in *Poems Written in Early Youth*, 36.

53. T. S. Eliot, *The Cocktail Party*, in *The Complete Plays of T. S. Eliot* (New York: Harcourt, Brace, 1967), 134, 153.

54. T. S. Eliot, *The Elder Statesman*, in *The Complete Plays of T. S. Eliot* (New York: Harcourt, Brace, 1967), 337, 340–41.

what they say, but some have a further meaning / For you and me only."[55] Instead of the straightforwardness of unembarrassed old age, Eliot suggests that the personal is essentially *secret*. And as personal confession hides itself, "the words" of the play signify autonomously and tautologously: "They mean what they say." In fact, Lord Claverton echoes none other than J. Alfred Prufrock. He alludes to "Moments we regret in the very next moment," like Prufrock's "decisions and revisions which a minute will reverse" (*CP*, 4). He also enjoins his daughter's fiancé to confess everything, even "situations which are simply ridiculous, / When he has played the fool (as who has not?),"[56] surely a deliberate allusion to Prufrock's admission of being "At times, indeed, almost ridiculous— / Almost, at times, the Fool" (*CP*, 5). Although these last plays relinquish the disruptive techniques that had been Eliot's hallmark up through *Four Quartets*, they continue to represent figures hovering between objecthood and personhood, conjoining themes of impersonality and lateness.

The continuities between these last works and Eliot's earliest work show the poetic productivity he found in late style. In 1916 he wrote to his brother:

> I had a very good review in the London *Nation* which I will send you. I feel a sort of posthumous pleasure in it. I often feel that "J.A.P." is a swan song, but I never mention the fact because Vivien is so exceedingly anxious that I shall equal it, and would be bitterly disappointed if I do not. So do not suggest to anyone how I feel. The present year has been, in some respects, the most awful nightmare of anxiety that the mind of man could conceive, but at least it is not dull, and it has its compensations.[57]

To the Eliot of 1916, at least in his most discouraged moods, even his debut poem was already in late style. It is also an occasion for concealing feelings ("do not suggest to anyone how I feel"). More than that, critical success is a "posthumous pleasure," putting the poem at a radical distance from the life of its author. What matters here is not the symptomatology of Eliot's depression but the possibility that the "compensations" included, along with—or rather, as part of—his succès d'estime, a way of developing aesthetic autonomy: the method in which, like every poem to follow, "Prufrock" *was* a swan song.

---

55. Eliot, *The Elder Statesman*, 294. Perhaps some hedge was needed against the embarrassing interpretation in which the love between Lord Claverton and his daughter stands for that between Eliot and his much younger second wife. What matters is that the hedge Eliot chooses is the aesthetic autonomy of impersonality.

56. *The Elder Statesman*, 340.

57. Letter to Henry Ware Eliot, September 6, 1916, in Eliot, *Letters*, 1:165–66.

Eliot was already drafting the line in "Little Gidding": "Every poem an epitaph" (*CP*, 208). After Eliot published *The Waste Land*, he deemed it, too, "a thing of the past" only a few months later.[58] *Ash-Wednesday* begins with the announcement that "I do not hope to turn again" and proceeds to spin obsessive variations on silence, particularly in section V, with its "unheard, unspoken / Word" and its assertion that "there is not enough silence" (*CP*, 85, 92).[59] Denis Donoghue remarks that the first readers of "Burnt Norton," finding it at the end of *Collected Poems, 1909–1935*, "might have thought Eliot's career as a poet was finished .... 'Burnt Norton' had an air of finality about it."[60] As a poet Eliot specialized in conjuring this effect repeatedly; the result, however, is not simply his own version of Adorno's "fatal aging of the modern." This form of lateness furnishes the poetry's escape from the poet's personality into the ideal order of monuments Eliot had imagined in "Tradition and the Individual Talent." If every work is a last work, every work leaves its author's life behind.

Four Quartets and Musical Lateness

Although lateness was a persistent obsession in Eliot's poetry, his sequence *Four Quartets* (*CP*, 173–209) offers his most extended meditation on artistic late style. In claiming, in its title and its occasional musical imagery, a kinship with music, the poem combines a musical ideal of poetic impersonality with its fictions of aging as depersonalization. This combination prompts Eliot to write poetry with strong resemblances to Adorno's description of musical late style. More than an analogy, this resemblance testifies to a shared enterprise in which both Adorno and Eliot transform high-cultural ideas of music's purity and spirituality—ideas of which Beethoven was an important icon—into a way of indicating the residue of personality that remains within the objective forms of late style.

Eliot's musical allusions—in titles like *Four Quartets* and "Preludes," or in moments of longing like Prufrock's "music from a farther room" (*CP*, 5)—hark

---

58. Letter to Richard Aldington, November 15, 1922, in ibid., 1:786–87.

59. Compare Adorno's reading of Goethe's "Wanderer's Night Song": "as in all authentic works ... the subject wants to fall silent by way of the work." *Aesthetic Theory*, 73. "Eher möchte es [das Subjekt], wie in jedem authentischen Gebilde, durch dieses hindurch darin verstummen." *Ästhetische Theorie*, 114.

60. Denis Donoghue, "On 'Burnt Norton,'" in *Words in Time: New Essays on Eliot's "Four Quartets*," ed. Edward Lobb (London: Athlone, 1993), 1.

back to earlier forms of aestheticism. Pater's famous epigram in *The Renaissance* sums up the aestheticist program at its most radically formalist:

> *All art constantly aspires towards the condition of music.* For while in all other kinds of art it is possible to distinguish the matter from the form, and the understanding can always make this distinction, yet it is the constant effort of art to obliterate it. That the mere matter of a poem, for instance, its subject, namely, its given incidents or situation—that the mere matter of a picture, the actual circumstances of an event, the actual topography of a landscape—should be nothing without the form, the spirit, of the handling, that this form, this mode of handling, should become an end in itself, should penetrate every part of the matter: this is what all art constantly strives after, and achieves in different degrees.[61]

Music, as the purest aesthetic form, has the power to annihilate the "mere matter." That matter would include, in poetry, "the subject"—and it is not mere wordplay to suppose that this word implies the vanishing of the writing subject, his or her moods and dispositions, as well. Pater devotes the rest of his essay to defending the view that, even though the attribution of specific paintings to Giorgione is uncertain, the "Giorgionesque," the style or "mode of handling" of the paintings attributed to Giorgione, is real. The author lives on as a function of the work. Pater declares the autonomy of form, but he also equates form with "spirit."

Adorno's theory belongs to this kind of aestheticism, too. Even the insistent social orientation of *Aesthetic Theory* does not preclude a celebration of form that reproduces Pater's dialectic:

> Although nothing counts in artworks that does not originate in the configuration of their sensual elements—all other spirit in the artworks, particularly injected philosophical thematics and putatively expressed spirit, all discursive ingredients, are material like colors and tones—the sensual in artworks is artistic only if in itself mediated by spirit.[62] (*Aesthetic Theory*, 87)

---

61. Walter Pater, "The School of Giorgione," in *The Renaissance: Studies in Art and Poetry*, ed. Adam Phillips (Oxford: Oxford University Press, 1986), 86 (emphasis in original).

62. "So wenig ein Geistiges an ihnen [den Kunstwerken] zählt, das nicht aus der Konfiguration ihrer sinnlichen Momente entspränge—aller andere Geist an den Kunstwerken, zumal der philosophisch hineingestopfte und angeblich ausgedrückte, alle gedanklichen Ingredienzien sind darin Stoffe gleich den Farben und Tönen—, so wenig ist ein Sinnliches an den Werken künstlerisch, das nicht in sich durch Geist vermittelt wäre." *Ästhetische Theorie*, 135.

Music occupies an iconic position in Adorno's aesthetic; as Richard Leppert points out, more than a third of Adorno's written output concerns music.[63] *Minima Moralia* states the case directly: "Perhaps the strict and pure concept of art is applicable only to music." The qualifying "perhaps" is important, though, for Adorno goes on to say that "great poetry or great painting—precisely the greatest—necessarily brings with it an element of subject-matter transcending aesthetic confines, undissolved in the autonomy of form."[64] This version of the impurity of poetry and painting, which denigrates the idea that they might aspire to the condition of music as pure form, bears a striking resemblance to Adorno's concept of cross-artistic late style. Within a few pages of the declaration in *Aesthetic Theory* that "nothing counts" in art except perceptible form, Adorno makes late style the exception: "If there is something like a common characteristic of great late works, it is to be sought in the breaking through of form by spirit. This is no aberration of art but rather its fatal corrective. Its highest products are condemned to a fragmentariness that is their confession that even they do not possess what is claimed by the immanence of their form" (*Aesthetic Theory*, 90).[65] The Adornian twist on Pater's aestheticist trope is, then, to establish lateness itself as the point at which all the arts can meet, as an aesthetic mode in which pure form is both essential—recall Adorno's insistence on Beethoven's "formal law"—and overcome by subjectivity breaking through.

The insistent, self-conscious lateness of *Four Quartets* affects the meaning of its appeal to music in a parallel fashion. Though the relation of Eliot's sequence to music has been considered many times, critics and scholars have not explored the links between musical lateness and aesthetic impersonality. Instead, they have offered various analogies between some aspect of (say) Beethoven's late string quartets and Eliot's sequence. These comparisons are now so hackneyed

63. Richard Leppert, introduction to *Essays on Music*, by Theodor W. Adorno, ed. Richard Leppert (Berkeley: University of California Press, 2002), 13.

64. Theodor W. Adorno, *Minima Moralia: Reflections from Damaged Life*, trans. E. F. N. Jephcott (London: Verso, 1974), 223. "Vielleicht ist der strenge und reine Begriff von Kunst überhaupt nur der Musik zu entnehmen, während große Dichtung und große Malerei—gerade die große—notwendig ein Stoffliches, den ästhetischen Bannkreis Überschreitendes, nicht in die Autonomie der Form Aufgelöstes mit sich führt." *Minima Moralia: Reflexionen aus dem beschädigten Leben* (Frankfurt: Suhrkamp, 1975), 298.

65. "Gibt es etwas wie eine übergreifende Charakteristik großer Spätwerke, so wäre sie beim Durchbruch des Geistes durch die Gestalt aufzusuchen. Der ist keine Aberration der Kunst sondern ihr tödliches Korrektiv. Ihre obersten Produkte sind zum Fragmentarischen verurteilt als zum Geständnis, daß auch sie nicht haben, was die Immanenz ihrer Gestalt zu haben prätendiert." *Ästhetische Theorie*, 139.

in criticism that even the gesture of dismissing them as hackneyed (pioneered by Hugh Kenner in 1959) has become hackneyed.[66] Indeed, the analogy-building criticism has been dominated—and limited—by Eliolatry, which puts the musical model to work in a celebration of artistic craft and putative structural perfection.[67] Instead, our analysis should assume that, far more than any specific analogy, including the ones Eliot himself proposed, precisely this celebration is the reliable effect of Eliot's allusions to chamber music on the reception of his poem within the literary world. Rather than generate more ad hoc analogies, I want to link Eliot's invocation of a late music to Adorno's as corresponding position-takings within their cultural fields—as tactical moves on behalf of the artwork's autonomy.[68]

Eliot draws on the aestheticist and symbolist celebration of music as the paradigmatic art, which was articulated hand in hand with the doctrine that all art aspires to pure form, to objective being rather than subjective expression. In the terminology of Bourdieu's *The Rules of Art*, such doctrines of autonomy are part of the doxa, or shared founding belief, of a literary field—in Eliot's oft-reiterated credo, "poetry as poetry."[69] Eliot was quite self-conscious about this aspect of his

66. Kenner wrote, "There is an empty custom of referring here to the 'late' quartets of Beethoven, a parallel which impedes understanding by suggesting that the *Quartets* offer to be an Olympian's transfinite testament." Hugh Kenner, *The Invisible Poet: T. S. Eliot* (New York: McDowell, Oblensky, 1959), 306.

67. Helen Gardner, *The Art of T. S. Eliot* (New York: Dutton, 1950); Keith Alldritt, *Eliot's "Four Quartets": Poetry as Chamber Music* (London: Woburn, 1978); John Holloway, "Eliot's *Four Quartets* and Beethoven's Last Quartets," in *The Fire and the Rose: New Essays on T. S. Eliot*, ed. Vinod Sena and Rajiva Verma (Delhi: Oxford University Press), 145–59; and, more recently, David Barndollar, "Movements in Time: *Four Quartets* and the Late String Quartets of Beethoven," in *T. S. Eliot's Orchestra*, ed. John Xiros Cooper (New York: Garland, 2000), 179–94.

68. In an important reconsideration of Eliot within a British late-modernist context, "Insular Time: T. S. Eliot and Modernism's English End," chap. 3 in *A Shrinking Island: Modernism and National Culture in England* (Princeton, NJ: Princeton University Press, 2004), Jed Esty discusses *Four Quartets* in terms of the end of England's empire and the consequent newfound emphasis on the particularity of national culture. For Esty, the formalist, impersonal aesthetic of music serves Eliot's ideal of self-effacement before the English nation. However, though this explains the English nationalism of Eliot's poem, it cannot fully account for its atmosphere of lateness, because lateness was central to Eliot's work from the very start. Where Esty sees the *Quartets'* "musicality" evoking a "new method" of impersonality (246 n81), one based in adherence to traditional native culture, I argue that late Beethovenian musicality leads back, once more, to the contradictory foundation of formal freedom in bodily aging.

69. In, for example, "The Frontiers of Criticism," in Eliot, *On Poetry and Poets*, 124; "Dante," in *Selected Essays*, new ed. (New York: Harcourt, Brace, 1950), 219; or, most famously, "Preface to the 1928 Edition," in Eliot, *The Sacred Wood*, viii.

invocation of music. When he wrote to his friend John Hayward in September 1942 about his idea for a title for the whole sequence, he said:

> The title I have always had in mind for it was KENSINGTON QUAR-
> TETS .... How great is the resistance to "quartets"? I am aware of general
> objections to these musical analogies: there was a period when people
> were writing long poems and calling them, with no excuse, "symphonies"
> (J. Gould Fletcher even did a "Symphony in Blue" I think, thus achiev-
> ing a greater *confusion des genres*). But I should like to indicate that these
> poems are all in a particular set form which I have elaborated, and the word
> "quartet" does seem to me to start people on the right tack .... It suggests
> to me the notion of making a poem by weaving in together three or four
> superficially unrelated themes: the "poem" being the degree of success in
> making a new whole out of them.[70]

Eliot knew perfectly well that he was harking back to the musicophilia of aestheticism, symbolism, and early modernism (Fletcher's "The Blue Symphony" first
appeared in *Poetry* in September 1914[71]); and he also knew the relation between
the musical analogy and a formalist reading which would attend to structure, the
"weaving" into a "whole." Eliot's practice, then, invites a readerly concentration
on the impersonal level of poetic craft, and, in doing so, seeks to encourage a
belief in aesthetic autonomy. His scholarly readers have frequently obliged. Yet we
should not regard Eliot simply as a cold-blooded aesthetic tactician.[72] As we will
see, the *Quartets* also *thematize* the autonomy they invoke, questioning its nature
and extent.

Adorno's theory of late Beethoven carries out the same questioning; instead
of a triumphant invocation of lateness as a pure, impersonal autonomy, Adorno's
dialectic brings out the latent personality within that form of autonomy. A similar
dialectical turn from musical autonomy to late personality makes *Four Quartets*
comparable to "Beethoven's Late Style" and to Adorno's aesthetics more broadly.
I am not claiming that Adorno and Eliot jointly perceived and expressed the true

70. Letter of September 3, 1942, quoted in Helen Gardner, *The Composition of "Four Quartets"* (New York: Oxford University Press, 1978), 26.

71. John Gould Fletcher, "The Blue Symphony," *Poetry* 4, no. 6 (September 1914): 211–15.

72. For an extensive account of Eliot's work as a cultural stratagem, see John Xiros Cooper, *T. S. Eliot and the Ideology of "Four Quartets"* (Cambridge: Cambridge University Press, 1995), esp. 116–17. Cooper sees the poem's aestheticism as a political alibi for quietism; but Eliot's poem, like his criticism, uses late style to define a more socially embedded and consequential version of aesthetic autonomy.

essence of the late Beethoven quartets. Adorno's writings on Beethoven are fragmentary and incomplete; they have more often been valued by musicologists for their suggestiveness than for their concrete analyses. Michael Spitzer, whose *Music as Philosophy* makes a book-length attempt to use Adorno's ideas on Beethoven within a contemporary musicological framework, remarks that "the analytical portions of Adorno's *Beethoven* are primitive."[73] Nor is it likely that Eliot could have harbored or put into poetry anything like Adorno's understanding of Beethoven's late style. Eliot more or less lacked classical musical culture and training. In a 1942 lecture, Eliot said he did not have "technical knowledge of musical form," though he opined that "a poet may gain much from the study of music."[74] His published letters have very few references to classical music, though he seems to have paid more attention to such music in later life.[75] And the poet's comments on Beethoven echo late Romantic clichés of Beethovenian spirituality and transcendence. In his memoir of Eliot, Stephen Spender quotes a letter from the poet: "I have the A minor Quartet [op. 132, a signal late work] on the gramophone, and find it quite inexhaustible to study. There is a sort of heavenly or at least more than human gaiety about some of his later things which one imagines might come to oneself as the fruit of reconciliation and relief after immense suffering; I should like to get something of that into verse before I die."[76]

73. Michael Spitzer, *Music as Philosophy: Adorno and Beethoven's Late Style* (Bloomington: Indiana University Press, 2006), 5. Significantly, Spitzer does confirm impersonality as an important aspect of Beethoven's late style: "Regarding the individual manner of the style (S2), there is a corresponding sense that Beethoven loses himself in this wealth of material, rather than blending the conventions into a unified voice" (25).

74. T. S. Eliot, "The Music of Poetry," in *On Poetry and Poets*, 32.

75. In a 1957 essay, Herbert Howarth claims that Eliot knew J. W. N. Sullivan's book *Beethoven: His Spiritual Development* (New York: Knopf, 1927). The evidence is circumstantial, and even if Eliot knew the book, he would have found in Sullivan an unabashedly biographical interpretation of the composer, dwelling on his aging, deafness, and illness as preconditions for "a higher degree of consciousness, probably, than is manifested anywhere else in art" (223). See Herbert Howarth, "Eliot, Beethoven, and J. W. N. Sullivan," *Comparative Literature* 9, no. 4 (Autumn 1957): 322–32. Knittel places Sullivan in the reception history of the late string quartets as one among several early twentieth-century "effusive" popularizers of Beethoven in terms of his soulfulness. See Knittel, "From Chaos to History," 231–32.

76. Letter of March 28, 1931, quoted in Stephen Spender, "Remembering Eliot," in *T. S. Eliot: The Man and His Work*, ed. Allen Tate (New York: Delacorte, 1966), 54. Eliot free-associates on Beethoven's inscription for the central third movement: "Hymn of thanksgiving to the divinity, from a convalescent, in the Lydian mode."

There is good reason to suppose that Eliot had long-established associations between the late Beethoven quartets and such ideas, for he could hardly have avoided encountering them in the Boston of his Harvard years. At the turn of the century, Boston followed, in the phrase of Joseph Horowitz's *Classical Music in America*, a "cult of Beethoven": Beethoven's name was enshrined in a medallion above the stage at Symphony Hall, which opened in 1900 with a dedicatory performance of the (late) *Missa solemnis*.[77] The cult was particularly strong in the Brahmin stratum of society in which Eliot moved; he was friendly with the Symphony's chief patron, Isabella Stewart Gardner.[78] Boston musical culture, dominated by the Boston Symphony Orchestra, rested on the belief in the superiority of German instrumental music generally and Beethoven in particular, which were regarded as epitomizing the spiritual, pure value of music. In turn-of-the-century Boston, according to Horowitz, "Music was honored as queen of the arts, said to range higher and probe deeper than mere words, to grasp truths more essential, sublime, or otherwise ineffable. Beethoven was enthroned as no writer could be."[79] However much time Eliot subsequently spent listening to Beethoven string quartets, he needed no musical sensibility to regard them as epitomes of a pure music striving to get beyond itself; such a conception was in the cultural air in which he came of age.

There may seem to be a contradiction between the significance of music in the Paterian tradition as a pure, impersonal form and its tenor in the Boston cult of Beethoven as transcendent spirituality. But I am arguing that Eliot's impersonal poetic, also the product of his Boston years, embodies the same contradiction. Likewise, Adornian late style is nothing other than a synthesis of aesthetic impersonality and the late Romantic mythoi of the aging artist and of music, mythoi of which Beethoven had been the prime example for a long time.[80] This synthesis,

77. Joseph Horowitz, *Classical Music in America: A History of Its Rise and Fall* (New York: Norton, 2005), 13, 73, 75.

78. For his gossipy letter to her of November 7, 1918, see Eliot, *Letters*, 1:290–92. On "Mrs. Jack's" Symphony patronage, see Horowitz, *Classical Music in America*, 90, 112.

79. Horowitz, *Classical Music in America*, 97.

80. Kristin Knittel, like other reception historians, credits Wagner's 1870 essay *Beethoven* as the most influential articulation of these tropes. According to Knittel, it was Wagner who devised the first biographical interpretation of Beethoven's late period to celebrate rather than regret his deafness and other infirmities, seeing in them so many more instigations to inwardness and uncompromising artistry. Knittel, "From Chaos to History," 8, 118, and passim. Adorno belongs in the Wagnerian line, but he has no patience for Wagner's idea of Beethoven as a titanic, all-mastering soul—nor, of course, for the triumphalist German nationalism Wagner linked to his idea.

taking place throughout the careers of Eliot and Adorno, yielded a dialectical version of autonomy, one that depends on its connection to an artistic personality.

The crucial moment for an Adornian late style in *Four Quartets* is also, not coincidentally, one of its extended evocations of old age. "East Coker" II opens with a stanza of apocalyptic vision in irregularly rhymed tetrameters. After the stanza break, the poem jolts into a conversational register:

> Comets weep and Leonids fly
> Hunt the heavens and the plains
> Whirled in a vortex that shall bring
> The world to that destructive fire
> Which burns before the ice-cap reigns.
>
> That was a way of putting it—not very satisfactory:
> A periphrastic study in a worn-out poetical fashion,
> Leaving one still with the intolerable wrestle
> With words and meanings. The poetry does not matter.
> It was not (to start again) what one had expected.
> What was to be the value of the long looked forward to,
> Long hoped for calm, the autumnal serenity
> And the wisdom of age? Had they deceived us
> Or deceived themselves, the quiet-voiced elders,
> Bequeathing us merely a receipt for deceit? (*CP*, 184)

Eliot discursively carries out one of Adorno's characteristic late-style moves: having written a stanza according to the rules of an older period (rhyme, meter, astrological symbolism), he makes a visual caesura and adverts to the fact that the convention was only a "worn-out poetical fashion," leaving it, in Adorno's terms, "naked." Such caesuras, according to Adorno, are what make the late Beethoven impersonal: "The work falls silent as it is deserted, turning its hollowness outwards. Only then is the next fragment added, ordered to its place by escaping subjectivity and colluding for better or worse with what has gone before" ("BLS," 126).[81] Eliot's stanza break hollows out the tetrameter performance, turning it from expression into a convention the poet impersonally orders to its place.

What follows the break tells us, in startlingly direct terms, that aging lies behind this rhetorical move: the rhyming stanza was a "periphrastic study" of the bitterness

---

81. "Das Werk schweigt, wenn es verlassen wird, und kehrt seine Höhlung nach außen. Dann erst fügt das nächste Bruchstück sich an, vom Befehl der ausbrechenden Subjektivität an seine Stelle gebannt und dem voraufgehenden auf Gedeih und Verderb verschworen." "SB," 184.

of growing old. Yet indications remain that Eliot has not forsaken poetic form for personal expression. He avoids the first person singular in favor of an impersonal third person ("one"), a neutral plural ("us"), or short passives ("the long looked forward to, / Long hoped for calm"). He dismisses one stylistic mode only to reemphasize the poem's engagement with problems of verbal craft, "the intolerable wrestle / With words and meanings"; the enjambment of the prepositional phrase calls attention to the fact that we are still reading verse. So does an ambiguity in pronoun reference, again making use of a line break: after "The poetry does not matter," "It" seems at first to refer to the poetry. Only once the parenthesis intervenes and the mode of questioning returns from the beginning of the first stanza ("What is the late November doing?") does it become clear that "It" has the same referent as in "That was a way of putting it." In the flicker of referents, poetry returns as the subject of the poem at the same moment it is dismissed.

In fact, a strange continuity joins the putatively "poetical" performance and the apparently unmediated personal statement. The first line of the second verse paragraph consists of sixteen syllables, with a midline caesura—to the ear, an unrhymed couplet, scannable in the iambic tetrameter norm of the preceding lines with some looseness in the opening feet. We can mark the metrical beats, some of which fall on secondary stresses or unstressed syllables, thus:

> That wás a wáy of pútting ít—
> Not véry sátisfáctorý[.]

Adorno's way of putting it is to say that between two fragments on either side of a caesura, "a secret is shared … and can be exorcized only by the figure they form together" ("BLS," 126).[82] The metrical continuity reminds us that the plain style of the second stanza is as much a style as the symbolist rhymes of the first; nonetheless, the blank forms a reverse image of the artist's subjectivity, the agency that ruptures the style. That agency's secret lies in the match between the old man's plain-spokenness of the second stanza and the "worn-out" style of the first. By associating the aging theme of "East Coker" II with the challenge of finding "ways of putting it," Eliot, like Adorno, makes the impersonal problem of form itself a locus of personality.

For the rigidity of imposed form is not, it turns out as Eliot's poem continues, an impersonal cure for personal whims but the product of them. "There is, it seems to us," says the speculative, prosy voice of the poem, with its impersonal "us,"

---

82. "Das Geheimnis ist zwischen ihnen, und anders läßt es sich nicht beschwören als in der Figur, die sie mitsammen bilden." "SB," 184.

> At best, only a limited value
> In the knowledge derived from experience.
> The knowledge imposes a pattern, and falsifies,
> For the pattern is new in every moment
> And every moment is a new and shocking
> Valuation of all we have been. We are only undeceived
> Of that which, deceiving, could no longer harm. (*CP*, 185)

The accumulation of personal experience appears to offer settled, structured knowledge: personality is pattern. But forward-moving time constantly escapes such a pattern, disintegrating the forms of experience. This disintegration takes place from the perspective of lateness—from the backward look at "all we have been." Eliot uses the rhetorical figure of climax—the ladder of repeated terms, "knowledge ... knowledge ... pattern ... pattern ... every moment ... every moment"—only to disavow the power of logical progression.

What remains, after this dizzying chain of pseudo reasoning, is a return to symbolism and personal affect, again under the sign of aging: "In the middle, not only in the middle of the way / But all the way, in a dark wood, in a bramble" (185). Knowing that imposing a pattern on life falsifies it does not prevent Eliot from imposing the poetic and religious pattern of Dante, including Dante's allegorization of the details of his aging, the *cammin di nostra vita*. The *Divina Commedia* offers Eliot a pattern for the kind of aging he prefers—one beset by darkness and uncertainty on all sides—and it draws on that uncertainty as the occasion for religious vision. But at this moment Eliot forsakes spiritual allegory, allowing the aging poetic self passionate speech:

> Do not let me hear
> Of the wisdom of old men, but rather of their folly,
> Their fear of fear and frenzy, their fear of possession[.] (185)

The first person singular appears here for the first time in "East Coker" II, after the coolly rational discourse of the early part of the stanza, embracing an alliterating series of powerful, negative affects: folly, fear, frenzy. Like Adornian lateness, then, this version of Eliotic lateness rejects false reconciliation in favor of discontented intransigence.

These affective traits also bring Eliot into alignment with an aesthetic position carved out by another late-style poet: William Butler Yeats. Eliot's evocation of the old man's "frenzy" echoes Yeats's "An Acre of Grass" (1938). In that poem, Yeats prays for the transformative power of the state of frenzy:

Grant me an old man's frenzy.
Myself must I remake
Till I am Timon and Lear
Or that William Blake
Who beat upon the wall
Till truth obeyed his call;

. . .

Forgotten else by mankind
An old man's eagle mind.[83]

Helen Gardner argues that Eliot is consciously alluding to Yeats in "East Coker" II.[84] Consciously or not, Eliot's late poem converges in tone with the works of Yeats's late period. Although Gardner contrasts Yeats, the outsize personality and idiosyncratic spiritualist, with Eliot, the Anglican ascetic, I argue that these differences cloak fundamental similarities of practice. In Yeats, "frenzy" is an expression of old age, but it is also a power to remake the self, to fully assume dramatic or poetic masks. The Yeatsian impersonality of the mask has all the freedom and pathos of aesthetic autonomy for the inhabitant of the quiet acre of grass, "Forgotten else by mankind." Like the Eliot of *Four Quartets*, the late Yeats does not simply voice extreme passions; rather, the force of personality in his last poems consists in his transformation of individual dispositions into an impersonal aesthetic.

This understanding of Yeats's lateness may seem to go against the grain of Eliot's nearly contemporaneous lecture on the Irish poet. Indeed, "Yeats" (1940) even claims to revise his notion of impersonality.[85] Praising Yeats for developing, in his later work, "that sense of a unique personality which makes one sit up in excitement and eagerness to learn more about the author's mind and feelings," Eliot assumes a retrospective stance on his own early period:

> I have, in early essays, extolled what I called impersonality in art, and it may seem that, in giving as a reason for the superiority of Yeats's later work the greater expression of personality in it, I am contradicting myself. It may be that I expressed myself badly, or that I had only an adolescent grasp of that

83. W. B. Yeats, "An Acre of Grass," in *New Poems*, in *The Collected Poems of W. B. Yeats*, 2nd ed., ed. Richard J. Finneran (New York: Scribner, 1989), 301–2.

84. Gardner, *The Composition of "Four Quartets,"* 68.

85. Lyndall Gordon accepts this claim, as I do not; see *T. S. Eliot*, 483. In general Gordon's biography treats impersonality as a strategy of concealment, to be overcome in order to detect the hidden personal revelations.

idea ... but I think now, at least, that the truth of the matter is as follows. There are two forms of impersonality: that which is natural to the mere skilful craftsman, and that which is more and more achieved by the maturing artist .... The second impersonality is that of the poet who, out of intense and personal experience, is able to express a general truth; retaining all the particularity of his experience, to make of it a general symbol.[86]

This revised exposition invokes the universality of the poet's experience as though it were self-evident what "general truth" Yeats's late poetry expressed. Yet by emphasizing lateness, Eliot retains all the paradoxical strangeness of the earlier doctrine of impersonality articulated in "Tradition and the Individual Talent." For the artist becomes general by "maturing"—recall that "maturity" was also the term of evaluation the young Eliot had used—and his putatively universal experience is precisely that of unpleasant aging. Quoting Yeats's "The Spur," with its defiant confession that "lust and rage" underlie his later writing, Eliot asks, "To what honest man, old enough, can these sentiments be entirely alien?" ("Yeats," 302). That a poem about an aging male poet should seem universal to another aging male poet from a closely related milieu is not surprising. But Eliot is not simply confusing himself with the universal; he also says that Yeats "*in his work* remained in the best sense always young, ... even in one sense became young as he aged" ("Yeats," 302; emphasis added). Thus the process of aging itself divorces the person in the work and the man outside, so that they age in opposite temporal directions. This vision of an autonomous, impersonal person inhabiting the poetry reproduces Adorno's idea of late style—and the young Eliot's idea of "mature" impersonality.

Once again, aesthetic autonomy forms the center around which the changing ideas rotate. Eliot rather gleefully emphasizes Yeats's ability to shock audiences with his late work, the "not very pleasant" quality of "The Spur" and the late play *Purgatory*. And his oration reaches its height with an aestheticist credo: "Born into a world in which the doctrine of 'Art for Art's sake' was generally accepted, and living on into one in which art has been asked to be instrumental to social purposes, he held firmly to the right view which is between these ... [that] an artist, by serving his art with entire integrity, is at the same time rendering the greatest service he can to his own nation and to the whole world" ("Yeats," 307). Eliot's formulation, with its emphasis on artistic "integrity" and on Yeats's survival, as a late-style artist, into the 1930s of politicized poetry, chimes with Adorno's dialectic of autonomy,

---

86. T. S. Eliot, "Yeats," in *On Poetry and Poets*, 299. Henceforth cited as "Yeats" in the text.

in which only the autonomous work can approach to critical truth about the world. Adorno dwells on the same complex of themes in *Aesthetic Theory*:

> The emancipation of the artwork from the artist is no *l'art pour l'art* delusion of grandeur but the simplest expression of the work's constitution as the expression of a social relation that bears in itself the law of its own reification: Only as things do artworks become the antithesis of the reified monstrosity. Correspondingly, and this is key to art, even out of so-called individual works it is a We that speaks and not an I—indeed all the more so the less the artwork adapts externally to a We and its idiom.[87] (167)

Like Eliot and the Yeats of Eliot's reading, Adorno dismisses late-nineteenth-century aestheticism to erect his own modernist aestheticism in its place. No matter how much his commitment to a Marxist critique of reification compels him to draw out the social aspect of the production of art, the heart of his model is still the heroically self-sacrificing individual artist.

At the level of form, however, the late Yeats and the Eliot of *Four Quartets* might seem strikingly different. Yeats was a formalist to the last, a master of the very rhyme and esoteric symbolism "East Coker" II stigmatizes as a "worn-out poetical fashion." Eliot's 1942 lecture on "The Music of Poetry," however, construes even a prosaic style as a test of formal virtuosity in the long poem. Eliot carries out this dialectical reversal by means of an analogy to music. "Dissonance, even cacophony, has its place," he says: "just as, in a poem of any length, there must be transitions between passages of greater and less intensity, to give a rhythm of fluctuating emotion essential to the musical structure of the whole; and the passages of less intensity will be, in relation to the level on which the total poem operates, prosaic."[88] Eliot rejects musicality at one level—the melodiousness of words—only to recuperate it at another: the "rhythm" of stylistic transitions. The prosaic, like other indications of "fluctuating emotion," remains only one effect among others. This Adornian concept of emotion as one more element of the form had been one of Eliot's theoretical mainstays since "Tradition and the Individual Talent," with its

---

87. "Die Verselbständigung des Kunstwerks dem Künstler gegenüber ist keine Ausgeburt des Größenwahns von l'art pour l'art, sondern der einfachte Ausdruck seiner Beschaffenheit als eines gesellschaftlichen Verhältnisses, das in sich das Gesetz seiner eigenen Vergegenständlichung trägt: nur als Dinge werden die Kunstwerke zur Antithesis des dinghaften Unwesens. Dem ist gemäß der zentrale Sachverhalt, daß aus den Kunstwerken, auch den sogenannten individuellen, ein Wir spricht und kein Ich, und zwar desto reiner, je weniger es äußerlich einem Wir und dessen Idiom sich adaptiert." *Ästhetische Theorie*, 250.

88. Eliot, "The Music of Poetry," 24–25.

image of the feelings chemically combining. In 1942, Eliot was still coaxing readers to regard prosaic lines like those in "East Coker" II not, in Adorno's dismissive
formula, as "a 'personality' ruthlessly proclaiming itself, which breaks through the
roundedness of form for the sake of expression, exchanging harmony for the dissonance of its sorrow" ("BLS," 123), but as the transformation of even the candid
admissions of late middle age into a dissonant but functional element of "musical
structure."

Reading Eliot in Adorno's terms therefore helps reconcile one of the abiding contradictions in the reception of Eliot: the mismatch between Eliot's *critical*
emphasis on organic unity and his *poetic* exploitation of the shock effects of disruption and juxtaposition. In "The Music of Poetry," Eliot emphasizes the musical
poet's "mastery" of the prosaic and dissonant. Adorno's position is quite similar.
He devises a theory of late style across the arts in terms of dissonance in *Aesthetic
Theory*:

> It is hardly an improper generalization of what is all too divergent if one
> derives the antiharmonic gestures of Michelangelo, of the late Rembrandt,
> and of Beethoven's last works not from the subjective suffering of their
> development as artists but from the dynamic of the concept of harmony
> itself and ultimately from its insufficiency. Dissonance is the truth about
> harmony. If the ideal of harmony is taken strictly, it proves to be unreach-
> able according to its own concept. Its desiderata are satisfied only when such
> unreachableness appears as essence, which is how it appears in the late style
> of important artists.[89] (*Aesthetic Theory*, 110)

Eliot's version might run: "Prose is the truth about poetry." According to
F. O. Matthiessen, in a 1933 lecture about Keats's and Lawrence's letters, Eliot
remarked:

> This speaks to me of that at which I have long aimed, in writing poetry; to
> write poetry which should be essentially poetry, with nothing poetic about
> it, poetry standing naked in its bare bones, or poetry so transparent that we
> should not see the poetry, but that which we are meant to see through the

---

89. "Kaum generalisiert man unziemlich … allzu Divergentes, wenn man die antihar-
monisch Gesten Michelangelos, des späten Rembrandt, des letzten Beethoven, anstatt aus
subjektiv leidvoller Entwicklung, aus der Dynamik des Harmoniebegriffs selber, schließlich
seiner Insuffizienz ableitet. Dissonanz ist die Wahrheit über Harmonie. Wird diese streng
genommen, so erweist sie nach dem Kriterium ihrer selbst sich als unerreichbar. Ihren
Desideraten wird erst dann genügt, wenn solche Unerreichbarkeit als ein Stück Wesen
erscheint; wie im sogenannten Spätstil bedeutender Künstler." *Ästhetische Theorie*, 168.

poetry, poetry so transparent that in reading it we are intent on what the poem *points at*, and not on the poetry, this seems to me the thing to try for. To get *beyond poetry*, as Beethoven, in his later works, strove to get *beyond music*.[90]

Late Beethoven provides Eliot with the model for poetry that becomes "essentially poetry" by eliminating everything "poetic," just as he provides Adorno the model for an aesthetic harmony "satisfied only when [its] unreachableness appears as essence." Eliot's ideal of visionary transparency contrasts drastically with Adorno's advocacy of an opaque art that would point at the wrongs of the bad social totality; yet the shared musical touchstone of Beethoven's late work brings them both back to lateness as the basis for a pure aesthetic consisting, paradoxically, in disruptions of aesthetic purity.

The works only integrate those disruptions by "the figure they form together" ("BLS," 126); as I have been arguing, the aesthetic of lateness always brings the putatively impersonal work back to the person of the aging, dying artist. *Four Quartets* thematizes this paradox in one of its few direct mentions of music. In the last section of "The Dry Salvages," after proclaiming that "to apprehend / The point of intersection of the timeless / With time, is an occupation for the saint" (*CP*, 198), the poem's discourse slides from preaching into sensuous evocation:

> For most of us, there is only the unattended
> Moment, the moment in and out of time,
> The distraction fit, lost in a shaft of sunlight,
> The wild thyme unseen, or the winter lightning
> Or the waterfall, or music heard so deeply
> That it is not heard at all, but you are the music
> While the music lasts. (198–99)

The idea of losing oneself in music furnishes one more version of the aesthetic of impersonality, this time from the perspective of the audience. Yet that audience, apparently a general "most of us" and "you," narrows down to a remembering Eliot

90. F. O. Matthiessen, *The Achievement of T. S. Eliot: An Essay on the Nature of Poetry* (London: Oxford University Press, 1935), 89–90. The authenticity of the exact wording of this much-cited passage has not been verified. On the other hand, Matthiessen's devotion to Eliot, attested throughout his book, gives good reason for supposing he paid attention to and faithfully recorded his key phrases. Stephen Spender's report of Eliot's letter about listening to late Beethoven in 1931, together with the *Quartets* themselves, at least makes the basic elements of Matthiessen's quotation plausible.

with the unexplained specificity of the chain of images that precedes it. In particular, the punning "wild thyme unseen" recurs from "East Coker" III, where "The wild thyme unseen and the wild strawberry, / The laughter in the garden, echoed ecstasy / Not lost" (187); the reference to the garden sends us back further, to "Burnt Norton" I and its scene of reminiscence. Yet here the poem's self-analogy to music proposes that such sequences of recollection do not establish the self but displace it by impersonal aesthetic forms, by "music."

Eliot returns to musical forms in the second part of the final quartet, "Little Gidding." In this climactic episode, however, he does not speak of music directly; instead, he puts the allusion in the mouth of a supernaturally aged, prophetic persona. The episode narrates the strange meeting between the speaker and a "familiar compound ghost" (203). This ghost, blurred and insubstantial, embodies an Eliotic ideal of impersonality: he is introduced contradictorily as "one walking, loitering and hurried," "both intimate and unidentifiable" (203). The ghost's only certain attribute is that he is, as Eliot vaguely puts it, "some dead master"—a poet, in the section's Dantesque idiom. As the ghost later says, alluding to Mallarmé, "Our concern was speech, and speech impelled us / To purify the dialect of the tribe" (204).[91] Thus Eliot turns once more to a Tiresias-like figure for the poetic speaker, a body whose capacity for insight depends on its aging and its attenuated personhood.[92]

The principal sign of the ghost's blurred impersonality is his and the speaker's shifts between singular and plural. Although the episode begins with the apparently personal speaker—Eliot the air-raid warden on "dead patrol"—speaking with a comfortable "I," he soon starts to dissolve: "I fixed upon the down-turned face / That pointed scrutiny with which we challenge / The first-met stranger" (CP, 203). This generalizing "we" anticipates the full confusion of voices and persons that follows:

91. The Mallarmé allusion has often been discussed. John Adames treats Eliot's relation to Mallarméan symbolism in the context of musical aesthetics in "Eliot's Ars Musica Poetica: Sources in French Symbolism," in Cooper, T. S. Eliot's Orchestra, 129–46.

92. Nancy Gish has argued that the recurrent figure of "the double as vile or dirty or mad old man" belongs to the repertoire of Eliot's "distinctive poetics of dissociation." Gish shows how Eliot derived some of his ideas about impersonality and the "dissociation of sensibility," including this figure of the double, from turn-of-the-century theories about the psychological malady of dissociation. The ghost of "Little Gidding" II is a late version of this depiction of a personal disorder as a depersonalizing process. Nancy K. Gish, "Discarnate Desire: T. S. Eliot and the Poetics of Dissociation," in Laity and Gish, Gender, Desire, and Sexuality in T. S. Eliot, 110.

So I assumed a double part, and cried

And heard another's voice cry: 'What! are *you* here?'

Although we were not. I was still the same,

Knowing myself yet being someone other—

And he a face still forming[.] (203)

This dream-vision encounter is, among other things, a straightforward metaphor for the poet's depersonalization in writing: far more explicitly than in earlier poems, Eliot narrates both the yielding of the poet's personality to the poem and the persistence of that personality, the assumption of a double part. He literalizes Adorno's dictum that "Even out of so-called individual works it is a We that speaks and not an I."

It should be no surprise, then, when the talk of these two intermingled figures turns directly from the purification of speech to old age:

'Let me disclose the gifts reserved for age

To set a crown upon your lifetime's effort.

First, the cold friction of expiring sense . . .

Second, the conscious impotence of rage

At human folly . . .

And last, the rending pain of re-enactment

Of all that you have done, and been . . .

From wrong to wrong the exasperated spirit

Proceeds, unless restored by that refining fire

Where you must move in measure, like a dancer.' (204–5)

Reworking Yeats's "The Spur,"[93] Eliot borrows from Yeats the powerful suggestion—which was also essential to the reception of late Beethoven from Wagner on[94]—that all the depredations of age set the poet apart from other persons. The "rage / At human folly" recalls Yeats's cult of Swift's *saeva indignatio*, and with it the implication that this rage, by its very impotence, becomes an inexhaustible provocation to poetry. Rage, like the "rending pain" of memory, coexists with the coldness of "expiring sense": the inner world of the poet is reinforced by the attenuation of the outer one. Yet Eliot's invocation of purgatory allows him to transfigure this idea of intensified late subjectivity into an image of depersonalizing musicality: the "refining fire" restores the spirit by burning away the weight of past wrongs,

93. Helen Gardner also notes the connection; see *The Composition of "Four Quartets,"* 188.

94. See n. 80.

replacing it with the measured movement of musical meter.[95] But, of course, one has to have something to be purged *of* in order to gain these aesthetic benefits.

Helen Gardner's *The Composition of "Four Quartets"* makes clear the deliberateness with which Eliot set about to produce such effects of lateness. Early drafts of "Little Gidding" lacked the ghost's speech on age; in its place was a catalog of images like the list of "unattended / moment[s]" in "The Dry Salvages" V: "Remember ... The wild strawberries eaten in the garden, / The walls of Poitiers [etc.]."[96] Eliot wrote in discontent to John Hayward: "The defect of the whole poem, I feel, is the lack of some acute personal reminiscence (never to be explicated, of course, but to give power from well below the surface) and I can *perhaps* supply this in Part II."[97] In the final version of the poem, Eliot filled the lack by *thematizing* the process of selecting an "acute personal reminiscence" and converting it into inexplicable aesthetic "power": the ghost, instead of invoking a chain of mysterious symbols, describes how the acute pains of personal aging are or should be purged away by the refining fire of poetic meter and Dantesque structure—a purgation whose completion sounds in the All Clear that ends the section (*CP*, 205). When the next section of "Little Gidding" proclaims, "This is the use of memory: / For liberation" (205), the aphorism is almost redundant. Liberation from the person has already entailed the self-reflexive description of the memory-laden, late poet who, becoming something other, ghostly, compound, living and dead, strives to free the work under his hands.

Though Eliot's gesture toward chamber music in the title of *Four Quartets* may have been a self-conscious attempt to lead readers to accept the work as a fully impersonal, completely autonomous form, the working out, within the poem, of a musical late style yields, as in Adorno, a more complex, more realistic version of the autonomy of the work. The poem's references to itself as an aesthetic object—as poetry, or as a dance, or as music—carry us back to the scene of its making. They deliver their own, unexpectedly nuanced hints about the poem's place in the world as the product of a late subjectivity. For Adorno, too, lateness guides us to see not a sealed-in artwork but a relationship between an artistic producer and the product he is striving to make autonomous. Our awareness of the affective

95. This renewal of the impersonal aesthetic as the product of lateness chimes with the echo of Yeats here: "Among School Children," beginning with a stanza describing the poet as "A sixty-year-old smiling public man," works its way to the final question, "How can we know the dancer from the dance?" Yeats, "Among School Children," in *Collected Poems*, 215–17.

96. Gardner, *The Composition of "Four Quartets,"* 183.

97. Quoted in ibid., 24. Gardner gives the date of the letter as August 5, 1941.

particularity of the late-style artist becomes a dialectical part of the relative, contextually embedded, impersonal autonomy of the late artwork.

The Late Style and the Intentional Fallacy

Impersonality has acquired, like other versions of modernist autonomy doctrine, a bad critical reputation. As an invitation to regard the artwork as a free-standing object, divorced from its creator's intent and experience, modernist impersonality has seemed in recent years to lead only to the New Critical attack on the "intentional fallacy" and the forced separation of artworks from their contexts in the service of an ideology of aesthetic transcendence. "New Critical impersonality," writes Cassandra Laity, effects writers' "removal from space and time." [98] Other ways of critiquing personality, subjectivity, and expression remain influential in the cultural and academic fields: Foucauldian, antihumanist accounts of the production of the subject; antiexpressive avant-garde poetics (Oulipo, Language poetry); queer theoretical arguments for breaking down stable personal identities. But the *modernist* rejection of personality in favor of the impersonal work, closely identified with Eliot and the heights of "high" modernism, is still under a cloud. Modernist impersonality seems less like an ambitious social-cultural critique than a claim for the autonomy of the artwork—as in fact it is. But as a result, Eliotic impersonality has been vulnerable to arguments like Maud Ellmann's in her classic *The Poetics of Impersonality*. For skeptics like Ellmann, impersonality is ideological and political; it not only distorts the critical discussion of artworks but serves as an alibi for political quietism or, worse, political reaction.[99]

Given impersonality's bad name, it is hardly surprising that the minor revival in the critical fortunes of Eliot has typically attempted to rescue him from impersonality and other versions of the idea of autonomy.[100] This tendency fits in with the

98. Cassandra Laity, "Introduction: Eliot, Gender, and Modernity," in Laity and Gish, *Gender, Desire, and Sexuality in T. S. Eliot*, 4. The locus classicus for New Critical antiintentionalism is W. K. Wimsatt Jr. and Monroe C. Beardsley, "The Intentional Fallacy," in *The Verbal Icon: Studies in the Meaning of Poetry*, by W. K. Wimsatt Jr. (Lexington: University of Kentucky Press, 1954), 3–18.

99. Maud Ellmann, *The Poetics of Impersonality: T. S. Eliot and Ezra Pound* (Cambridge, MA: Harvard University Press, 1987).

100. Hence Rainey's emphasis on the "histrionic" in *Revisiting "The Waste Land"* and Chinitz's defense of Eliot's thinking about popular culture in *Eliot and Popular Culture*. Laity summarizes this turn as follows: "Eliot's reinsertion into modernity corresponds with

larger recuperative project of recent modernist studies, which, as I remarked in the introduction, has sought to restore modernists to their contexts at the expense of their claims to autonomy. The comparison of Eliot and Adorno I have made in this chapter, however, vitiates the equation of impersonality with a reactionary belief in the immortal transcendence of art. For Eliot and Adorno, impersonality is more than a denial or a cover-up; indeed, the choice between autonomy and engagement, impersonality and contextualization, is artificial. In late style they find an aesthetic strategy of depersonalization that reveals rather than hides the relations of the artistic work to authorial intention, biographical personality, and historical context. That strategy, unlike a more straightforwardly expressive aesthetic, points up the way personal stances and authorial labors give rise to a work which can seem to stand on its own. Late-style impersonality is an effort not of concealment but of disclosure. I hypothesize that such a disclosure may be necessary to the pursuit of a relative autonomy for modernist art: for Eliot and Adorno, whether they fully intend it or not, that pursuit entails the self-reflexive representation of the late artwork's relationship to the persona of its maker.

The pathos of late style, however, matters. It gives Eliot's and Adorno's fictions of impersonal autonomy their characteristic dialectical form. Accounts of Eliot's impersonality that have, quite rightly, related it to ideas of professionalism and the emerging social institutions of autonomous art tend to leave the impression of Eliot as an opportunistic manipulator of literary preconceptions, motivated mostly by the quest for preeminence within the world of letters.[101] Such accounts provide a useful corrective to views of Eliot as a spiritual sage, but they do not explain the personal intensity and the atmosphere of lateness that accompany the images and techniques of impersonality in his poetry. In the same way, readers of Adorno should not have to choose between accepting his theories as universally valid or reducing them to the irascible opinions of an aggravated, disappointed exile. Late style, by contrast, implies both impersonalizing autonomy *and* subjectivity, social

---

a larger, all-encompassing project ... to dissolve the boundary between aesthetics and society in various venues, including the academy's methodological divides, for which Eliot long stood." Laity, "Introduction: Eliot, Gender, and Modernity," 5. However, Tim Dean's essay in the same collection, cited in n. 41, is, in its sympathetic approach to impersonality, an exception to the rule.

101. In addition to the critics cited in n. 11, see Lawrence Rainey, "The Price of Modernism: Publishing *The Waste Land*," chap. 2 in *Revisiting "The Waste Land"* (which expands upon the corresponding chapter of Lawrence Rainey, *Institutions of Modernism: Literary Elites and Public Culture* [New Haven, CT: Yale University Press, 1998]). Rainey does not fully explain how his later, textually intensive reading of *The Waste Land* squares with his sociology of its publication.

position-taking *and* personal expression—but only when the latter augments and modifies the former. In this version of high modernism, all art does aspire to the purely formal, impersonal condition of music; but for Eliot and Adorno, in their late periods from the beginning, the partial, painful conversion of personal experience into musical form is itself well worth making into art.

3. Expatriation as Autonomy
Djuna Barnes, James Joyce, and Aesthetic Cosmopolitanism

There are other ways to live aesthetic autonomy besides lateness. Of these, one modernist lifestyle has been particularly consequential for twentieth-century world literature: writerly exile. Or rather, the mode of life or art that James Joyce, through his character Stephen Dedalus, christened "exile"; in the period of modernism, its practitioners—Joyce included—were, in general, voluntary expatriates.[1] To leave the homeland for Paris, London, or Berlin was supposedly to reject convention and devote oneself to artistic freedom. Later writers living in the Joycean mode, from Vladimir Nabokov to Gao Xingjian, have truly been political exiles, so that alongside this sense of aesthetic autonomy, they acquire a degree of moral or political authority from their circumstances; modernist expatriates have a much less certain claim on such authority. Even Joyce, who did a great deal to promote his own image as an intransigent hero driven out of Ireland by a stifling culture, registers his ambivalence about expatriation in his depiction of Stephen Dedalus. At the end of *A Portrait of the Artist as a Young Man* (1916), Stephen declares for exile and sets off for Paris; we meet him again in the opening sections of *Ulysses* (1922), back in Dublin, creatively frustrated and in despair. If *Ulysses* itself is understood, by Joyce and many others, to be the product of the liberating, generative connection between the writer's expatriate circumstances and his work, why does Joyce leave

1. James Joyce, *A Portrait of the Artist as a Young Man*, ed. Jeri Johnson (Oxford: Oxford University Press, 2000), 208.

his alter ego—who, though often ironized, is never entirely disavowed—with nothing to show for his stay on the Continent? Putting the heroic model of artistic exile in question, these doubts compel us to seek a truer account of the relation between the expatriate mode of life and the modernist modes of literary production.

To develop such an account, I turn to the U.S. born writer Djuna Barnes. Whereas Joyce represents expatriation only in fleeting glimpses, Barnes's work constitutes an extensive, fiercely antiheroic analysis of modernist expatriation. Barnes, who spent most of the years between the wars in Europe, has often appeared to be a Joycean "exile" novelist, above all in the formally experimental, phantasmagorical *Nightwood* (1937). Unlike Joyce, Barnes, in her fiction and journalism, devotes many pages to the world of the expatriates. Yet despite the grimly sardonic tone of her writing, Barnes is not simply a critic or satirist of expatriation. Like the Joyce of *Portrait*, she associates expatriation with aesthetic freedoms: in her work, imaginative play, dreaming, affectation, pleasure, and verbal invention depend on and help create a liberating distance from national and other group identities.

These freedoms, however, do not settle magically on the artist as soon as she steps off the boat to Europe. In Barnes's writings, they are secured only through the exhausting, lonely performance of the aesthete role; to forge a literary style, to gain a foothold in the field of international modernism, she must also insist on a certain lifestyle, that of the detached cosmopolitan writer who refuses group affiliations and political solidarities. In my reading of Barnes, I argue that expatriation offers the modernist writer an opportunity to assert a form of autonomy for her art; but, like the forms of autonomy delineated by those other émigrés, Henry James, T. S. Eliot, and Theodor Adorno, Barnes's does not deny the connections among the work, the writer, and her social scene. Indeed, Barnes, with Joyce, exemplifies one important branch of the family tree of the socially self-reflexive, aestheticist modernism I traced from Huysmans and Wilde to James and Proust in chapter 1. In Barnes's version of this modernism, the assertion of autonomy calls forth detailed representations of the role she must play—and the artistic techniques she must use—within the world of the expats in order to transform expatriation into a relative aesthetic autonomy.

These representations trouble the most familiar accounts of modernism and exile. A long-standing critical tradition, exemplified by Terry Eagleton, George Steiner, and Raymond Williams, sees the disruptions of modernist form as the result of authors' real—or metaphorical—displacement.[2] This experience is also

2. Terry Eagleton, *Exiles and Émigrés: Studies in Modern Literature* (New York: Schocken Books, 1970); George Steiner, *Extraterritorial: Papers on Literature and the*

supposed to afford those who undergo it a convention-breaking artistic freedom; in the most extreme versions of this idea, literal alienation is redeemed in the aesthetic realm. But as another exile writer, Edward Said, has pointed out, the twentieth century's countless refugees and displaced peoples might not be so quick to embrace the redemptive aesthetic value of the exilic experience: "You must first set aside Joyce and Nabokov and think instead of the uncountable masses for whom UN agencies have been created."[3] In this chapter, I show how Barnes, far from mystifying exile as an essentially aesthetic experience, points up the performance through which she *makes* an expatriate lifestyle function as part of a literary claim to autonomy. In her life and work, Barnes creates a space for herself as a modernist writer in the literary field. Her personal and narratorial detachment from national and sexual identities, from coteries and communities, is not a consequence of alienation but a chosen literary position.

This position is, as we shall see, a form of aesthetic cosmopolitanism. But Barnes's cosmopolitan style does not conform to the models of cultural and political cosmopolitanism that have recently been widely discussed in modernist studies and beyond. The "new" or "critical" cosmopolitanisms seek to connect literary themes and styles of transnationalism with a political-ethical project of reform and solidarity on a supranational scale. Whereas earlier scholars of international modernism like Richard Ellmann and Hugh Kenner celebrated writers' exilic disengagement from political conflict, the value of modernist transnationalism would, for the newer school of thought, lie in its engaged, "cosmopolitical" vision; the virtue of modernist style would be that it can also serve as a political ethos. Though Barnes also depicts cosmopolitanism as an always imperfect, socially specific practice rather than a state of perfect detachment, in her work the expatriate aesthete faces a choice between a relatively autonomous artistic practice and the solidarity of political community.

At this troubled juncture of aesthetics and political ethos, Barnes's relation to Joyce becomes important. Even more than Barnes, Joyce has seemed an exemplary cosmopolitan modernist writer, one whose anticolonial, humanist politics appears

---

Language Revolution (New York: Atheneum, 1971); Raymond Williams, "Metropolitan Perceptions and the Emergence of Modernism," chap. 2 in *The Politics of Modernism: Against the New Conformists*, ed. Tony Pinkney (London: Verso, 1989). Williams's argument, though more sociological, does not distinguish expatriation from other kinds of displaced experience of the metropolis.

3. Edward W. Said, "Reflections on Exile," in *Reflections on Exile and Other Essays* (Cambridge, MA: Harvard University Press, 2000), 175. Aijaz Ahmad is also attentive to the modernist connection as he pursues a severe critique of overgeneralizations of exile in cultural theory in his *In Theory: Classes, Nations, Literatures* (London: Verso, 1992).

to be woven into his aesthetic project. At the end of this chapter, however, I suggest that the Barnesian understanding of expatriation as autonomy is equally applicable to Joyce. Barnes shows how we must drive a wedge between Joycean aesthetics and Joycean politics precisely where they meet: in the theme of artistic exile. Joyce, like Barnes, makes the autonomy of his writing depend on the lifestyle of the artist, and Joyce's cosmopolitanism, like Barnes's, keeps communal political programs at a distance.

Nightwood: The Luminous Deterioration of Cosmopolitanism

The most prominent feature of Barnes's writing is not her expatriate themes but her startling prose style. Her phrasing leaps away from the expected word, as in the first description of the recumbent Robin Vote:

> About her head there was an effulgence as of phosphorus glowing about the circumference of a body of water—as if her life lay through her in ungainly luminous deteriorations—the troubling structure of the born somnambule, who lives in two worlds—meet of child and desperado.[4]

As the dashes and metaphors multiply, the text comes to resemble the "luminous deteriorations" it describes. Nothing is in place: life lies "through" or "around" instead of within, as though Robin's drunken haze has spilled into the narration. Barnes describes her character as a conjunction of unlikes, awake and asleep, child and outlaw. A related hybridity infects the word choice, as the sentence culminates in an illicitly male-gendered and Hispanophone "desperado." The strange, ungovernable, mysterious figure of Robin Vote, named in French as "la somnambule," is matched by an outlaw descriptive language framing its own rules, setting aside the norms of conventional English prose.

It is tempting to see in this prose style, which runs throughout Barnes's novel and her entire œuvre, an analogue for the themes of the novel and a symbol for Barnes's own turbulent expatriate career. *Nightwood*'s characters—expatriate Americans, together with one European Jew—wander the streets of Paris and Berlin, chasing after lovers and struggling to make sense of their own desires as their aspirations move incessantly out of reach. An account of modernist style as

4. Djuna Barnes, *Nightwood: The Original Version and Related Drafts*, ed. Cheryl J. Plumb (Normal, IL: Dalkey Archive, 1995), 33. Henceforth I cite this edition parenthetically in the text.

exile in language, in the manner of George Steiner, might describe Barnes's form as an imitation of the alienated condition of the author and her characters. But that account would not explain *why* Barnes would practice such an imitative form. It is true that the border-crossing metaphors—Robin's life as coastline, her birth not in one nation but in two worlds—like the multilingual vocabulary, simultaneously advertise the author's international experience and proclaim her willingness to adopt a difficult, unconventional idiom; and Barnes's style does give voice to a distinctly cosmopolitan sensibility, knowing, worldly, divided between empathic insight and wry detachment.[5] Yet these aspects of her style mark her not as a transcriber of her own experience in imitative form but as a writer committed to her own literary autonomy.

Indeed, instead of form imitating theme, the description of Robin thematizes form: Robin, the hybrid and transgressor of borders, offers a figure for Barnes's style. But if Robin seems to stand for aesthetic freedom in her roles as a dreamer and liberated spirit, a young woman on her own in Bohemian Paris, she is also isolated, outlawed, and, in an ambiguously gendered sense, desperate. Furthermore, Robin's aesthetic quality is the source of her pathos: her luminousness entails ungainly deterioration, and her ethereal somnolence leaves her unresponsive to others, even as it makes her the object of desire to those, like Baron Felix Volkbein, who look at her.

In light of this troubling combination of freedom and pathos, *cosmopolitan* becomes a particularly appropriate term for Barnes's style, because the term has an inescapable ambivalence. On one hand, cosmopolitanism bespeaks a high-minded idea of global community, a wide range of cultural reference, and an ethically even-handed interest in people of many kinds and places. But the word also indicates a leisurely, uncommitted, "rootless," and, indeed, aestheticist mode of life: a "lifestyle" in the pejorative sense that word sometimes implies, with its ties to consumerist superficiality. As the ethical ideal shades into the leisured pose, cosmopolitanism can seem quite at ease with the inequalities of power and the essentializing, restrictive notions of identity that a universalist global citizenship might be thought to oppose. Jessica Berman has captured this duality well in her analysis of the early years of the American magazine *Cosmopolitan*

---

5. In an essay on *Nightwood* and Barnes's *Ladies Almanack*, Monica Kaup analyzes similar features of Barnes's style in the context of a transnational, anti-authoritarian, anti-Enlightenment "Neobaroque." Though I share Kaup's sense of the fundamental significance of Barnes's style, I seek to interpret its implications for expatriation and cosmopolitanism rather than for modernity tout court. Monica Kaup, "The Neobaroque in Djuna Barnes," *Modernism/Modernity* 12, no. 1 (January 2005): 85–110.

at the end of the nineteenth century, when it was suspended between the sensibility of its 1886 masthead declaration, "The world is my country and all mankind are my countrymen," and "wanderlust and desire for exotica."[6] In a similar vein, David Damrosch finds that early twentieth-century world-literature anthologies like the Harvard Classics demonstrate that "cosmopolitanism itself showed elements of a higher form of nativism."[7] Describing Barnes's mode of writing as cosmopolitan, therefore, specifies its social range of significance, associating the aesthete's detachment—her flair for striking description, her wry or ironic narrative attitude to her characters, and her exuberant, disturbing dislocations of language—with an ethical detachment from limited, local, putatively fixed forms of identity and affiliation. But the label "cosmopolitan" also reminds us that this association of the political stance with an aesthetic mode is contingent at best.[8]

Just when and how cosmopolitan attitudes conduce to political engagement with local and global communities has been a central preoccupation for literary and philosophical defenses of cosmopolitanism. Bruce Robbins sets forth an exemplary version of this defense in *Feeling Global*. In mounting his case that culture, rather than political institutions, can create strongly felt, ethically significant transnational bonds, he finds that modernist aesthetic practice poses particular problems. In a critique of a Susan Sontag essay from 1995 about Bosnia, he faults that practice as a politically ineffective version of internationalism:

> As she tells it, her sojourn in Bosnia becomes a model of avant-garde aesthetic experience. Its aim is the modernist aim of disorientation, defamiliarization, making strange .... Sontag's contempt for the stay-at-home is the contempt of the coterie tastemaker for the mass of the tasteless or insensitive, those who are incapable of the latest, deepest, most strenuous

6. Jessica Schiff Berman, *Modernist Fiction, Cosmopolitanism, and the Politics of Community* (Cambridge: Cambridge University Press, 2001), 28, 30.

7. David Damrosch, *What Is World Literature?* (Princeton, NJ: Princeton University Press, 2003), 123.

8. This uncertain association is a primary concern of work on the new cosmopolitanism. In addition to Berman, I have drawn on three writers in particular: Rebecca Walkowitz, *Cosmopolitan Style: Modernism beyond the Nation* (New York: Columbia University Press, 2006); Amanda Anderson, *The Powers of Distance: Cosmopolitanism and the Cultivation of Detachment* (Princeton, NJ: Princeton University Press, 2001); and Bruce Robbins, *Feeling Global: Internationalism in Distress* (New York: New York University Press, 1999) and "The Newspapers Were Right: Cosmopolitanism, Forgetting, and 'The Dead,'" *Interventions* 5, no. 1 (January 2003): 101–12. In what follows I return to each of these writers.

self-alienation, the most rigorous self-problematizing—those incapable, in short, of modernism's version of aesthetic experience.[9]

Robbins's argument makes clear why a cosmopolitan politics should find itself in tension with a Barnesian modernist style. As an engine of artistic distinction that separates the convention-busting writer from the conventional "mass," the dislocating aesthetic technique Robbins calls "disorientation" or "self-alienation" jars against feelings of community or shared concern. It might seem, then, that to adopt the disruptive techniques of modernist cosmopolitanism is also to condone the elitism Robbins sees in Sontag.

At times, it is true, Barnes also struck a haughtily elitist pose, as when she responded to a *Little Review* questionnaire about her personal opinions with a flat refusal, adding, "Nor have I that respect for the public."[10] Yet even that statement might better be seen as a performance of impersonal, solitary autonomy for an avant-garde audience that expects and values such declarations from its writers. More significantly, in *Nightwood* and elsewhere, Barnes shows none of the self-satisfaction of the elitist, dwelling instead on the frustrated yearnings that beset the cosmopolitan aesthete. Though she chooses the pursuit of aesthetic autonomy, she nonetheless registers the appeal of transnational community. The first chapter of *Nightwood* describes the kinship that Baron Felix, perpetually ill at ease over his fraudulent claim to Austrian nobility, feels with the people of the circus. The narrative conjoins a self-reflexive affirmation of aesthetic artifice with the possibility, quickly withdrawn, of a fellowship of outcasts:

> Early in life Felix had insinuated himself into the pageantry of the circus and the theatre. In some way they linked his emotions to the higher and unattainable pageantry of Kings and Queens. The more amiable actresses of Prague, Vienna, Hungary, Germany, France and Italy, the acrobats and sword-swallowers, had at one time or another allowed him their dressing rooms—sham salons in which he aped his heart. Here he had neither to be capable nor alien. He became for a little while a part of their splendid and reeking falsification.
>
> The people of this world, with desires utterly divergent from his own, had also seized on titles for a purpose. There was a Princess Nadja, a Baron von Tink, a Principessa Stasera y Stasero, a King Buffo and a Duchess of

---

9. Robbins, *Feeling Global,* 15.

10. Quoted in Mary Lynn Broe, ed., *Silence and Power: A Reevaluation of Djuna Barnes* (Carbondale: Southern Illinois University Press, 1991), 66.

Broadback: gaudy, cheap cuts from the beast life, immensely capable of that great disquiet called entertainment. They took titles merely to dazzle boys about town, to make their public life (and it was all they had) mysterious and perplexing, knowing well that skill is never so amazing as when it seems inappropriate. Felix clung to his title to dazzle his own estrangement. It brought them together. (10–11)

Placed at the opening of the novel, the circus functions as the model for all the other arenas in which the novel unfolds—its cafés, parties, and junk-filled apartments.[11] Like Barnes's text, the circus provides the stage for fantastic "acts" that straddle the boundary between pleasure and horror in their exaggeration, whimsy, and grotesquerie. Its performers possess only "stage" identities: their public life is "all they have." They anticipate the novel's most flamboyant performer, Doctor Matthew O'Connor, who calls himself "damned, and carefully public" (134). The people of the circus, like the characters in a fiction, have no offstage lives, only the aesthetic ones that people pay to see. They are condemned to continuous falsification and affectation, attempting to confer value on their act through the "dazzlement" of their unlikely names. For Barnes, however, this is—in a twist that looks ironically at her own stylistic performance—simply the nature of entertainment itself, which, disquietingly, depends on "splendid and reeking falsification."

Nonetheless, the circus provides a refuge for the wandering Felix, a realm in which his inability to belong and the falseness of his claim to titled blood finds its comforting double among people for whom authenticity has no importance. The comfort and discomfort of the circus, in other words, are equally due to its aesthetic nature.[12] That aesthetic is specifically nonnational. Barnes's description, following the traveling circus, makes it seem as though the circus dressing rooms of both cities and countries across Europe—"Prague, Vienna, Hungary, Germany, France and Italy"—are all one continuous, transnational "world." In this it matches Felix, "for the Jew seems to be everywhere from nowhere" (8). These multiple places can be conflated because they always map onto the single otherworld of the aesthetic; even the circus dressing rooms, where the truth under the costume might be

11. For a discussion of the circus in Barnes's New York journalism as well as her fiction, see Laura Winkiel, "Circuses and Spectacles: Public Culture in *Nightwood*," *Journal of Modern Literature* 21, no. 1 (Fall 1997): 7–28.

12. Barnes elsewhere depicts nobility as an equally stylized form of being. In a 1927 *McCall's* magazine piece on "American Wives and Titled Husbands," she quotes an American-born, "real" principessa as saying of her Italian husband: "Manners rule his life." "American Wives and Titled Husbands," in *Interviews*, ed. Alyce Barry (Washington, DC: Sun & Moon, 1985), 316.

revealed, are only "sham salons." Those rooms are associated with the artificiality of the aesthetic twice over, as shams and as salons. Felix joins this realm as a performer himself; in a characteristically Barnesian phrase, he "apes his heart" rather than merely expressing or exposing it.

But the same loneliness Barnes associates with Robin Vote's aesthetic quality also disrupts the hopeful dream of the circus as a cosmopolitan refuge. The narrator stresses the temporariness of Felix's ease with the circus people: "he became *for a little while* a part of their ... falsification"; their desires are "utterly divergent from his own." The circus is therefore a model for the novel's other cosmopolitan communities not only in its welcoming characteristics but in its inhospitality, transience, and alienation. If Barnes represents a place of allegiance of radically diverse people in which the idea of the nation, like the idea of authenticity itself, has no value except in parody, she does so only to withdraw the utopian appeal it might have. Still, she is not simply satirizing the circus world and the other aestheticized realms for which it stands. The circus in *Nightwood* makes Barnes's best case for the aesthetic as a socially redemptive domain including both expatriated life and autonomous art: its style of life permits extravagant freedoms of performance and transnational mobility. But the community of durably shared aims and desires that those freedoms seem to promise cannot hold together.

For readers of Barnes, the community of desire has seemed particularly important. Needless to say, the novel's attention to the people of the circus—like the love story of Nora Flood and Robin Vote and the monologues of the cross-dressing Doctor O'Connor—represents an exploration of queer sexuality just as much as they interrogate a cosmopolitan lifestyle. Barnes's relation to lesbianism and queerness has been extensively debated by readers from her work's first appearance. Especially since the recuperative work of Shari Benstock in *Women of the Left Bank*, Barnes has been increasingly understood as a lesbian or a queer writer at the level of technique as well.[13] But as Scott Herring argues convincingly in *Queering the Underworld*, the scholarly tendency to link Barnes to affirmations of minority

13. Shari Benstock, *Women of the Left Bank: Paris, 1900–1940* (Austin: University of Texas Press, 1986). Joseph Allen Boone argues for *Nightwood* as a queer novel in *Libidinal Currents: Sexuality and the Shaping of Modernism* (Chicago: University of Chicago Press, 1998). Other theoretical approaches to Barnes have also tended to see her as affirming queer sexuality; see, for example, Dianne Chisholm's Benjaminian reading, "Obscene Modernism: *Eros Noir* and the Profane Illumination of Djuna Barnes," *American Literature* 69, no. 1 (March 1997): 167–206, and Merrill Cole's Lacanian treatment, "Backwards Ventriloquy: The Historical Uncanny in Barnes's *Nightwood*," *Twentieth-Century Literature* 52, no. 4 (Winter 2006): 391–412.

sexual identity or subculture ignores the "deeply anticommunitarian" tendency of her work.[14] Herring shows how Barnes's modernist stylistic choices—her antirealism, her cultivation of "*dis*articulation on levels both formal and thematic"—makes her novel a "blueprint for an illegible queer diaspora" rather than a rallying cry for queer identity.[15] The disquieting solitude of *Nightwood*'s circus makes the incompatibility between Barnes's literary work and a queer identity politics particularly clear.

Barnes's procedures dissolve sexual solidarities at the same time as they trouble other cosmopolitan affiliations. But her modes of life and art do not have sexual-identity critique as their principal aim or content. Without denying the complex connections among aestheticism, expatriation, and queerness in Barnes's writings and her social contexts, I want to emphasize her significance as an exemplary modernist cosmopolitan over and above her relation to the politics of sexual identity. I seek to explain her disdain for community—lesbian and queer as well as national and transnational—in terms of the conflict between the social role of the would-be autonomous modernist writer and the field of group-identity politics. For Barnes, solidarity in that field, appealing though it might be, will have to be realized through other than aesthetic means.

French Nights and the Artist's Lifestyle

Though the aesthetic cosmopolitan may refuse the bonds of political community, she does not claim to take leave of the social world altogether. There *is* a social context for Barnes's work, and *Nightwood*'s most conspicuously lonely figure, Doctor O'Connor, can point us to it. In the novel's central chapter, "Watchman, What of the Night?," Nora Flood comes to him to find out what has become of the absconded Robin Vote. The doctor talks to her at length, but his wide-ranging rhapsody strays further and further from her desperately pointed questions:

> "But," Nora said, "I never thought of the night as a life at all—I've never lived it—why did she?"
>
> "I'm telling you of French nights at the moment," the doctor went on, "and why we all go into them." (72)

14. Scott Herring, *Queering the Underworld: Slumming, Literature, and the Undoing of Lesbian and Gay History* (Chicago: University of Chicago Press, 2007), 181.

15. Ibid., 174, 187 (emphasis in original).

The doctor's meditation stubbornly avoids his interlocutor's concerns. Just as other moments of self-reflexivity in the novel are invaded by loneliness, here too O'Connor's—and Barnes's—stylistic display occurs under the sign of frustrated expectation and erotic loss for both characters: when Nora appears at his apartment the doctor is "extremely put out, having expected someone else" (69), presumably a lover. But if Barnes's expatriates once again find themselves unable to find common ground in queer desire, the doctor is quite clear on what they do share: "French nights."

Whereas the pursuit of cosmopolitan aesthetic autonomy disrupts many forms of community, it harmonizes with a shared sense of the meaning of France, and of Paris in particular, for those who devote themselves to literature and the artistic expat lifestyle. Later I discuss Barnes's nonfiction accounts of Paris, but here I emphasize the city's broader cultural significance. In the early decades of the twentieth century, Paris was internationally understood as standing for aesthetic liberty. It was imagined, Pascale Casanova writes in her sociology of *The World Republic of Letters*, to be "the capital of a republic having neither borders nor boundaries, a universal homeland exempt from all professions of patriotism, a kingdom of literature set up in opposition to the ordinary laws of states, a transnational realm whose sole imperatives are those of art and literature: the universal republic of letters."[16] Malcolm Cowley's memoir of the 1920s, *Exile's Return*, describes this notion as pervasive among his generation of American expatriates: "At last hundreds and thousands of them became veritable exiles, living in Paris or the South of France and adhering to a theory of art which held that the creative artist is absolutely independent of all localities, nations or classes."[17] Or, as Gertrude Stein hyperbolically puts it in her 1940 book *Paris France*, "So Paris was the place that suited those of us that were to create the twentieth century art and literature, naturally enough."[18]

The truth of claims made on behalf of Paris's artistic preeminence and cosmopolitan openness is far less important than the fact that those claims were widespread.[19] The mythology of Paris gives significance to Doctor O'Connor's

16. Pascale Casanova, *The World Republic of Letters*, trans. M. B. DeBevoise (Cambridge, MA: Harvard University Press, 2004), 29.

17. Malcolm Cowley, *Exile's Return: A Literary Odyssey of the 1920s*, ed. Donald W. Faulkner (New York: Penguin, 1994), 206.

18. Gertrude Stein, *Paris France* (New York: Liveright, 1940), 12.

19. For the historian Patrice Higonnet, after 1889 the prevailing cultural conceptions of Paris detached themselves from reality; the city, he says, "became the phantasmagoric, falsely mythical capital of pleasure, sex, and (in 1931) European colonialism." Nonetheless, "for thousands of Americans from the American Revolution until at least the 1960s … Paris

preference for discussing French nights over Nora's despair, making his non sequitur a version of the Barnesian turn toward cosmopolitan aesthetic autonomy. The aesthetic detachment of the doctor's cosmopolitanism becomes tied to the notion of Paris as a world capital: " 'French nights are those which all nations seek the world over—and have you noticed that? Ask Doctor Mighty O'Connor, the reason the doctor knows everything is because he's been everywhere at the wrong time and has now become anonymous'" (71). The more outlandishly stylized and fictional an understanding of the geographical context the doctor articulates, the better it serves as an icon of aesthetic autonomy, of a life which can be freely cosmopolitan because it takes place wholly within an aesthetic realm.[20]

To write in the expatriate mode is, according to the doctor, to be untimely, migratory, and "anonymous." By submerging himself in the Parisian nightworld, the doctor imagines that he can slough off the contingencies of location, history, and personality. As *Nightwood* makes clear, this performance of artistic independence nourishes itself on the conventions of the Parisian milieu. But the more the doctor succeeds in cultivating this expressive freedom, becoming almost a word-producing device, the less he can stick to the topics that matter to his friends. He becomes ever more reminiscent of *Nightwood* itself; readers have often described its own distance from its flattened or grotesque characters, its flair for recherché vocabulary, and its occasionally archaizing style.[21] The doctor is a grotesque, too, a melodramatic, self-pitying egotist; but if Barnes thereby establishes a certain distance from this character, he still indicates what kind of social life the expatriate aesthete chooses when she goes into the French night.

If style is not simply something the cosmopolitan practices in her books but something she lives as well, the ramifications of Barnes's cosmopolitan style should be visible in her own expatriate life. In fact, the pressure of aesthetic distinctiveness against communal belonging does have suggestive resonances in Barnes's biography. In 1932 Barnes left her Paris apartment to live in a manor house in Devonshire rented by Peggy Guggenheim, who had supported her intermittently

---

has been a Mecca of high culture." Patrice Higonnet, *Paris: Capital of the World*, trans. Arthur Goldhammer (Cambridge, MA: Harvard University Press, 2002), 15, 319.

20. Higonnet notes with disgust the "superficial nature" of the relation the "Lost Generation" had to the Paris they lived in, but Barnes cannily incorporates such superficiality into her aesthetic. Higonnet, *Paris*, 338.

21. See, for example, Kaup, "The Neobaroque in Djuna Barnes," and Louis F. Kannenstine, *The Art of Djuna Barnes: Duality and Damnation* (New York: New York University Press, 1977). Kannenstine dwells at length on Barnes's "effort of literary detachment" (xv) in *Nightwood* and throughout her career.

for at least a decade. Guggenheim describes Barnes's living situation at Hayford Hall in her memoirs:

> One bedroom, however, was rather dressed up in rococo style, and it looked so much like Djuna that we gave it to her. It was in this room, in bed, that she wrote most of *Nightwood*. Later she did not agree, and said we gave her this room because nobody wanted it.[22]

The "rococo" probably called Barnes to mind at least in part because of her elaborate, mannered literary style.[23] In any case, "we"—Guggenheim and John Ferrar Holms, *Nightwood*'s dedicatees—see Barnes herself as a kind of style personified: Guggenheim does not say that the room, "rather dressed up" and "rococo," reminds her of Barnes but that it "looked so much like her." The artist thus becomes interchangeable, in the patron's eyes, with the interior decorations.

Guggenheim's remark sums up Barnes's position in expatriate circles. Invited into the house, Barnes is assigned a room—which she, with an outsider's resentment, takes to be the one everyone else rejected. Guggenheim's "rather dressed up" might be a dig at Barnes's well-known sartorial extravagances; on the other hand, Barnes's taste for "very beautiful French gowns" appears in a different light when Guggenheim unself-consciously remarks a few pages later that Barnes "had no suitable clothes for the country .... I usually wore riding pants."[24] In a quasi-utopian artist's retreat, an idyll of expatriate autonomy on the Dartmoor, Barnes has become her style—in dress and in writing. The result is her uncomfortable sense that she lives at the mercy of a patron, who, with her friends, lovers, and cronies, has typecast her and hemmed her in precisely because of the style that makes her distinctive. Guggenheim remarks that Barnes "was afraid to leave the house. She felt it necessary to guard her manuscript."[25] According to Guggenheim, Barnes feared that their friend Emily Coleman would burn her manuscript, but such a fear over her text blends in with social unease. Of course this does not mean that Guggenheim, whatever her possible condescension, was anything other than a patient friend and supporter of Barnes. Rather, the social-aesthetic position Barnes

---

22. Peggy Guggenheim, *Out of This Century: Confessions of an Art Addict* (New York: Universe, 1979), 114.

23. "The term *rococo*," writes Louis Kannenstine of *Nightwood*, "is crucial in describing the book's manner ... as an art of ornamentation, where a sense of pattern is uppermost." Kannenstine, *The Art of Djuna Barnes*, 100. Compare also Kaup's term "neobaroque."

24. Guggenheim, *Out of This Century*, 116–17.

25. Ibid., 116.

occupied together with her writing left her subject to "a feeling of 'removal'" even where she might have been at home.[26]

This same displaced, outsider status makes Barnes's stylistic investment in autonomy far riskier and socially more meaningful. Her gender already puts her at odds with the norm of male modernism in expatriate Paris.[27] Within specifically female and lesbian circles, Barnes does not fit neatly into any coteries, even those of her patrons. Karla Jay writes about the class difference that separated Barnes—raised in impoverished conditions, lacking formal education, and supporting herself through journalism and friends' occasional patronage—from other expatriate American women artists with independent incomes, like Stein and Natalie Barney, and describes Barnes as "half in and half out of the club."[28] Whereas the aesthetics of Stein and Barney are linked to their sense of creating and participating in their own avant-garde communities, Barnes's aestheticism, the work of someone not in a position to join the "club," has a different significance. It becomes the foundation of her claim to be taken seriously as a distinctive modernist writer. By no means am I suggesting that Barnes's social alienation, to whatever degree she experienced it, is merely *reflected* in *Nightwood* at the level of plot or style. Nor do I mean to imply any judgment about her social habits and friendships. Instead, I suggest that Barnesian style, in the expatriate context, is simultaneously a literary and a social mode, offering a measure of aesthetic autonomy at the price of comfortable group belonging.

For Barnes, literary aesthetics and lifestyle are interwoven; to invoke a Bourdieuean term, her literary mode and her mode of life are expressions of one habitus. As Bourdieu describes it in *The Logic of Practice* [*Le sens pratique*], habitus

26. The phrase is from the description of Jenny Petherbridge (*Nightwood*, 83). Barnes's biographer Phillip Herring describes Hayford Hall as "a critical community that provided both intellectual stimulation and editorial input for her novel-in-progress." *Djuna: The Life and Work of Djuna Barnes* (New York: Viking, 1995), 186. For more details on the Guggenheim–Barnes relationship at Hayford Hall, see Mary Lynn Broe, "My Art Belongs to Daddy: Incest as Exile, the Textual Economics of Hayford Hall," in *Women's Writing in Exile*, ed. Mary Lynn Broe and Angela Ingram (Chapel Hill: University of North Carolina Press, 1989), 41–86.

27. See Benstock's classic recuperation of women expatriate modernists in *Women of the Left Bank*, as well as Bonnie Kime Scott, *Refiguring Modernism*, 2 vols. (Bloomington: Indiana University Press, 1995). The masculine tone of the American artist cliques in Paris is indicated by the almost complete absence of women from Malcolm Cowley's book—with the exception of dismissive references to "unhappy ex-débutantes wondering whether a literary career wouldn't take the place of marriage." Cowley, *Exile's Return*, 240.

28. Karla Jay, "The Outsider among the Expatriates: Djuna Barnes' Satire on the Ladies of the *Almanack*," in Broe, *Silence and Power*, 193.

is a system of "durable, transposable dispositions, structured structures predis-posed to function as structuring structures"; this system, more often expressed through practical sense than in conscious reflection, can explain patterns of "stylis-tic unity" in a given person's behavior in multiple domains of practice.[29] The idea of habitus, with its element of the involuntary, may seem to conflict with any affirmation of autonomy. But one of Bourdieu's key insights into the problem of aesthetic autonomy is that the would-be autonomous artist occupies a spe-cific social position with its own associated habitus, its own practical sense and lifestyle; literary autonomy, like other forms of autonomy, can be meaningful, be real, precisely because it can be founded in a habitus. Bourdieu makes his case for this theory of autonomy in *The Rules of Art*, where he analyzes how Gus-tave Flaubert carved out the position of the autonomous artist in the Paris of his time, not only by his literary choices but also by his social mannerisms and positions in cultural controversies; "'Art for art's sake,'" Bourdieu argues, "is a *posi-tion to be made*."[30] To seek autonomy, the artist must take possession of a specific habitus.

Bourdieu's hypothesis can help us understand why Barnes's prose and her social manner with Guggenheim and other American expatriates are related—whether Barnes wished it or not. To pursue autonomy in literature requires work not just on a literary product but on a social persona as well. I return to Bourdieu's theory of the literary work when I say more about Barnes's stylistic methods. For now, it is enough to see that Bourdieu's theory of a habitus linking a lifestyle and an aspi-ration to autonomy can illuminate Barnes's expatriate life. Not that Barnes simply confirms Bourdieu's Flaubertian paradigm. Barnes, socially marginal even among the American expatriates, has more occasion to notice the burdens of this artistic life than Bourdieu's Flaubert does. Whereas the sociologist emphasizes Flaubert's heroic "conquest of autonomy," Barnes and her cast of outsiders keep up the per-formance of cosmopolitan aesthetic freedom only by doing without communities of sexuality, class, nationality, even friendship. But Barnes also knows that this per-formance makes her distance from these communities meaningful for her position in the literary field.

29. Pierre Bourdieu, *The Logic of Practice*, trans. Richard Nice (Stanford, CA: Stanford University Press, 1990), 53, 13.

30. Pierre Bourdieu, *The Rules of Art: Genesis and Structure of the Literary Field*, trans. Susan Emanuel (Cambridge: Polity Press, 1996), 76 (emphasis in original). Henceforth I cite this translation parenthetically in the text. All emphases are original unless otherwise noted; brackets mark my occasional modifications to the translation.

Wandering Jews, Wandering Americans

Barnes's cosmopolitan detachment extends even to an ambivalence about cosmopolitans themselves. The most conspicuous form of this ambivalence is also the least ethically appealing—the representation of *Nightwood*'s Felix Volkbein in terms of the anti-Semitic cliché of the Jew as a rootless wanderer:

> No matter where and when you meet him you feel that he has come from some place—no matter from what place he has come—some country that he has devoured rather than resided in, some secret land that he has been nourished on but cannot inherit, for the Jew seems to be everywhere from nowhere. When Felix's name was mentioned, three or more persons would swear to having seen him the week before in three different countries simultaneously. (8)

This characterization poses serious problems for any ethical claim on behalf of Barnes's cosmopolitanism. In speaking with a generalizing "you," she seems to endorse the stigmatization and exclusion of an entire ethnic group from any community—hardly a generous ethical stance. Worse yet, those stereotypes denigrate Jews precisely because they are seen as mobile, landless cosmopolitans. To be "from nowhere" is not (as some expatriates might have it) to achieve freedom from the confines of one's own homeland and national identity; it is to be a predator on someone else's. Although we might believe that Barnes would accept the cosmopolitan loneliness of Doctor O'Connor or Robin Vote for herself, it is hard to imagine her choosing to be an exile in the manner of Felix.

So troubling is Barnes's treatment of her Jewish character that admiring readers of *Nightwood* have tried to minimize its anti-Semitism in various ways. Many significant readings have argued for the novel's feminist or queer or—in a recent formulation due to Alex Goody—"minoritarian" politics, claiming that it lodges a protest against bad kinds of social authority and speaks for oppressed groups, Jews included.[31] Jane Marcus's influential essay on *Nightwood* and abjection offers an exemplary version of such claims: "Barnes's portraits of the abject constitute a political case, a kind of feminist-anarchist call for freedom from fascism."[32] Marcus dismisses the charge of anti-Semitism, claiming that "Djuna Barnes identifies

---

31. Alex Goody, *Modernist Articulations: A Cultural Study of Djuna Barnes, Mina Loy and Gertrude Stein* (Houndmills, UK: Palgrave Macmillan, 2007), 192.

32. Jane Marcus, "Laughing at Leviticus: *Nightwood* as Woman's Circus Epic," in Broe, *Silence and Power*, 221.

with all outsiders."[33] Goody concedes that Barnes's "representation of Jews remains equivocal," but still maintains that "Barnes does include Jews in her attempt to write out a minoritarian politics."[34] But Barnes's aesthetic position precludes her calling for these forms of political solidarity. Indeed, her treatment of Felix harmonizes with that aesthetic, marking her archly distanced narrative position with distinctive, rococo rhetorical flair in a ladder of noun phrases: "some place ... some country ... some secret land."

If the narrator's antipathy for Felix suits the novel's style, so does Felix's own mode of life. For all the distance between Barnes and Felix, he is a primary representative of aestheticism in a novel powerfully shaped by aestheticism. The baron is an aesthete in his obsession with forms and his complete devotion to a pure affectation. His claim to nobility is false, its only basis consisting in two portraits of putative noble ancestors his father, Guido, had made (8); Felix's identity is constituted through art. His obsession with the books and paraphernalia of the "great past" (9) transforms his life into a work of (futile) imagination. Though he may be a wandering Jew, he is also deeply akin to his aesthete creator. Barnes in fact announces this kinship with the first sentence of the novel, which describes Felix's birth and the death of his (non-Jewish) mother, Hedvig: Barnes stages her authorship of her character as a birth—and then disavows it by killing off the mother, her surrogate. But this disavowal of someone related to her is also something the author has in common with the ersatz baron.

The importance of the anti-Semitism in the characterization of Felix lies, then, in its resemblance to other disquieting moments of self-reflexivity in the novel, like the description of the circus.[35] The prejudiced treatment of Felix represents one more attempt to work out the consequences of a cosmopolitan aesthetic as a lifestyle. But I do not mean to suggest that this connection to Barnes's aesthetic completely redeems the expression of prejudice in her novel. Ethical ambivalence of this kind is probably a regular feature of this mode of literary cosmopolitanism. Scholarship has certainly noticed it frequently; advocates of the new cosmopolitanisms often find themselves arguing that some cosmopolitan writer's expression of racial or national prejudice is nonetheless part of a redeeming global orientation.

33. Ibid, 229.

34. Goody, *Modernist Articulations*, 192.

35. Phillip Herring puts the case this way: "The national and racial stereotypes of *Nightwood* ... express the intense alienation from both family and nation that Barnes felt during her adult life, for one would be hard put to make the case that she saw herself as a truly American writer." But Barnes's writing manifests alienation as part and parcel of her aesthetic position—not as an an unmediated expression of her psyche. Herring, *Djuna*, 85.

Amanda Anderson's *Powers of Distance* sees a sophisticated ethical cosmopolitanism alongside the sometimes crude stereotypes in Matthew Arnold's study of Celtic literature; Jessica Berman argues for an inclusive vision of community amid the expressions of anti-Semitism in Henry James's "The Question of Our Speech."[36] Indeed, according to the geographer David Harvey, awkward conjunctions of universalist outlook and particular prejudice—especially imperial prejudice toward dominated and colonized peoples—have dogged cosmopolitanism at least since Kant.[37]

Barnes furnishes an additional example of this conjunction, but her case helps underscore the importance of aesthetics—of writerly technique—to the modernist version of the problem. The preconceptions about the wandering Jew that surface in the treatment of Felix contribute to *Nightwood*'s thematization of its own expatriate style. In *Nightwood*, that style is, like Felix himself, incompatible with national or transnational political community. Thus, he points to the place where we can *distinguish* cosmopolitan aesthetics from cosmopolitan politics in Barnes's account of expatriation as part of the practice of aesthetic autonomy. This distinction arises not because of any essential alienation of the modern artist from society, nor because of the nature of art, but because Barnes's particular style is also a social tactic of disidentification. If that tactic sometimes works through ethically unappealing prejudice, it also grants to her work an insight into the social and political implications of autonomy in her milieu, troubling as these sometimes are.

This version of autonomy, marked though it is by a compatibility with anti-Semitism, also differentiates Barnes from the contemporary American literary tendency Walter Benn Michaels has described as "nativist modernism" in *Our America*. Nativist modernism, including that of Faulkner, Hemingway, and William Carlos Williams, was, according to Michaels, "deeply committed to the nativist project of racializing the American." This project occurred in tandem, Michaels claims, with an attempt to develop a literature that would be autonomous by virtue of being nonreferential and tautologically self-identical in the same way Americans supposedly possessed a racialized Americanness. In this context, an anti-Semitic rejection of putatively unassimilable Jews seemed to be "an essential aspect of

36. See Amanda Anderson, "The Powers of Distance: Revisiting Matthew Arnold," chap. 3 in *The Powers of Distance*, and Jessica Schiff Berman, "Henry James," chap. 2 in *Modernist Fiction, Cosmopolitanism, and the Politics of Community*.

37. David Harvey, "Cosmopolitanism and the Banality of Geographical Evils," *Public Culture* 12, no. 2 (Spring 2000): 529–64.

American identity."[38] As we see in the next chapter, the idea of a tautological modernist poetry has different implications in the hands of Wallace Stevens, suggesting that Michaels's rather dismal picture of American modernism may be incomplete. However, his account provides a useful contrast with Barnes's cosmopolitan modernism. American nativism links modernist style with an attempt to create a particular political community—not, in this case, a cosmopolitan community but a national one. Though Barnes shares the nativist fascination with racial and national identity, her work does not participate in this communal political project. Her novel, in simultaneously likening itself to and distancing itself from the cosmopolitanism it attributes to Felix, limns not a nativist but an outsider or migrant aesthetics. Its definitive account of identity describes it as a circus performance, ungrounded, grotesque, self-created, transient. And *Nightwood*'s version of aesthetic autonomy—dispersive, exorbitant, caustically negative—suggests not a self-identical racial grouping with modernist writers at its heart but an atomizing social vision.

This divergence from nativist trends within modernism also appears in Barnes's treatment of the Americanness of American expatriates. Barnes first crossed the Atlantic on assignment for *McCall's* magazine; the article she eventually produced was "American Wives and Titled Husbands" (1927). In this piece, American noblewomen by marriage make a series of mannered statements about national characteristics in even more mannered surroundings. The women she interviews have succeeded where Baron Felix Volkbein fails: they have acquired real titles and grounded themselves in a European past, becoming "lost to [their] native land."[39] In the article, the results of their expatriation appear mostly in the leisurely style of living and affected style of speech Barnes attributes to her interview subjects—as should hardly be surprising in an article for what we would now call a *lifestyle* magazine. At one moment Barnes interrupts her transcriptions of the pronouncements of a principessa to observe "a bee, flinging himself crisply from crystal grape to crystal plum, searching for the essence of that nature so exactly reproduced" (318). The rhetorical extravagance of the aside, cast in the characteristic Barnes style—especially the difficult-to-parse, nested syntax of "searching [for the essence [of that nature [[so exactly] reproduced]]]"—calls attention to the luxurious artificiality of the setting and the subject, as exemplified by the crystal fruit.

38. Walter Benn Michaels, *Our America: Nativism, Modernism, and Pluralism* (Durham, NC: Duke University Press, 1995), 13, 10.

39. Barnes, "American Wives and Titled Husbands," 315. Henceforth I cite this article parenthetically in the text.

The leaping bee itself figures the women's expatriation, but it also, for all its movement, shares their restriction to a world of sugary, crystalline artifice. Like Felix Volkbein's barony, the American princess's claim on nobility turns out to be an aesthetic confection. For Barnes, a European diadem exhibits the aesthetic nature of American expatriate lifestyle.

The recurring theme of all the wives' speeches is the impossibility of Americans becoming fully rooted. The Duchess of Clermont-Tonnerre gets the last word in the article:

> "A Jew, yes. They make an ideal marriage the world over, because they have no land. You say, well, the American is the outcome of so many races that she too should be easily assimilated. Yes, but the mixture is too new, like some new wine, not yet justly proportioned." (324)

If this declaration hints at nativism—Americans can't become something else—it is not because they are American but because they are everything at once. The Jew and the American resemble one another, but in another paradox of anti-Semitic identification, the Jew is *more* adaptable. Barnes's article, then, only increases the irony of Felix's announcement to the doctor that, in looking for a wife to legitimate his nobility, he will choose an American: "With an American anything can be done" (*Nightwood*, 37). In fact, according to Barnes's Duchess of Clermont-Tonnerre, Americans are so hybridized, "the outcome of so many races," that nothing can be done with them—as Felix quickly discovers in the course of his marriage to Robin Vote. Expatriate Americans and Jews are alike in being too cosmopolitan to form the social bonds that come with a stable identity.

This implicit comparison between wandering Jews and cosmopolitan Americans makes clear that *disidentification*, not communal belonging, marks aesthetic autonomy for Barnes the journalist as much as for Barnes the novelist. As an artistic tactic, disidentification operates both in the artist's social life and in her work. Bourdieu's theory of literary style is again useful for making sense of this tactic. According to Bourdieu's analysis of *L'éducation sentimentale*, Flaubert creates his relatively autonomous position outside the existing social possibilities by means of "the *very ambiguity of viewpoint*" in his novel; the author manufactures this ambiguity through the "methodical" use of free indirect discourse (*Rules of Art*, 108), placing him at a distance from his characters without pinning him down. Bourdieu argues that this literary technique of distance enabled Flaubert to "invent ... that unprecedented social personage who is the modern writer or artist, a full-time professional, dedicated to [his or her] work in a total and exclusive manner, indifferent to the exigencies of politics and to the injunctions of morality, and not recognizing any jurisdiction other than the norms specific to [his or her] art" (76–77). Bourdieu's vocabulary, not coincidentally, likens the social task to the novelist's: the artist "invents" a position that exists only potentially, filling it with a "social personage" or *personnage*, meaning also a character in a novel.[40] A habitus and a social position are articulated *through* a literary style, for the artistic professional is in turn defined by a commitment to the artistic work—work which Flaubert's rigorous devotion to style leads Bourdieu to describe as concerned above all with form (108).

Barnes in her novels is not an ironist in the dry, Flaubertian mode, but her tactics of expatriate disidentification do make the narrative point of view of *Nightwood* indeterminate. Barnes is no more identical with any of her lonely characters than Flaubert is with Frédéric Moreau. As Tyrus Miller remarks in his study of late modernism, Barnes's work is both socially and narratively "marked by a minimal 'positionality' of the authorial subject."[41] Even her most autobiographical character, Nora Flood, is described from a distance: "She was known instantly as a Westerner. Looking at her, foreigners remembered stories they had heard of covered wagons" (46). The narrative adopts the foreigners' perspective on the American, in case there were any doubt that Barnes the cosmopolitan artist claims to stand apart from Americans and Europeans alike in the expat nightworld she depicts. Indeed, the author's distance from her characters marks the estranging and artistically liberating power of her style.

By standing apart in her work, Barnes rules out participating in an inclusive political program, nationalist or internationalist. A political cosmopolitanism should, according to David Harvey, spurn the "the passive contemplation of global citizenship" in favor of "a political project that strives to transform living, being, and becoming in the world."[42] Barnes's cosmopolitan modernism does not strive for world-spanning transformation. Neither, however, is it merely contemplative in the self-satisfied manner Harvey scorns; Barnes's style does have real-world effects. Her achievement was to create, in the teeth of considerable social obstacles, an autonomous space for herself within the field of literary modernism. The evidence of the success of Barnes's position-taking (to use Bourdieu's term) as a pure artist consists in T. S. Eliot's introduction to the first American edition of

40. Pierre Bourdieu, *Les règles de l'art: Genèse et structure du champ littéraire*, rev. ed. (Paris: Seuil, 1998), 131.

41. Tyrus Miller, *Late Modernism: Politics, Fiction, and the Arts Between the World Wars* (Berkeley: University of California Press, 1999), 62.

42. Harvey, "Cosmopolitanism and the Banality of Geographical Evils," 560.

the book, proclaiming Barnes's "great achievement of a style" and declaring the value of the "whole pattern" of the book as an autonomous aesthetic object.[43] In 1937, such a pronouncement marked the highest consecration to which an Anglophone literary work might aspire to, a certification of its status as authentic modernism. In its wake came *Nightwood*'s definitive canonization, by means of Joseph Frank's seminal 1945 *Sewanee Review* essay "Spatial Form in Modern Literature"; Frank groups *Nightwood*, *Ulysses*, and the *Recherche* together as exemplars of the experimental, autonomous, unified form of modernist fiction.[44] For the outsider Barnes to reach this inner circle of "modern literature" was no mean social and literary feat.

The point is not that Eliot's standards of aesthetic value were necessarily correct. In fact his and Frank's idea of Barnes's swerving, flagrantly inconclusive narrative as a geometrically balanced "pattern" is quite strange. More importantly, the celebration of *Nightwood*'s putatively autonomous form elides all of the novel's specific analysis of expatriate Paris and the cosmopolitan lifestyle—an analysis that suggests how the appearance of autonomous aesthetic form actually depends on a social performance by the artist.[45] Nonetheless, Eliot's approval measures the effectiveness, as social action, of the style in *Nightwood*. If that action ruled Barnes out of political communities, the Barnes-Eliot relationship shows exactly what kind of community her expatriate autonomy does *not* disable: the constitutively nonpolitical community of modernism and its relatively autonomous aesthetic practices.[46]

43. T. S. Eliot, introduction to *Nightwood*, by Djuna Barnes (New York: Harcourt, Brace, 1937), xiv, xii. This introduction is reprinted in *Nightwood* (New York: New Directions, 2006).

44. Frank writes, "The structural principle of *Nightwood* is the same as of *Ulysses* and *A la recherche du temps perdu* . . . . We are asked only to accept the work of art as an autonomous structure giving us an individual vision of reality." Joseph Frank, "Spatial Form in Modern Literature," in *The Widening Gyre: Crisis and Mastery in Modern Literature* (Bloomington: Indiana University Press, 1963), 28. The article was originally published in *Sewanee Review* 53 (1945): 221–40, 433–56, 643–53.

45. As we saw in chapter 2, the London expatriate Eliot, though far better endowed with social, cultural, and economic capital than Barnes ever was, knew this performance intimately in the personal labors of his lifelong late style. Langdon Hammer's *Hart Crane and Allen Tate: Janus-Faced Modernism* (Princeton, NJ: Princeton University Press, 1993) describes the import of Eliot's "de-naturalization" (14) in his English context.

46. For an account of the collaboration of Barnes and Eliot in preparing *Nightwood* for publication, see Georgette Fleischer, "Djuna Barnes and T. S. Eliot: The Politics and Poetics of *Nightwood*," *Studies in the Novel* 30, no. 3 (Fall 1998): 405–37.

"Vagaries Malicieux": Losing All Connection at the Deux Magots

More than a decade before *Nightwood*, Barnes represented her first arrival on the Parisian scene of the modernist community in an essay, "Vagaries Malicieux," for the New Orleans little magazine *The Double Dealer*. Barnes describes her first sights of Paris in skeptical terms:

> It took me several days to get over the sensation of dangerous make-believe, and as a matter of fact I am not yet quite sure that a Frenchman is not gaming when he talks to me, and I am almost ready to swear that the Bon Marché is a fraud, and that the Louvre is a somewhat flawless production of something French.[47]

This description leaves ambiguous whether the source of inauthenticity is France (the "gaming" Frenchman) or the expatriate herself and her "sensation of dangerous make-believe." Barnes ironizes herself even further when she goes on to imagine a friend indicating with a smile that "you can begin to be authentic as soon as you like" (252). Everything is hedged about with characteristic Barnesian qualification and paradox: "almost ready to swear," "a somewhat flawless production." Far from undermining Barnes's credentials as a reporter, however, such stylistic gambits reinforce her stance (or pose) as a knowing aesthete. Later in the essay, this aestheticism will reach Wildean heights: "Three times in my life, no more I think, have musical instruments been either covered or uncovered in such a way as to change my life" (255).

Such a stance suits a magazine whose title announces its interest in artifice and trickery, and whose arch tone would not conduce to an innocent tourist's appreciation of Paris in any case. Elsewhere in this same issue of *The Double Dealer*, Arthur Moss writes from Paris, "One cannot sit in the Café de la Rotonde five minutes without being hailed by Americans of all varieties of the seven arts."[48] Indeed, Barnes herself, at the end of her essay, throws up her hands at giving a straight description of Paris: "How many times I have tried to do it for my Greenwich Village friends (who can always be found at the Rotonde in the afternoons) and have failed" (260). Such a remark simultaneously advertises her affiliation with an expatriate avant-garde in-crowd and defensively mocks her own parochialism

---

47. Djuna Barnes, "Vagaries Malicieux," *Double Dealer* 3, no. 17 (May 1922): 251–52. Henceforth cited as "Vagaries" in the text.

48. Arthur Moss, "Paris Notes," *Double Dealer* 3, no. 17 (May 1922): 279.

in spending her Paris time with Greenwich Village friends. Barnes the newcomer must take care not to indulge in too much cheerful esprit de corps.

Shadowing Barnes's essay is the sense that expatriation may *already* be a hackneyed gesture, something that can only be cited or performed. Malcolm Cowley writes of his own departure for Paris in 1921: "When we left New York hardly anyone came to say good-by. Most of our friends had sailed already; the others were wistful people who promised to follow us in a few months."[49] Indeed, "Vagaries Malicieux" registers Barnes's sense, shared with others of her generation, that she must remain under the suspicion of merely having copied the heroically liberating artistic programs of earlier "exiles," Stein and Joyce among them. Bourdieu suggests that "the further the process of autonomization [of the field of cultural production] advances, the more possible it becomes to occupy the position of 'pure' producer without having the properties—or at least without having them all or to the same degree—that had to be possessed to *produce* the position" (*Rules of Art*, 257).[50] Barnes thus faces the challenge of having to distinguish herself aesthetically when, as Jay says, "far from having opened the show, however, Barnes made the last entrance when she disembarked in France in the early 1920s."[51]

Responding to the challenge, Barnes is at pains to keep conventionalized versions of American artistic expatriation at a distance. Even within the confines of an advanced periodical (the same number of *The Double Dealer* has pieces by Ezra Pound, Hart Crane, and Allen Tate), she marks out a liminal status through her aestheticized, rigorously indefinite cosmopolitanism. The magazine's editorial apparatus takes note of Barnes's unreliability as a team player. The inside cover of the issue describes her with a wry tone: "Djuna Barnes is identified with the *Little Review* group of enthusiasts. This has not seriously interfered with her entrée to *Vanity Fair* and other prosperous organs of the bourgeoisie."[52] Barnes in fact published "James Joyce; A Portrait of the Man Who Is, at Present, One of the More

---

49. Cowley, *Exile's Return*, 80.

50. Casanova remarks of Beckett that even Parisian exile, after Joyce, looked like a form of imitation (*The World Republic of Letters*, 319). The same suspicion falls on expatriates in general, who tread a moral path already blazed by involuntary exiles. As Caren Kaplan comments, "A not-so-subtle strain of puritanism runs through critiques of expatriates and cosmopolitans—if not literally forced out of their place of origin by formidable political opponents, the faux exiles are seen to be reaping the social and artistic benefits of displacement without *paying* for them, without undergoing the anxiety, fear, and uncertainty that 'true' exiles must always experience." *Questions of Travel: Postmodern Discourses of Displacement* (Durham, NC: Duke University Press, 1996), 106–7 (emphasis in original).

51. Jay, "The Outsider among the Expatriates," 184.

52. "Notes on Contributors," *Double Dealer* 3, no. 17 (May 1922): inside front cover.

Significant Figures in Literature" in the April 1922 issue of *Vanity Fair*.[53] A free-lancer in both the large-circulation and avant-garde periodical spheres, Barnes once again finds herself "half in and half out of the club," as Jay says. But this uncertain affiliation only gives more point to the scrupulously ironized description of Barnes's own expatriation in "Vagaries Malicieux," keeping the aesthetically autonomous writer at a distance from any compromising identification.

Alongside her irony, Barnes has another strategy of autonomy in "Vagaries": wandering attention. On arriving in Paris, she sets out for some dangerously clichéd sight-seeing, but she heads off any assumption that she doesn't see the cliché for what it is:

> And so it was I came to Paris, and a few hours later was leaning out of my window in the Rue Jacob, and thinking in my heart of all unknown churches, and so thinking, I put on my cloak and went out to Notre Dame in the sad, falling twilight, and wandered under the trees and thought of another city, in a truly traitorous fashion. (251)

As in the style and plot of *Nightwood*, here too Barnes brings us to one location, Paris, only to jolt us to another. Her walking to the church is only purposeless "wandering," her thinking not serious and devoted but "traitorous" and trivial. Then Notre Dame turns out not to be the real destination at all, but the church of Saint-Germain-des-Prés, which Barnes finds more appealing. That appeal, however, lies in the fact that "it is a place for those who have 'only a little while to stay'" (251). In other words, it is a church for traitorous wanderers, who find a temporary stopping point only within a set of hedging quotation marks. As an ephemeral refuge, Barnes's Saint-Germain anticipates *Nightwood*'s circus. Of course, Barnes does not enter the churches as a worshiper but as a follower in the footsteps of half a century's worth of aestheticist admirers of church architecture.

Wandering attention enacts the writer's imaginative autonomy: refusing to be captured by present surroundings or by the worn-out patterns of touristic sight-seeing, Barnes affirms this knowing, cosmopolitan mode as a form of freedom in her writing. Rebecca Walkowitz has argued for the importance of wandering attention for modernist cosmopolitanism in her book *Cosmopolitan Style*. There, discussing "Joyce's Triviality," Walkowitz describes Joyce's representation of vagrant minds as implicitly criticizing both British imperial domination of Ireland and too-narrow versions of Irish nationalism. "Joyce's project is cosmopolitan," she

53. Djuna Barnes, "James Joyce; A Portrait of the Man Who Is, at Present, One of the More Significant Figures in Literature," *Vanity Fair* 18, no. 2 (April 1922): 65, 104.

writes, "in two important ways: it is critical of authenticity as a measure of belonging and it promotes intellectual vagrancy, what I call 'triviality,' as a condition of materialist critique and social transformation."[54] Walkowitz emphasizes the liberating potential of affectation and inauthenticity—much as Barnes's "Vagaries," archly ironic, guards her own independence. But unlike Barnes, Walkowitz's Joyce has a specific political program: the promotion of a liberated, democratically pluralist Ireland, achieved by "transform[ing] the consciousness of his readers"; that transformation is effected through "literary strategies," formal tactics of distraction and irreverence.[55] For Walkowitz, Joyce's style has the extraordinary power of teaching his readers to be members of a new, cosmopolitan community.

The Barnes of "Vagaries Malicieux," by contrast, may use a "trivial" style to critique and distinguish herself from clichés of Paris tourism, but that use is individualist, not community-building. In Barnes, the aesthetic autonomy that wandering style creates and enacts—the freedom of "intellectual vagrancy"—may help secure her standing as an avant-gardist, but it refuses to invite her readers to join in any shared political purpose. Barnes's essay ends with the narrator asking herself, "Shall I tell the world what Paris meant to me, or shall I let it sit in its clubs?" and answering, "I do not know" (260). The essay could have had no other conclusion, because it disclaims the possibility of an authentic relationship to Paris or to expatriation in favor of the "sensation of dangerous make-believe." Although Barnes's wandering, "traitorous" attention and preference for refuges for those who have "'only a little while to stay'" *do* disrupt the established expatriate framework for Paris, they leave her in the position of the outsider, the position later described by *Nightwood*. Indeed, the convergence between Barnes's position-taking as a journalist and her technique as a novelist gives strong evidence for the operation of a single habitus in her career—generating a correspondence between mode of art and mode of life, between the fictional performance and the personal performance. Irony and aestheticism allow Barnes to keep her distance in both fiction and nonfiction genres.

Barnes's essay enacts this withdrawal from interpersonal bonds in the expatriate modernist encounter at its heart: a quirky, informal interview with none other than James Joyce. Barnes's vagrant, perpetually disruptive style structures her response to this central icon of expatriate artistry—and treats him with the same nonseriousness Walkowitz attributes to Joyce's project:

54. Walkowitz, *Cosmopolitan Style*, 57.

55. Ibid., 58.

> Coming from this church [Saint-Germain-des-Prés] one evening I stopped
> a moment at the cafe of the 'Deux Magots' and had a glass of wine,
> while Joyce, James Joyce, author of the suppressed 'Ulysses,' talked of the
> Greeks. (251)

The sentence begins as seemingly one more stage in her touristic journey, taking as long as possible to arrive at Joyce; Barnes makes their meeting casual, as
though, having stopped at the famous expat café for a solitary drink, she had discovered Joyce talking away there by accident. After tantalizing *The Double Dealer*'s
readers with the prospect of fresh news about the recent scandal of the suppression of the *Little Review*—with which this magazine had "identified" her—for
publishing *Ulysses* in serialization, Barnes reveals that the conversation turned to
the deliciously not-quite-relevant Greeks. Whereas Barnes's *Vanity Fair* interview
with Joyce quotes Stephen Dedalus proclaiming his devotion to "silence, exile and
cunning," in the New Orleans little magazine she wanders away from the familiar
images of Joyce the avant-gardist.[56]

Barnes does transcribe several striking declarations: Joyce's claim to have told
Synge that "Ireland needed less small talk and more irrefutable art," his mockery
of the Celtic revivalists for not knowing "that Gaelic is not the tongue of Dublin!"
("Vagaries," 252). But she deflates them by noting his "strangely spoiled and appropriate teeth" (252) and his tendency to "drift from one subject to the other" (253).
For Barnes, Joyce does not possess the Olympian hauteur of the heroic artistic exile;
instead, he "lives in a sort of accidental aloofness" (252–53). The unmistakable
marks of Joyce's aesthetic autonomy and cosmopolitanism—his aloofness, his disdain for Irish revivalism, even the triviality of his discourse—become the quirks of
Bohemian personal style. By representing Joyce's style in this comical, bodily way,
Barnes's interview mocks its own premise: why take such interest in Joyce the man
if his importance lies in the autonomy of his work—the convention-defying rigor
that caused *Ulysses* to be suppressed?

Such interest was indeed widespread: Cowley recalls the writers of his generation wondering, "How did a man live who had written a masterpiece?"[57] This
obsession expects the writer, even one with as impersonal a style as Joyce, to live as
his masterpiece implies he does. Barnes humorously reduces the idea to absurdity.
Just as her deliberately affected treatment of her arrival in Paris subverts expatriate conventions, so, too, her sly transformation of the crucial attributes of Joycean
technique into comic aspects of Joyce the interview subject punctures her readers'

56. Barnes, "James Joyce," 104.
57. Cowley, *Exile's Return*, 118.

overinflated expectations of the man. When Joyce tells Barnes, "A writer should never write about the extraordinary, that is for the journalist" (253), his affirmation of the importance for his art of the everyday and the trivial only underscores the fact that here he is the extraordinary subject of a journalistic article. But if Barnes undermines the martial myth of Joyce as the exiled leader of a cosmopolitan artistic vanguard, she still documents the way his artistic performance extends off the page and into his social life.

Having taken in the performance, Barnes finds that she must leave Joyce alone. In the end, his talk does not hold her attention: "My mind wandered a little," she says, and then, after one further short snatch of Joyce, she tells us, "Here I lost all connection with this man, sad, quiet, and eternally at work" (253–54). As in *Nightwood*, though in a more comic vein, the liberating effects of aestheticized style and wandering attention come with the loss of personal attachment. With the author of *Ulysses*, Barnes remains, as she says about her relations with the French, "the stranger past the threshold" (254). I do not mean to imply that she critiques and mocks Joyce in order to present a superior, alternative aesthetic or political program, or that the purpose of "Vagaries Malicieux," despite its title, is simply to tear down the idols of modernist expatriate culture. Whereas scholars of Barnes like Tyrus Miller and Monika Kaup see her as attacking the dogmas of high modernism, in fact Barnes has learned Joyce's lessons well.[58] Disidentification dialectically gives rise to another kind of identification: Barnes treats Joycean authority with Joycean irreverence and aloofness—a pattern she repeats in the treatment of the aesthetes of *Nightwood*, the baron, the doctor, and Nora Flood.[59] She anticipates Walkowitz's understanding that Joyce's trademark modernist stylistic tactics are also the attitudes and practices of a sophisticated cosmopolitanism. But Barnes's reflections on those tactics and her own uses of them do not fit the communal political project of the new cosmopolitanisms. Her aesthetic cosmopolitanism, precisely because the artist finds herself living as well as writing it, appears less a method for building

58. Miller writes of Barnes's implicit "attack on the redemptive mission attributed to artistic form ... by modernist writers and critics" (*Late Modernism*, 125), Kaup of Barnes's "deviat[ion] from the mainstream of modernism" ("The Neobaroque in Djuna Barnes," 98).

59. This same pattern appears in a later evocation of Joyce for an American audience, in Barnes's nostalgic "Lament for the Left Bank," a 1941 elegy for occupied Paris published in *Town and Country*. After the publication of *Ulysses*, Barnes says, "Expatriate pens stood still .... This time writers were floored. They wept in joy and copied in despair .... [Joyce] had, overnight, changed the perspective of all who embraced the hope of a literary career." Djuna Barnes, "Lament for the Left Bank," in "Vantage Ground," *Town and Country* 96, no. 4230 (December 1941): 138.

an activist political solidarity than an individuating, and isolating, mode of artistic achievement.

Stephen Dedalus's Hat

Let us now turn the analysis of expatriation carried out by Barnes's work on the most mythologized of all modernist expatriates: Joyce himself. I offer neither a comprehensive account of Joyce's expatriation nor a full discussion of his modernism. But I will show how the Barnesian perspective allows us to challenge the assumptions underlying one of the central debates about Joyce: the debate on his relationship to Ireland in general and Irish politics in particular. For scholars concerned with these questions, it has seemed necessary to deny that Joyce claims any aesthetic autonomy for his work in order to link that work meaningfully to its social and political contexts. With the rejection of the putative detachment from politics once attributed to his "exile," the social significance of Joyce's expatriation has also receded from view. Yet the image of Joyce the committed political thinker is as mythic, in its way, as the notion of Joyce the nonpolitical humanist. Both views pay insufficient attention to the nature of the social role Joyce constructs for himself as an expatriate artist. Barnes helps us see how Joyce's work takes that role into account; in brief glimpses of the expatriate's lifestyle, Joyce analyzes the worldly significance of that lifestyle for his work. The writer's social performance as a cosmopolitan is part and parcel of the effort to maintain that work's relative aesthetic autonomy.

In linking Barnes and Joyce, I do not mean to suggest that their forms of cosmopolitanism or modernism are identical. They belong to overlapping but different contexts. Joyce was an expatriate from a European colony that decolonized as he wrote his major works; his intervention into that cultural situation confronts both Britain's imperial hegemony and the demands of an emergent, powerful—and eventually itself hegemonic—Irish cultural nationalist movement. Barnes's United States was not politically dominated, and she herself—an outsider by class, gender, and sexuality—worked for autonomy even within expatriate circles, including those that saw themselves as resisting a confining American national culture. Indeed, American cultural nationalism, though an important force in the 1920s and 1930s, is hardly the most important context for understanding Barnes, even if her cosmopolitan style contrasts with other, more nativist literary projects.[60] Nonetheless, Barnes's and Joyce's expatriate positions have important

---

60. See the earlier discussion of Michaels's *Our America*.

features in common. If the United States was no colony, its literature was nonetheless still relatively lacking in stature. As David Shumway shows, at the turn of the twentieth century American writing had still "not yet attained a clear evaluation as literature."[61] In the subsequent decades the United States remained, according to Casanova, "literarily a dominated country that looked to Paris in order to try to accumulate resources it lacked."[62] For Barnes, as for Joyce, Parisian expatriation offered the prospect of wider literary horizons. For the readers who placed them in the international modernist canon, from T. S. Eliot to Joseph Frank, they both seemed to have produced, in that capital of literary space, works that rose above their national origins and biographical contexts into the realm of aesthetic forms. Limited as the canonizing reading is, it nonetheless attests to the distinct combination of stylistic virtuosity and cosmopolitan sensibility in their writings.

In Joyce as in Barnes, style and cosmopolitanism depend on one another. Joyce, like Barnes, creates a figure for artistic autonomy in his cosmopolitan characters, particularly the artistic alter ego Stephen Dedalus. Furthermore, the "arms" with which Stephen claims he will fight for freedom, "silence, exile, and cunning," are also figures for Joycean technique, particularly his devious irony and ambivalent parody.[63] Although ironic distance and detachment separate Joyce from Stephen, the relationship between Joyce and his character resembles Barnes's relation to her aesthete cosmopolitans—the American wives with titled husbands, Baron Felix, Doctor O'Connor, Nora Flood, and even her own portrayal of Joyce. These authors share with their characters the same detached manner by which they separate themselves from them. If Felix is a homeless aesthete who cannot attach himself securely to anyone, so is the Barnesian cosmopolitan writer; if Stephen cannot shake his aloof mannerisms, Joyce cannot do without his styles of aloofness.[64]

For scholars of modernist cosmopolitanism like Rebecca Walkowitz and Jessica Berman, Joyce demonstrates how the cosmopolitan can also be politically engaged. They therefore differentiate Stephen's rejection of political causes from Joyce's stance. According to Walkowitz, Joyce approves of a "flexible" mentality that

---

61. David R. Shumway, *Creating American Civilization: A Genealogy of American Literature as an Academic Discipline* (Minneapolis: University of Minnesota Press, 1994), 15.

62. Casanova, *The World Republic of Letters*, 42.

63. Joyce, *Portrait*, 208.

64. This paradox of cosmopolitan style helps make sense of the persistent difficulties Joyce's attitude to his character has posed to readers. The standard account of those difficulties in *Portrait* is Wayne C. Booth, "The Problem of Distance in 'A Portrait of the Artist,'" in *The Rhetoric of Fiction*, 2nd ed. (Chicago: University of Chicago Press, 1983), 323–36.

differentiates him from Stephen's "definitive and unyielding" exile.[65] Berman, comparing Joyce to another novelist of decolonization, Mulk Raj Anand, argues that the ironic use of Stephen as a focalizer only underscores Joyce's rejection of a "retreat into a personal aesthetics" and his openness to communal political engagement.[66] But though Joyce's technique invites us to reflect on the artist's relation to community in the colonial context, the author's superiority to Stephen, evidenced in terms of irony, humor, and the other devices of aesthetic distance that mark Joyce as a successful expatriate writer, has little to do with an affinity for political collectivity, even of the anti-imperial, cosmopolitan kind. Instead, it is, like Barnes's sardonic narration—or Flaubert's impersonal style—a tool for marking out the modernist's relatively autonomous position. Paradoxically, the exaggeration of Stephen's exilic drive in *Portrait* marks Joyce's attempt to secure aesthetic autonomy by differentiating himself from his hero. Indeed, Richard Ellmann writes of Joyce in his university days that "it would be a mistake to see Joyce as already buying a ticket for Paris; he probably still expected he could live in Ireland."[67] Stephen's intransigence is *not* wholly biographical but rather a device of the cosmopolitan novelist.

Although Joyce, however unlike Stephen he may be, remains something of a political nonparticipant, that does not mean we should regress to the "humanist" reading of Joyce. In that critical narrative of Joyce's artistic exile, his expatriation and his devotion to his work went hand in hand, lifting him away from the bonds of nationality and the conflict-ridden Irish political scene. Richard Ellmann's work did much to establish this narrative. In his biography of Joyce, he wrote, "Writing was itself a form of exile for him, a source of exile for him, a source of detachment."[68] Though Joyce's subject matter was Irish, his work depended, in this reading, on his removal from Ireland to become a cosmopolitan artist on the world stage. According to Ellmann, "When Philippe Soupault asked Joyce, 'Why not go back to Dublin?', he answered, 'It would prevent me from writing about Dublin.'"[69] At the culmination of Joyce's œuvre one would then find the universalist ambition, the uncompromisingly experimental form, the polylingualism, and the myth-making of *Finnegans Wake*, with Joyce himself identified as a

65. Walkowitz, *Cosmopolitan Style*, 65.

66. Jessica Berman, "Comparative Colonialisms: Joyce, Anand, and the Question of Engagement," *Modernism/Modernity* 13, no. 3 (September 2006): 477.

67. Richard Ellmann, *James Joyce*, rev. ed. (Oxford: Oxford University Press, 1982), 66.

68. Ibid., 110.

69. Ibid., 643n.

world-spanning Shem the Penman, "an Irish emigrant the wrong way out" and a "Europasianised Afferyank!"[70] The exiled artist and the fully autonomous work seemingly come to share in a cosmopolitan freedom from local political concerns.

But the partiality of this Franco-American humanist interpretation has become apparent, particularly through the contributions of Irish studies and the application of postcolonial approaches to Irish culture and history. It has become hard to credit a picture of Joyce that gives short shrift to Irish contexts. Though Declan Kiberd, in his important treatment of Joyce as a fundamentally Irish and postcolonial writer, is still able to say that "for Joyce, writing was a measure of his own exile from Ireland," he also makes Joyce a part of a widespread cultural revival and a member of "a nation of exiles and migrants."[71] For Derek Attridge and Marjorie Howes, in their introduction to *Semicolonial Joyce*, "the critical practice of contrasting Joyce's tolerant, cosmopolitan modernism with the narrow Irish nationalism he rejected is reaching the limits of its usefulness."[72] Scholars like Berman and Walkowitz—as well as students of the similarities between Joyce's work and early twentieth-century nationalism like Emer Nolan and Pericles Lewis[73]—have worked to overcome this contrast in productive ways. While the earlier critics explained Joyce's stylistic virtuosity as evidence of his rejection of local ties in favor of universal aesthetic pursuits, later literary historians recast his writerly project as a politically charged intervention in Irish culture.

This view is also partial, for if Irish culture is one Joycean social context, the international literary field, with its center on the Continent, is another. As Barnes's writing helps us see, the spectacles of imaginative freedom and verbal artistry in Joyce's work insistently point back to this transnational context in ways that complicate his connection to Irish politics. Joyce concludes his 1907 Trieste lecture "Ireland: Island of Saints and Sages" by speculating on the possibility of a reborn, economically and culturally vibrant Ireland, but his final remarks put such hopeful notions at a distance:

> It is high time Ireland finished once and for all with failures. If it is truly capable of resurgence [*capace di risorgere*], then let it do so or else let it

70. *Finnegans Wake* (New York: Penguin, 1939), 190.36, 191.04.

71. Declan Kiberd, *Inventing Ireland* (Cambridge, MA: Harvard University Press, 1996), 333, 328.

72. Derek Attridge and Marjorie Howes, introduction to *Semicolonial Joyce*, ed. Derek Attridge and Marjorie Howes (Cambridge: Cambridge University Press, 2000), 11.

73. Pericles Lewis, *Modernism, Nationalism, and the Novel* (Cambridge: Cambridge University Press, 2000); Emer Nolan, *James Joyce and Nationalism* (London: Routledge, 1995).

cover its head and decently descend into the grave forever. "We Irish," Oscar Wilde said one day to a friend of mine, "have done nothing, but we're the greatest talkers since the days of the ancient Greeks." But, though the Irish are eloquent, a revolution is not made from human breath, and Ireland has already had enough of compromises, misunderstandings, and misapprehensions. If it wants finally to put on the show for which we have waited so long, this time, let it be complete, full and definitive .... I, for one, am certain not to see the curtain rise, as I shall have already taken the last tram home [*sarò già tornato a casa coll'ultimo tram*].[74]

A Barnes-like irony arises from Joyce's disparagement of Irish talk in the peroration to his own talk on Ireland. That irony pulls apart the anticolonialist, enlightened, nationalist dream of a revived homeland, revealing it to be—in Joyce's mouth—only rhetoric. Joyce invokes Wilde, the patron saint of aestheticism and a martyr to the philistine public, when he reflects bitterly on the limitations of such imaginative freedoms in the cause of Ireland. The possibility of an authentic Irish revival becomes no more than a theatrical "show" in which Joyce can have no part. Locating his "home"—really, after all, a Triestine *casa*—at a distance from the spectacle, Joyce implicates his own exile in the aesthetic vacuity of his Irish Risorgimento fantasy. Importantly, Joyce does call for an Irish revolution; but he sees little role for his free, imaginative talk within it.

Of course, the politics of the Trieste lecture need not correspond to those of Joyce's later fiction.[75] Yet the lecture has an important continuity with the central Joycean treatment of the expatriate aesthete and his relation to political community: the depiction of the repatriated Stephen Dedalus in *Ulysses*. Wilde returns to haunt Stephen when, in the opening of the novel, Stephen must literally face what his expatriation has made him. Buck Mulligan offers him a mirror, which, he explains, he has "pinched ... out of the skivvy's room":

74. "Ireland: Island of Saints and Sages," trans. Conor Deane, in *Occasional, Critical, and Political Writing*, ed. Kevin Barry (Oxford: Oxford University Press, 2000), 125–26, 259. The "friend," according to Barry, is Yeats, whose poetic cultural nationalism is, by implication, scornfully dismissed. John McCourt argues that this lecture, though nationalist, draws on Catholic history to overturn the clichés of the Celtic revival; see "Joyce's Well of the Saints," *Joyce Studies Annual* 2007 (Winter 2007): 109–33.

75. Seamus Deane emphasizes the shift from the Parnellite hauteur of Joyce's early career to the new tactics of *Ulysses* and *Finnegans Wake*, in which, claims Deane, "The Irish people have found their voices." Introduction to *A Portrait of the Artist as a Young Man*, by James Joyce, ed. Seamus Deane (New York: Penguin, 1992), xxxvi.

—The rage of Caliban at not seeing his face in a mirror, he said. If Wilde were only alive to see you!

Drawing back and pointing, Stephen said with bitterness:

—It is a symbol of Irish art. The cracked lookingglass of a servant.[76]

This exchange is *Ulysses*'s gloss on Stephen's credo of exile in *Portrait*, "I will not serve."[77] The passage is also, as I remarked in chapter 1, evidence of the continuing entwinement, in modernism, of aestheticism and domestic service. The aestheticist lineage is prominent here, for of course Stephen, responding to Mulligan's mocking allusion to Wilde, has adapted his line from "The Decay of Lying":

> CYRIL: I can quite understand your objection to art being treated as a mirror. You think it would reduce genius to the position of a cracked looking glass. But you don't mean to say that you seriously believe that Life imitates Art, that Life in fact is the mirror, and Art the reality?[78]

Wilde's figure of the cracked looking-glass rebukes realism for the limits it places on artistic autonomy: if art is only a mirror, the artistic genius is "cracked" if it departs from faithful representation. In inserting a servant into the figure, Stephen keeps to the pattern set by Wilde's treatment of domestics—they appear when social realism presses in on aesthetic autonomy.[79]

On the other hand, Stephen has probably not forgotten that the cracked looking glass is also a symbol for genius. Scoring a point against Buck Mulligan, Stephen goes from being Caliban to being an artistic prodigy, reduced but liberated, by the very fact of being damaged, from the constraints of plodding, mimetic realism. For it is *himself* Stephen beholds in the mirror. The cracks remind him of his frustration and despair, but they also recall Wilde's celebration of aesthetic liberty from reality. Indeed, as a figure of imperfect, secondhand representation—Mulligan has

76. James Joyce, *Ulysses*, ed. Hans Walter Gabler (New York: Vintage, 1986), 1.138, 143–46. Henceforth I cite this edition by episode and line number parenthetically in the text.

77. "I will not serve that in which I no longer believe whether it call itself my home, my fatherland or my church." *Portrait*, 208.

78. Oscar Wilde, "The Decay of Lying: An Observation," in *Intentions*, in *The Soul of Man under Socialism and Selected Critical Prose*, ed. Linda Dowling (London: Penguin, 2001), 179.

79. Margot Norris's extended reading of this passage focuses on themes related to my own, but Norris argues, as I would not, that Wilde's aestheticism is not as self-critical as Joyce's. See *Joyce's Web: The Social Unraveling of Modernism* (Austin: University of Texas Press, 1992), 63–66.

stolen the mirror from his aunt's servant—the mirror forecasts the devices of parody and stylistic disruption that will take over the form of *Ulysses*.[80] Sordid as this "symbol" is, then, it has a celebratory aura of aesthetic freedom about it, a stylistic kinship to Joyce's own work. This combination of denigration and celebration strikingly resembles Barnes's treatments of the aesthete. And Barnes can teach us to see that though Stephen's other embellishment of Wilde's figure—"a symbol of *Irish art*"—seems at first to represent his scornful disavowal of Irishness and Irish culture, it also constructs an analogy between Stephen's damaged genius and Ireland's damaged culture.

But the example of Barnes, like that of Wilde, also cautions us to stop short of triumphantly reinserting Stephen's Joycean art back into the Irish political community. His Irishness serves his declaration of aesthetic autonomy from reality, Irish reality included. As the novel makes clear, this declaration leaves Stephen on the outside of more communal Irish cultural endeavors. He is, like the Joyce of "Ireland: Island of Saints and Sages," a great Irish talker who only watches the spectacle of nationalist struggle from the sidelines. Certainly Stephen's verbal virtuosity does nothing to deter Buck Mulligan's jovial hostility or the ethnographic condescension of their bien-pensant English housemate Haines, who proposes to make a collection of Stephen's sayings. In fact, this minor incident sets the pattern for the scene at the library in "Scylla and Charybdis": the novel stages Stephen's Wildean display of speculative bravura, his biographical theory of *Hamlet*, in the context of his feelings of alienation from the Irish literary revival.[81]

In *Ulysses* as in *Portrait*, Stephen lives Joycean aesthetic freedom as a stylistic performance which prevents him from joining the various communities that are offered to him. By imposing this experience on his character, Joyce registers the position the expatriate artist must take up, the taxing social role that undergirds the work's claim to cosmopolitan independence. *Ulysses* links Stephen's frustrated artistic mode to expatriation through the visible mark of his French excursion: his "Latin quarter hat" (1.519)—as Buck Mulligan mockingly names it. Later,

80. Hugh Kenner gives the standard account of Joyce's parody and ventriloquism in *Joyce's Voices* (Berkeley: University of California Press, 1978). See also Karen Lawrence, *The Odyssey of Style in "Ulysses"* (Princeton, NJ: Princeton University Press, 1981).

81. Clare Hutton argues that Joyce makes the revival out to be less hospitable to him than it really was—precisely for the sake of affirming his autonomy: "It suited Joyce's aesthetic self-fashioning to portray Literary Revivalism as a movement that could not cater for the interests of gifted young intellectuals such as Dedalus. But the facts of Irish literary history do not bear out this undeniably powerful fiction." Clare Hutton, "Joyce, the Library Episode, and the Institutions of Revivalism," in *Joyce, Ireland, Britain*, ed. Andrew Gibson and Len Platt (Gainesville: University Press of Florida, 2006), 134.

in "Proteus," alone and thinking about his time in Paris, Stephen takes the gibe to heart:

> My Latin quarter hat. God, we simply must dress the character. I want puce gloves. You were a student, weren't you? ... Just say in the most natural tone: when I was in Paris, *boul' Mich'*, I used to. (3.174–79)

Heroic exile has become the expatriate mode: a costume and some verbal affectations of cosmopolitanism.[82] "*Prix de Paris*," Stephen thinks ironically: "beware of imitations" (3.483). But the imitative, affected character of the hat and the "natural tone" has the same force as the cracked looking glass, or the titles of Barnes's circus performers: it enhances the cosmopolitan style's claim to autonomy. By making expatriation into a performance, Stephen may appear a ridiculous, self-pitying poseur—after "Proteus," readers probably turn to Bloom with relief—but he also creates a compelling image for Joyce's artistic practices of distance, polyglot verbal play, and stylistic imitation. Indeed, in "Scylla and Charybdis," Stephen thinks of his hat as "*Stephanos*, my crown" (9.947): he identifies himself with this accoutrement of his pose. For Stephen, a cosmopolitan style, far from being a wholly autonomous technical achievement, ramifies in the life of the artist. But applying "your best French polish" to his manners, as he does in "Scylla and Charybdis," leaves Stephen alone rather than at home among fellow cosmopolitans (9.315). Ultimately, when he meets his sister Dilly buying a French primer in "Wandering Rocks," his response to this manifestation of their sibling resemblance as cosmopolitans is simply "Misery!" (10.880).

As Barnes's fictions of expatriation show, we need not identify Joyce with his aesthete character to see in these moments an analysis of the cosmopolitan modernist's lifestyle—a lifestyle Joyce shares. Rather, in accordance with the dialectic I have been tracing throughout this book, Joyce's fiction of expatriate autonomy puts his own stylistic strategies, his own work on novelistic form, back into a social context; it becomes apparent that the mode of art is a mode of life as well. In Amanda Anderson's terms, Joycean cosmopolitanism links method to ethos.[83] But the mode of life is *not* a mode of communal political identity and activism—and thus, despite some of the most powerful recent scholarly accounts of Joyce, neither is Joycean

---

82. *Finnegans Wake* condenses this development into a pun, when a drunken Shaun, about to leave home, berates his sister Issy: "What do ye want trippings for when you've Paris inspire your hat?" (453.24–25). Trips to Paris and the head-borne trappings of Paris start to seem as though they are one and the same.

83. Anderson sees the turn to personal practice as constitutive of cosmopolitanism in the nineteenth century: "Like the nineteenth-century tendency to fuse method and ethos,"

style. This point can be difficult to see, because scholarship has done so much to reject the myth of the apolitical Joyce. We now have a convincing and nuanced picture of the views of Joyce on the "Irish question"—nationalist in his commitment to an independent Ireland and his rejection of imperialism, cosmopolitan in his persistent refusal to acquiesce in ideologies of racial purity and isolationism.[84] Joyce appears, then, to have measured a critical distance between himself and less complex political alternatives for someone with his background: resignation, rigidly Gaelic or Catholic nationalism, pretentious West Britonism, various idealistic universalisms. With this picture before us, it becomes almost irresistible to connect Joyce's formal virtuosity to this appealingly critical political stance as two aspects of the same brilliant achievement.

Yet the critical distance bears a suspiciously neat resemblance to the distancing at the core of Joyce's *stylistic* practice in its various modes of irony, parody, and exuberant play. Enda Duffy, in *The Subaltern "Ulysses,"* and Rebecca Walkowitz, in *Cosmopolitan Style*, make particularly strong cases for the power of Joyce's aesthetics to confront the political problems of Irish decolonization through shocks, defamiliarizations, parodies, and novel juxtapositions. But the apparent harmony between aesthetic forms of distance and the rigors of political critique is really based on a confusion, because it assumes that artistic strategies for avoiding authorial commitment are good models of ethical commitment. As Joyce's account of Stephen—like Barnes's account of her expats—makes clear, the Parisian modernist can and must live his style of ironies and aesthetic disruptions, but in taking up his aesthetic position he forgoes the kind of communal commitments required of nationalist and cosmopolitan politics. Indeed, his habitus, his style of life, teaches him to regard the practices of political solidarity as threats to the position of the would-be autonomous artist.

Other politically attentive scholars have also argued that Joyce's aesthetic distance implies a refusal to propose political resolutions. Seamus Deane sees the

---

she writes, "cosmopolitanism is the expression of the need above all to enact or embody universalism, to transform it into a characterological achievement." Anderson, *The Powers of Distance*, 31.

84. See, for example, Kiberd, *Inventing Ireland*; Nolan, *James Joyce and Nationalism*; Enda Duffy, *The Subaltern "Ulysses"* (Minneapolis: University of Minnesota Press, 1994); and Derek Attridge and Marjorie Howes, eds., *Semicolonial Joyce* (Cambridge: Cambridge University Press, 2000). For a survey of Joyce's ambivalent treatment of universalist cosmopolitanism as a theme, see Vincent J. Cheng, "Nations without Borders: Joyce, Cosmopolitanism, and the Inauthentic Irishman," in Gibson and Platt, *Joyce, Ireland, Britain*, 212–33.

mature Joyce "surrender[ing] critique for aesthetics."[85] Andrew Gibson, though less disillusioned, also insists on Joyce's "refusal in principle of the 'quick fix', whether artistic, political, intellectual, or ethical."[86] Duffy qualifies his argument about *Ulysses* as a text of the postcolonial Irish community by suggesting that Joyce's distance—including his geographical distance from Ireland—leads him to question the very project of imagining that community.[87] With the example of Djuna Barnes in mind, we can add to these negative conclusions the affirmative claim that Joyce's work carries out a concrete analysis of his mode of literary auton-omy. We need not choose between seeing him as either compromised by political disengagement or as somehow conducting politics by aesthetic means. Instead, he reflects on the way the social role of the expat is constrained by the autonomous literary practice it supports.

We can agree—as Joyce himself might have—that the political positions attributed to Joyce's work in the contemporary scholarship I have mentioned can and should be justified. But those positions cannot be legitimately promoted by means of Joyce's tremendous prestige within the field of modernist culture, a prestige achieved partly by means of those very stylistic-social tactics of cosmopoli-tanism and relative aesthetic autonomy whose political content is in question. Derek Attridge argues that Joyce's success threatens to have a mystifying effect on contemporary Joycean scholarship: as he remarks about *Ulysses*, "its cultural supremacy, and the scholarly efforts which reflect and promote that supremacy, have turned it into a text that confirms us in our satisfied certainties."[88] Though we need not be so quick to scorn our own beliefs, political and otherwise, as satis-fied certainties, Joyce's work, alongside Barnes's, shows us why those beliefs need to be justified by means other than the aesthetic value or symbolic capital of the modernist masterpiece. Otherwise we fall into modernist studies's version of what Anderson calls the "charismatic fallacy," in which the personal and literary style of a cultural theorist is used by his later exponents to trump all other arguments.[89]

---

85. Seamus Deane, "Dead Ends: Joyce's Finest Moments," in Attridge and Howes, *Semicolonial Joyce*, 33–34.

86. Andrew Gibson, *Joyce's Revenge: History, Politics, and Aesthetics in "Ulysses"* (Oxford: Oxford University Press, 2002), 18.

87. See Duffy, *The Subaltern "Ulysses,"* 168–69.

88. Derek Attridge, "Envoi: Judging Joyce," in *Joyce Effects: On Language, Theory, and History* (Cambridge: Cambridge University Press, 2004), 185.

89. Anderson sees the fallacy at work in arguments about Foucault. See "Argument and Ethos," chap. 6 in *The Way We Argue Now: A Study in the Cultures of Theory* (Princeton, NJ: Princeton University Press, 2006).

In fact, Joyce and Barnes both demystify such a strategy by exhibiting, in their fictions, just what the ethos of their cosmopolitan style does amount to—and how little it carries them into collective political enterprises.

Barnes and Joyce, in thematizing expatriation as autonomy, dwell on the convergence between the artist's lifestyle and aesthetic style. They suggest, with Molly Bloom, "sure you cant get on in this world without style" (*Ulysses*, 18.466–67). Narrating expatriate loneliness with humor and melancholy, they analyze forms of aesthetic detachment as forms of social life. But they do not disguise the fact that in their world of transnational modernism, stylish artists must measure a considerable, often lonely and disappointing distance from political communities when they perform the aesthetic cosmopolitan's role. Barnes and Joyce represent this distance in cosmopolitan personae whose poses they imitate in the same strategies of irony and detachment that mark the distance between the writer and the literary creation. Unlike those personae, Barnes and Joyce are consecrated, productive modernist authors. But though they share membership, through their work and their lifestyles, in the social field of international modernism, they do not join any less individualistic communities of shared identity or shared political aims. If Barnes and Joyce envision a cosmopolitan community, they place Barnes- or Joyce-style writers on its margins.

4. Literature without External Reference

Tautology in Wallace Stevens and Paul de Man

The most expansive claims for autonomy may be those that seem not to claim anything at all. "My intention in poetry," wrote Wallace Stevens in 1938, "is to write poetry."[1] It is hard to imagine a less explicit literary program, or a less helpful explanation of a poetics. Given the chance to spell out his aims for the readers of the *Oxford Anthology of American Literature*—to demystify some of the most difficult and idiosyncratic verse readers would find in the volume or anywhere else—Stevens responds with the ultimate mystification: a tautology. He might as well have said, "I am what I am"; or, like Iago at the end of *Othello*, "Demand me nothing; what you know, you know." For tautology, which appears to be true simply by virtue of its form, seems to assert nothing at all about the world. Stevens does, to be sure, expand on his cryptic statement, adding that his intention is "to reach and express that which, without any particular definition, everyone recognizes to be poetry, and to do this because I feel the need of doing it."[2] But this tautological expansion of his statement—poetry is what everyone knows to be poetry—offers no clarification. Stevens considers his poetry to be definable only in terms of itself. This refusal to explain would seem to suit his

1. Wallace Stevens, "A Note on Poetry," in *The Oxford Anthology of American Literature*, ed. William Rose Benét and Norman Holmes Pearson (New York: Oxford University Press, 1938), 1325.
2. Ibid.

long-standing image as a poet with an opaque, even willfully obscure idiolect.[3] Worse yet, the statement taunts readers with the syntactic and logical *form* of an explanation, in the same way that Stevens's poetry frequently takes the form of expository and descriptive sentences while rarely yielding to straightforward understanding.

Yet Stevens's self-explanation in the *Oxford Anthology* is not so vacuous as all that. We can infer what he means when he says that he writes poetry in order to write poetry. In ordinary speech and writing, we use tautologies of this sort to indicate that a particular, specific case is wholly explicable in terms of a more general category: "boys will be boys"; "rules are rules." In the case of a tautology like "boys will be boys," the hearer assumes that the speaker did not intend a completely vacuous statement, and so searches for a relevant meaning from among the possible ways of understanding the sentence. In this case—on one plausible analysis—the hearer can make use of two possible ways of understanding "boys": "a given set of specific young male humans" on one hand, and "the general class of young male humans, supposedly possessing characteristics of unruliness, risk-taking, etc." on the other. Not only that, we understand the equation to carry an affect of resignation to the inevitable.

Saying that my intention in poetry is to write poetry, then, makes the concrete assertion that my specific poetry partakes of the essence of poetry; and it suggests, with underhand rhetorical force, that readers have no choice but to accept my poetic way of doing things. Stevens reinforces the point with his nonexplanatory expansion: poetry is what "everyone" knows to be poetry. These unforthcoming assertions amount to a defense of his poems' autonomy. Such a defense echoes, in its tautological form, the essential slogan of aestheticism: art for art's sake. As with that formula, Stevens's *Oxford Anthology* note implies that it is self-evident that there *is* a distinctive, essential "poetry" which one could pursue to the exclusion of other aims. Indeed, Stevens's rhetoric has a faintly coercive character, for the natural way to understand his declaration *requires* us to assent in advance to an idea of aesthetic autonomy.

Yet Stevens qualifies his declaration of autonomy: his phrase "what everyone understands" adverts readers to the social, consensual character of his concept of poetry. And he gives a clue to his particular poetic procedure: "To *reach and express*

---

3. John Timberman Newcomb's reception history of Stevens documents the beginnings of this image in the reviews of *Harmonium*: "Nearly all commentary on *Harmonium*," he says, concurred about "its formal brilliance and its obscurity." John Timberman Newcomb, *Wallace Stevens and Literary Canons* (Jackson: University Press of Mississippi, 1992), 52.

that which ... everyone recognizes to be poetry." Stevens's intention in poetry, his project, is not simply to write poetry but to write about poetry. He makes self-reference a crucial component of his poetry-for-poetry's-sake, and he understands that self-referential poetic as having a communal basis and a communal function. In fact, this understanding was already implicit in the choice of the figure of tautology itself: tautologies that appear to describe something only in terms of itself become intelligible precisely by relying on the common wisdom of readers, put to use in the inferences that make sense out of what would otherwise be a vacuous construction.

Stevens's use of tautology is not restricted to the particular occasion of the *Oxford Anthology*. It is a highly characteristic feature of his poetry, from first to last:

> Twenty men crossing a bridge,
> Into a village,
> Are
> Twenty men crossing a bridge
> Into a village.   ("Metaphors of a Magnifico," in *Harmonium*)[4]

>   Air is air.
> Its vacancy glitters round us everywhere.
>   ("Evening Without Angels," in *Ideas of Order*, *CPP*, 111)

> You as you are? You are yourself.
>   ("The Man with the Blue Guitar," XXXII, *CPP*, 150)

> One's grand flights, one's Sunday baths,
> One's tootings at the weddings of the soul
> Occur as they occur.
>   ("The Sense of the Sleight-of-Hand Man," in *Parts of a World*,
>   *CPP*, 205)

> I have not but I am and as I am, I am.
>   (*Notes toward a Supreme Fiction*, III.viii, *CPP*, 350)

> The water puddles puddles are
>   ("Poésie Abrutie," in *Transport to Summer*, *CPP*, 268)

> What has he? What he has he has.
>   ("In a Bad Time," in *The Auroras of Autumn*, *CPP*, 367)

---

4. Wallace Stevens, *Collected Poetry and Prose*, ed. Frank Kermode and Joan Richardson (New York: Library of America, 1997), 15. Henceforth cited as *CPP* in the text.

> The enigmatical
>
> Beauty of each beautiful enigma
>
> > ("An Ordinary Evening in New Haven," X, *CPP*, 402)
>
> Required, as a necessity requires.
>
> > ("The Plain Sense of Things," in *The Rock*, *CPP*, 428)[5]

In this chapter I argue that Stevens's poetic tautologies consistently have the same implications as his *Oxford Anthology* statement—that they imply a particular declaration of poetry for poetry's sake. The declaration relies on the presentation of an ostensibly self-referential, logically impervious language of poetry. At the same time, these tautologies are surrounded by reminders that they only have meaning by virtue of socially shared common knowledge. "I am one of you," says the "Angel Surrounded by Paysans," "and being one of you / Is being and knowing what I am and know" (*CPP*, 423).[6]

I am emphasizing tautology, in this final chapter, as a limit case among modernist autonomy tactics. Here, it might seem, is a version of autonomy that is too absolute to yield to reformulation as a worldly fiction of autonomy. Tautology presents the appearance of unqualified truth, of language certifying itself in a virtuous circle that depends on nothing else. Furthermore, it differs from the ways of writing which, in scholarly accounts, emerge as characteristic of Stevens: his language of qualification, his dialogic forms, his love for finding a rhetorical middle way. These latter features dominate two of the most significant works on Stevens, Helen Vendler's *On Extended Wings* and James Longenbach's *Wallace Stevens: The Plain Sense of Things*.[7] Yet such a generalized centrism tends to

5. As these examples indicate, I am using "tautology" as a rhetorical term that covers not only tautological propositions in a strict logical sense but also a larger class of redundant expressions.

6. My emphasis on the common knowledge of tautology complements the argument of Liesl Olson's "Wallace Stevens's Commonplace," chap. 4 in *Modernism and the Ordinary* (New York: Oxford University Press, 2009). Olson describes Stevens as a theorist of the ordinary whose satisfaction with everyday existence extends to a basic contentment with what language can do. If this supplies one motivation for his uses of tautology, it nonetheless needs to be balanced with an explanation of how Stevens continued to maintain his works' poetic distinction, their claim to purity and autonomy, through the very same devices.

7. Helen Hennessy Vendler, *On Extended Wings: Wallace Stevens's Longer Poems* (Cambridge, MA: Harvard University Press, 1969); James Longenbach, *Wallace Stevens: The Plain Sense of Things* (New York: Oxford University Press, 1991). Longenbach speaks of Stevens's "achievement" of "a middle ground ... a position from which extremes, aesthetic and political, were clearly assessed" (viii). Alan Filreis's influential microhistories defend an alternative view, limited in a different way, of Stevens as a thoroughly political poet: *Wallace*

reinstate the assumption of the poet's autonomy by imagining him as floating at an equal distance from all ideological points. In what follows, I show that Stevens's tautologies do imply a commitment to the autonomy of poetry, but in a radically qualified, socially embedded form that depends on the consent of the poet's partners in dialogue, his audience. For Stevens, even when tautology seems to suspend outside reference altogether, his poetry still acquires its meaning through a social relation between conversation partners.

To account for the meanings and implications of tautology in such conversational situations, I have drawn on ideas from the field of linguistic pragmatics. This field has attracted little notice within literary studies, which, when it thinks about questions of language use in a systematic way, has tended to rely on traditional rhetoric and some fragments from the theory of speech acts. In many quarters Saussurean ideas, in which language is an objectively existing code and language users are coders and decoders, still prevail. This model is inadequate to actual language use, which is far more elliptical and context-dependent than any coding scheme could explain. Since the work of H. Paul Grice, linguists and philosophers of language have instead understood the cognitive task of utterance interpretation as a basically collaborative process by which hearers or readers *infer* speakers' or writers' meanings on the basis of both a decoded sentence meaning and assumptions about shared contexts and shared intentions of relevance and informativeness.[8] This inferential model of communication helps me clarify how

---

Stevens and the Actual World (Princeton, NJ: Princeton University Press, 1991) and *Modernism from Right to Left: Wallace Stevens, the Thirties, and Literary Radicalism* (Cambridge: Cambridge University Press, 1994). I discuss Filreis's work further later.

8. For Grice's exposition of this theory and a brief application to tautology, see his "Logic and Conversation," chap. 2 in *Studies in the Way of Words* (Cambridge, MA: Harvard University Press, 1989). For an account of the difference between code-based and inferential models of utterance processing, see Dan Sperber and Deirdre Wilson, *Relevance: Communication and Cognition*, 2nd ed. (Oxford: Blackwell, 1995), esp. 1–64. Sperber and Wilson's Relevance Theory has done much to shape my thinking here; see also their "Relevance Theory," in *The Handbook of Pragmatics*, ed. Laurence R. Horn and Gregory Ward (Oxford: Blackwell, 2005), 607–32. Steven Pinker treats tautologies in his survey of semantics and pragmatics for a general audience, *The Stuff of Thought: Language as a Window into Human Nature* (New York: Penguin, 2007), 163–67. The linguist Anna Wierzbicka argues that some of the content of tautological statements is culturally specific, particularly their affective overtones, in "Boys Will Be Boys: Even 'Truisms' Are Culture-Specific," chap. 10 in *Cross-Cultural Pragmatics: The Semantics of Human Interaction*, 2nd ed. (Berlin: Mouton de Gruyter, 2003). Her argument reminds us that despite its purely logical appearance, tautology actually depends on context to acquire a meaning.

Stevensian tautology can appear to be contained in its own self-reference even as it implicitly acknowledges the poet's relation to his social context.[9]

Of course, Stevens is not alone among modernists in his love of tautology. The iconic tautologist of modernism is not Stevens but the Gertrude Stein of "Rose is a rose is a rose is a rose." Nor do I mean to suggest that Stevens's writing constitutes the limit point of nonreferential language. Movements in experimental writing from Futurism to Dada to Concrete poetry to Language poetry have gone much further in refusing everyday linguistic referentiality, often in the name of aesthetic autonomy—though they have equally often, and sometimes simultaneously, claimed a radical political program. Stevens's poetry, however, insistently *represents* this linguistic autonomy in a way the other, more emphatically avant-garde lineage—including Stein—does not: Stevens's poems unfold at the boundary, where enough of the referential apparatus of language remains to assert the right of poetry not to refer. He does not adopt Stein's sometime program of producing free-standing, nearly nonreferential linguistic objects—but he never defends a poetics of representational transparency, either.[10] Rather, he tries to call autonomy forth by teasing and engaging our understanding, our reasoning processes, our linguistic capacity, and our conventional wisdom, not by assaulting understanding in an avant-gardist mode.

I compare Stevens's tautologies not with the radical experimentalism of other poets but with the modernism of a later language theorist: Paul de Man. De Man's essays in rhetorical reading outline a theory of literary language as doomed only ever to refer to its own inability to refer to anything other than this inability, in a quasi-tautological circuit strikingly analogous to the forms of poetic self-reference Stevens offers. One of de Man's discussions of Rilke offers a paradigmatic statement: "In conformity with a paradox that is inherent in all literature, the poetry gains a maximum of convincing power at the very moment that it abdicates any

9. A brief discussion of linguistic pragmatics in connection with Stevens's philosophical principles appears in Anca Rosu, *The Metaphysics of Sound in Wallace Stevens* (Tuscaloosa: University of Alabama Press, 1995), 4–5.

10. For an account of Stevens's relation to the idea of the poem-as-object, see Douglas Mao, *Solid Objects: Modernism and the Test of Production* (Princeton, NJ: Princeton University Press, 1998). Whereas Mao argues that Stevens "stressed art's immersion in life as against the repose of an artifact that never fails to gesture to its own gratuitousness" (211), I claim that Stevens's poetic effort attempts to reconcile gestures to gratuitousness with immersion in life. In a related argument, Michael Szalay contrasts the highly planned, would-be organic unity of Stein's (and Hemingway's) poetics with Stevens's "performative" embrace of contingency in an "admittedly autonomous" poetry. *New Deal Modernism: American Literature and the Invention of the Welfare State* (Durham, NC: Duke University Press, 2000), 82, 126.

claim to truth."[11] And de Man's project, like Stevens's, is both steeped in philosophical idioms and yet strangely unphilosophical, even obscure, as much a bravura
display of style as an argument. As an exhibition of modernist technique, however,
de Man's work does not always rest on the problematic affirmation of literature's
ontological autonomy. In particular, his reflections on tautology in *The Rhetoric
of Romanticism* suggest, like Stevens's tautologies, a peculiar correspondence relation between an ostensibly nonreferential poetic language and a social reality. I
trace this insight latent in de Man's theory to his defense of a modernist version of
aesthetic autonomy.

I am very far from proposing a deconstructive or "rhetorical" reading of Stevens.
Numerous such accounts exist, some of them directly inspired by de Man's work,
but, in my view, even when deconstructive themes contribute to appealing readings, those readings lack explanatory power.[12] On the contrary, de Man's appeal to
literary-critical readers should itself be explained in terms of his seductive vision
of autonomy—for both literature and the literary academic. I offer an explanation
that combines John Guillory and François Cusset's work on the sociology of de
Manian theory with an analysis of de Man's roots in high modernism, which are
attested from his first publications in Belgian newspapers. This explanation makes
sense of Stevens's own high standing within academic literary theory by showing
how theory followed in Stevens's conceptual, stylistic, and institutional footsteps.[13]
My description of de Man as a late modernist allows me to show how, despite

11. Paul de Man, *Allegories of Reading: Figural Language in Rousseau, Nietzsche, Rilke,
and Proust* (New Haven, CT: Yale University Press, 1979), 50.

12. De Man himself has little to say about Stevens in his own writings, except for a pass-
ing mention as one of Wordsworth's "descendants"; see "Wordsworth and the Victorians,"
chap. 5 in *The Rhetoric of Romanticism* (New York: Columbia University Press, 1984), 87–88,
92. Nonetheless, Stevens was the subject of deconstructionist criticism as soon as that practice solidified: as early as 1972, Joseph N. Riddel invokes de Man, together with Heidegger
and Derrida, in the course of a deconstructive reading of Stevens, "Interpreting Stevens:
An Essay on Poetry and Thinking," *boundary 2* 1, no. 1 (Fall 1972): 79–97. J. Hillis Miller's
deconstructive writings on Stevens began with "Stevens' Rock and Criticism as Cure," *Geor-
gia Review* 30 (1976): 5–31, 330–48; he gives a programmatically de Manian treatment of
Stevens in "Stevens's 'The Red Fern' as Example," *Yale French Studies* 69 (1985): 150–62. For
an even-handed overview and assessment of deconstructionist approaches to Stevens, see
Bart Eeckhout, *Wallace Stevens and the Limits of Reading and Writing* (Columbia: University
of Missouri Press, 2002), esp. 117–32.

13. Newcomb's assessment in his reception history is that "no single author was more
important to the rise of American critical theory than Stevens .... He was *the* modernist
poet to emerge as central to the development of this ambitious and influential discipline
between 1957 and 1966." *Wallace Stevens and Literary Canons*, 207.

differences in tone, sensibility, and genre, he and Stevens both seek ways for the affirmation of autonomy from external reference to reveal literature's social contexts. Far from needing to be saved from such real-world relations, poetry's autonomy depends on them. The stuttering, nearly nonsensical sound of tautological formulae becomes an essential reminder that literary autonomy, even autonomy from reference, is a social arrangement made by and for real-world audiences.

The Aesthete Is the Aesthete

Tautology offers Stevens one of his most flamboyant gestures of individual, imaginative autonomy—a gesture inherited from Romanticism, which in turn had inherited it, via any number of intermediaries, from the Old Testament:

> Not less because in purple I descended
> The western day through what you called
> The loneliest air, not less was I myself. (*CPP*, 51)

In these opening lines of "Tea at the Palaz of Hoon," Stevens gives an extended reworking of a classic assertion of individual intransigence: "I am that I am." His more modest version, "Not less was I myself," still insists on the tautological claim to personal identity, its ineffable, essential, unchangeable qualities. "I" was "myself" by *definition*; on the other hand, the inferable meaning is: "I remained what I essentially am and always have been, despite my changing circumstances." In the context of *Harmonium*'s stylistic extravagances, especially its fantastical imagery, "Tea at the Palaz of Hoon" also implies an apology for Stevens's poetics. Despite his gorgeous accoutrements and his evocations of a strange world, the speaker is only—as we say—being himself. By the time the poem works round to its final tercet, the apology's tautological quality has taken over the whole world:

> I was the world in which I walked, and what I saw
> Or heard or felt came not but from myself[.] (*CPP*, 51)

All those apparently external trappings, even though they seem to belong to the world, are only extensions of the same unchanging self. The poem moves from positing a fixed self in a changing world to positing a self which encompasses the changing world. Instead of Whitmanian expansiveness, Stevens finds a way to apprehend the sensuous variety of the world while remaining within a process of autonomous self-discovery.

Despite the unpromising solipsism of these propositions, "Tea" is framed as a social utterance. After all, it is teatime at Hoon's palaz. The poem's "I" addresses himself to a "you" in order to cast doubt on the epithet "loneliest air." The question-and-answer structure of the middle tercets—"What was the ointment sprinkled on my beard? ... Out of my mind the golden ointment rained" (51)—also suggests dialogue, though of course the questions are, in the poem's tautological idiom, only rhetorical. Nonetheless, the framing devices give a conversational, pragmatic meaning to what might otherwise have been the completely private statement that I am I and I will remain myself.[14] The opening "Not less ... was I myself" places the reader in the position of someone who *already knows* what the speaker is like, who can supply that knowledge in drawing out the meaning of the seemingly sense-less proposition. The teatime interlocutor must simply grant the poem's autonomy from reference external to the speaker's self, must yield to the seemingly inevitable logic of the claim that "I" remain truly "myself," no matter what strange hymns I hear or produce.[15]

Stevens returns to the dialogue setting to proclaim his self-identity again in the later poem "Re-statement of Romance" (*CPP*, 118). In this short lyric from *Ideas of Order*, he makes a sharp division between the poet's world of language and the external world:

> The night knows nothing of the chants of night.
> It is what it is as I am what I am[.]

As far as observation of nature goes, nothing could be more vacuous than the asser-tion that "it is what it is": Stevens uses tautology to draw our assent to what we *already think* about night. He seems to have nothing new to predicate of it, any more than he has anything to add about himself or his speaker. Far from the reve-latory metaphors posited by symbolist or imagist aesthetics, the simile "It is what it is as I am what I am" refuses to surprise us with an unexpected likeness.[16] Yet Stevens does stage a surprise, with an enjambment over a stanza break:

14. Thus I disagree with Longenbach's treatment of the poem as an example of the "aristocratic state of mind" of Stevens at his most aestheticist. *Wallace Stevens*, 35.

15. The poem's apologetic quality comes through particularly clearly in its print con-texts, where it appeared with a group of equally enigmatic, fantastic poems. The first publication was in *Poetry* in 1921, as part of the sequence "Sur ma Guzzla Gracile"; its sub-sequent appearances in *Harmonium* came between "The Cuban Doctor" and "Exposition of the Contents of a Cab."

16. This drama of nonsurprise is also the import of the tautological stanza in "Metaphors of a Magnifico": "Twenty men crossing a bridge, / Into a village, / Are / Twenty men crossing a bridge / Into a village" (*CPP*, 15). Eeckhout describes tautology here as "a mere blabbering formula that keeps us forever locked in the mind." *Wallace Stevens and the Limits of Reading and Writing*, 237. I am arguing for a more complex characterization of tautology in context.

And in perceiving this I best perceive myself

And you. Only we two may interchange
Each in the other what each has to give.

What seemed to be a hermetic poem of tautological statement turns out to be a direct address. The tautologies seem to deny relationships: "It is what it is as I am what I am" implies in the usual way that the night's essential nature explains everything about the night and that my essential nature explains me; thus, the two have nothing to do with one another. Yet the unfolding of the poem, especially through the disruption of the stanza break, implies a series of analogic relations: not only between the self-identical night and the self-identical speaker but also between the chants of night and the speaker and between the speaker and the addressee. Each of these terms is related to the others in its very tautological integrity. But the autonomy of the "chants" is especially stringent: they seem to have no intercourse with anything else, neither their apparent subject—night—nor the two persons who may be hearing or producing them, "I" and "you."

In "Re-statement of Romance," Stevens offers another nonexplanatory apology for a self-referential, inward poetics. At the same time, like "Tea at the Palaz of Hoon," "Re-statement" points up the social meaning that the seemingly empty apology affords. At night—when nothing can be seen anyway—this poem offers the opportunity for speaker and hearer to contemplate their shared experience of separateness. "Only we two are one," the speaker continues, "you and I, alone, / So much alone, so deeply by ourselves." And the poem ends with a shared light radiating from another nearly tautological phrase: "our selves, / Supremely true each to its separate self, / In the pale light that each upon the other throws." In other words, a capital-R Romantic poem about the relation between a human subject and Nature becomes a lowercase-r romantic poem about the relation between two people. The implication of poetry's referential autonomy, however, survives the transformation: Stevens does not state the necessity of turning from chants of night to chants of one another. Instead, he only restates his perception that "I am what I am," that he as person and poet is no more tractable than the night is. This seemingly empty statement may not be much of a sensory "perception," but it does turn out to produce an interpersonal connection, a shared sense of the symmetry between speaker and addressee.

Thus Stevens's oft-reiterated emphasis in essays and letters on the necessity of upholding and renewing the "romantic," in the sense of the capital-R Romantic imagination, is strangely irrelevant to this poem.[17] Instead, the poem depends for its "pale light" on the qualities of the lowercase-r romantic in what he called, in "Sailing After Lunch," its *"pejorative"* sense (*CPP*, 99): the commonplace, the already-assumed, the near-at-hand. This poetics offers not novel observations but restatements, exchanging the possibility of surprising descriptive referentiality for the unassailable autonomy of tautology. Commenting on "Sailing After Lunch" as he sent it to the first publisher of *Ideas of Order*, Ronald Lane Latimer, Stevens wrote: "When people speak of the romantic, they do so in what the French commonly call a *pejorative* sense. But poetry is essentially romantic, only the romantic of poetry must be something constantly new and, therefore, just the opposite of what is spoken of as the romantic."[18] This poetic attempt to root out sentimental cliché is, according to Stevens, the perpetual task of the poet: "What one is always doing," he writes, "is keeping the romantic pure."[19] So far this point of view would seem to be at odds with the implications I have set out in "Re-statement of Romance." Yet Stevens frames his explanation to Latimer by disavowing it: "I am against explanations," he says; "a poem, like anything else, must make its own way."[20] Stevens's sense of the poem's free-standing quality—reminiscent of Eliot's impersonality ("Let the author, at this point, rest in peace")—conflicts with his desire to transvalue the "romantic" so completely that the word will come to mean the opposite of its usual meaning. Just what the new romantic might be remains obscure: in speaking of the "pure" romantic, Stevens says only that the poet must keep the romantic romantic. He seems to maintain the purity of his poetic task precisely by refusing to specify it more exactly. "Re-statement of Romance" makes the same rhetorical gesture: far more important than any new perception or other form of defamiliarization is simply the abstract "perception" of poetic purity, treated as something with all the self-evidence of tautology. And this self-evidence itself

17. For this aspect of Stevens's theory, see, for example, his 1934 preface to William Carlos Williams's *Collected Poems 1921–1931*: "All poets are, to some extent, romantic poets" (rpt. in *CPP*, 770). Filreis chronicles Stevens's 1930s versions of the Romantic in *Modernism from Right to Left*, 139–79. Eventually, Stevens came to prefer the term *imagination* over "the romantic"; in "Imagination as Value," written in 1948 and printed in *The Necessary Angel*, he asserts that the romantic "is to the imagination what sentimentality is to feeling" (*CPP*, 728). This change of terms—possibly a nod to the prevailing anti-Romanticism of Eliot and the New Critics—does not, however, signal a real change in the theory.

18. Letter to Ronald Lane Latimer, March 12, 1935, in Wallace Stevens, *Letters of Wallace Stevens*, ed. Holly Stevens (Berkeley: University of California Press, 1966), 277. This volume is henceforth cited as *Letters*.

19. *Letters*, 277.

20. Ibid.

becomes something exchanged between poet and reader. As Stevens goes on to say to Latimer in the same letter: "It seems to me to be perfectly clear, with the explanation. I hope you will find it equally so without the explanation."[21]

Such protestations against explanation reappear throughout Stevens's letters, often right next to lengthy explications of his poems. In 1940, he wrote to Hi Simons, "A long time ago I made up my mind not to explain things."[22] In the same letter, he answers a question about the *Ideas of Order* poem "Gray Stones and Gray Pigeons" (*CPP*, 113–114):

> This is a perfect instance of destroying a poem by explaining it. I suppose that there is an abstraction implicit in what is actually on the page, and that it would be something like this: everything depends on its sanction; when its sanction is lost that is the end of it. But the poem is precisely what is printed on the page. The poem is the absence of the archbishop, who is the personification or embodiment of a world (globe) of today and tomorrow, among fireflies. The true explanation of this poem is not to expose its abstract shadow or double, but to expose the absence of the archbishop, etc. among the fireflies. (*Letters*, 347–48)

Thus the "true explanation" of the lines "The archbishop is away. The church is gray. / He has left his robes folded in camphor / And, dressed in black, he walks / Among fireflies" (*CPP*, 113) is "to expose the absence of the archbishop, etc. among the fireflies." Stevens tells Simons at length that the poem is the poem. This tautological explanation competes with Stevens's alternate, allegorizing reading, where the poem means that "everything depends on its sanction." Yet he is, precisely, denying that the poem depends on the sanction of an explanation.[23] The apparent

---

21. Ibid.

22. Letter to Hi Simons, January 9, 1940, in *Letters*, 346.

23. Shortly afterward, Stevens changed his mind, writing to Simons that "the thing and its double always go together." He encapsulates this thesis with yet another simile: "A poem is like a man walking on the bank of a river, whose shadow is reflected in the water. If you explain a poem, you are quite likely to do it either in terms of the man or in terms of the shadow, but you have to explain it in terms of the whole. When I said recently that a poem was what was on a page, it seems to me now that I was wrong because that is explaining in terms of the man. But the thing and its double always go together." Letter to Hi Simons, January 18, 1940, in *Letters*, 354. This complicated figure seems to confuse the shadow a man might cast on the water with his reflective image. Equally surprisingly, Stevens underscores the primacy of the text by making *it* the man, with the allegorical meaning as the shadow. He recapitulates metaphorically his own hesitation between explaining and refusing to explain. I am arguing that his efforts are primarily directed toward defending an inexplicability that itself carries pragmatic, explicable content. The meaning is the shadow of the poem, rather than the poem being merely the shadow of a man's intended meaning.

philosophical content—in this case, the experience of secularization rehearsed in Stevens's work again and again—may be "implicit," but the real function of the poem is to be itself.

Stevens is not simply waffling between trying to oblige an ingenuous reader and maintaining his high aesthetic line; he is taking the position of *relative* referential autonomy, in which the poem's tautological self-identity radiates a halo of suggestive implication *about* the poem as a communication between poet and reader. Thus Stevens can produce for Simons, under the heading of "*PARAPHRASES*" of "The Man with the Blue Guitar," the statement: "The poem is the poem, not its paraphrase."[24] As I argue later, such a statement itself paraphrases one of the central premises of the sequence. "I don't want these comments to be quoted," Stevens tells Simons, who had written a critical essay on Stevens and was planning a book; still, he adds: "they are meant to help you. A poem of symbols exists for itself."[25] Presumably Stevens imagines that Simons can then go on to write a critical essay which transmits all the symbolic resonance of the poem without violating its unparaphraseable qualities. But Stevens demonstrates, quite self-consciously, just how a tautological affirmation of poetic autonomy might produce a shared understanding of poetry.

The denial of explanation in "Re-statement of Romance"—and, as we will see, "The Man with the Blue Guitar"—was itself conventional poetic material. In particular, "Re-statement" restates a lyric Stevens read and copied over decades earlier by the British aesthete Laurence Binyon:

> Ask me not, Dear, what thing it is
> That makes me love you so;
> What graces, what sweet qualities,
> That from your spirit flow:
> For I have but this old reply,
> That you are you, that I am I.
>
> My heart leaps when you look on me,
> And thrills to hear your voice.
> Lies, then, in these the mystery
> That makes my soul rejoice?
> I only know, I love you true;
> Since I am I, and you are you.[26]

24. Letter to Hi Simons, August 9, 1940, in *Letters*, 362.
25. Ibid.
26. Laurence Binyon, *Lyric Poems* (London: Elkin Mathews and John Lane, 1894), 62.

Stevens quotes the first stanza of this poem of the 1890s in a courting letter to his future wife, Elsie Kachel Moll, in 1909.[27] Binyon's poem of romance shares with Stevens's its dialogue situation, its use of the tautological assertion that the speaker is the speaker, its avoidance of further explanations, and its paradoxical implication that it is nonetheless a relevant, and indeed romantic, communicative act. Binyon's admission that this speech act is an "old reply" also anticipates the weary embrace of reiteration found in Stevens's title. For the point of the tautology is that it can add nothing by way of further explanation: its relevance is in recalling to attention what speaker and hearer already know. Binyon's love poem rests on the supposition that the very inexplicability of the speaker's love can guarantee its authenticity. For Stevens, taking "the chants of night" and the theory of poetry as his poetic subjects, the inexplicability of the poem in terms of fresh observation serves as a guarantee of *its* purity.

I do not mean to imply that Binyon's poem was somehow the prime mover of Stevens's poem, written some twenty-five years after the letter to Elsie Moll. The tautologies "you are you" and "I am I" are, as Binyon's poem admits, well-worn expressions—of both ordinary speech and love lyrics. Versions of them appear in Shakespeare's Sonnets 84 and 121. But Stevens's acquaintance with and youthful affection for Binyon's poem—even his belief that it was suitable for a love letter—testify to the poet's disposition to redeploy and reiterate such tauto-logical materials. Such a disposition went together with Stevens's aestheticism: a month later, he wrote to his future wife: "Poetry for poetry's sake, 'debonair and gentle' has become difficult. The modern conception of poetry is that it should be in the service of something, as if Beauty was not something quite sufficient when in no other service than its own."[28] Though "Beauty" soon dropped out of Stevens's theory, the conceptual framework remained remarkably fixed over his career.

The kinship between Binyon's poem and Stevens's also points up the mod-ernist poet's continuing relationship to aestheticism, even during the decade in which scholars have found the most evidence of attempts by Stevens to produce more engaged, less flamboyantly aestheticist poetry.[29] "Re-statement of Romance" shows how he was indeed, as he claimed on the book jacket of the Knopf edition

27. Letter to Elsie Moll, May 9, 1909, in *Letters*, 143.

28. Letter to Elsie Moll, June 27, 1909, in *Letters*, 147.

29. See Filreis, *Modernism from Right to Left*. On Stevens and 1890s aestheticism, in particular the aestheticism of Wilde and Santayana, see Mao, *Solid Objects*, and Frank Lentricchia, *Modernist Quartet* (Cambridge: Cambridge University Press, 1994).

of *Ideas of Order*, writing "essentially a book of pure poetry."[30] As he continued to write such poetry, Binyon's "old reply" served him again in a more momentous context. "The Man with the Blue Guitar," in its explorations of the relation of poet to audience—and in particular of Stevens's poetry to leftist demands for politically engaged realism—draws again on tautology as the best reply to questions about what poetry says. The long sequence opens with a nameless group of people demanding "A tune upon the blue guitar / Of things exactly as they are" (*CPP*, 135); this initial problem reaches its seeming resolution in the penultimate section of the poem, whose ringing final couplet reprises the question-and-answer device Stevens has used before:

> You as you are? You are yourself.
> The blue guitar surprises you. (*CPP*, 150)

Stevens deflates the demand for realistic representation with his trivial, logically vacuous answer. Where tautology rules, there can be no surprise. Or, rather, Stevens invites us to imagine that the wielder of the blue guitar comes on "you" unawares, discovering "your" essence in a surprising way—but the particular figure of tautology precludes Stevens saying just what is surprising in this rediscovery. Instead, he leaves the guitarist and his language safely autonomous from the referential task. The offhand one-liner suggests a testy, mocking refusal to cooperate, as though all it took to reply to the demand for "A tune beyond us, yet ourselves" was this rhetorical commonplace.[31] The end-stopping in the sing-song tetrameter couplet heightens the rhetorical closure, particularly since it offers a strong contrast to the rest of section XXXII's enjambed, metrically irregular lines.

But this closure is not the last word. "The Man with the Blue Guitar" has a final section, the tortured lines of which suggest the consequences of accepting this tautological reasoning. Another quasi-tautological formulation gives a more chilling conclusion: "That generation's dream, aviled / In the mud ... // That's it, the only dream they knew" (*CPP*, 150). These final couplets elaborate the implications of resignation and stasis that already lay behind the guitar's "surprise": the dream is the dream, and that's it; it has nothing to do with the future. "Here is the bread of time to come," the poem continues—here and not there, later. The reiterative,

30. The jacket copy is reprinted in *CPP*, 997 n95.1. For the intellectual background of Stevens's use of this phrase, see Benjamin Johnson, "Pure Poetry, Ideas of Order, and the Problem of Poetic Solitude," *Wallace Stevens Journal* 32, no. 2 (Fall 2008): 181–205.

31. Already Binyon shows this same prickly self-assertion: "*Ask me not*, Dear"; "I only know, I love you true."

tautological assertions continue: "The bread / Will be our bread" (151). This pre-diction is hardly a revelation; the aforementioned bread is already the bread "here." Tautology becomes a rhetorical figure for a conservative vision of an unchanging world of things chained to their essences.[32] Against all this stony self-identity, the poem's final couplet makes a dramatic contrast:

> We shall forget by day, except
>
> The moments when we choose to play
> The imagined pine, the imagined jay. (151)

Play, choice, imagination, daytime, and nature all stand opposed both to the dreary, sleepy urban reality of things as they are and to the equally dreary "aviled" urban dreams of a future, better bread. Or so it seems. In moving from the poem's earlier I-you or he-they divisions to the inclusion of "we," Stevens hints that this playful freedom is available to blue guitarist and audience together. In other words—this is the burden of the entire sequence—the capacity for imaginative poetic play is a part of "you as you are," something the blue guitar only has to reveal, obviating the need for any revolutionary transformations. Indeed, such transformations are not only unnecessary, they are, in the world of the poem, unimaginable.[33]

Sections XXXII and XXXIII of "The Man with the Blue Guitar" thus reaffirm the propositions of the explicitly theoretical moment in the poem: "Poetry is the subject of the poem," says the twenty-second section:

> From this the poem issues and
>
> To this returns. Between the two,
> Between issue and return, there is
>
> An absence in reality,
> Things as they are. Or so we say.

32. Ordinary language tautologies, unlike those of propositional logic, *appear* to be logically unassailable but in fact are not. They play on hearers' or readers' assumptions and biases. There is nothing inarguable about the inferred meaning of, say, "boys will be boys": we know, or ought to, that specific boys are capable of deviating from the commonly accepted idea of boyishness.

33. Douglas Mao claims that "The Man with the Blue Guitar" avoids art for art's sake by suggesting that "poetry will have the definite use of refreshing reality or making it new, of renewing desire where desire had seemed exhausted"; but the "price" of this purposefulness is "an intensified emphasis on alienation from the object world under which the possibil-ity of thinking of the real as social simply disappears." Mao, *Solid Objects*, 221. Thinking about tautology in the poem leads, I am arguing, to just the opposite view: the *non*relevatory quality of poetry serves to reconcile its autonomy with a social reality.

> But are these separate? Is it
> An absence for the poem, which acquires
>
> Its true appearances there, sun's green,
> Cloud's red, earth feeling, sky that thinks?
>
> From these it takes. Perhaps it gives,
> In the universal intercourse.[34] (*CPP*, 144–45)

Stevens makes iconic use of the blanks between stanzas to map out the "absences" between the verses' issues and returns. "Things as they are" enter the poem only through their absence; reality is only invoked in the poem when poetry does not depart from the subject of poetry. Stevens holds out hope that this doctrine of separateness is compatible with "the universal intercourse"—an intercourse anticipated by the first-person plural in "Or so we say," and then elaborated in section XXIII's evocation of the "duet / With the undertaker" (145).

"The Man with the Blue Guitar" stands in continuity with "Tea at the Palaz of Hoon" and "Re-statement of Romance." Expanding on those two poems' use of tautology, it stages a dialogue in which the utterance of tautologies constitutes the only possible relation between a freely imaginative poetry and an unchanging reality ("things as they are," a redundant phrase in itself). The sequence's theatrical frame, the confrontation between guitarist and crowd, allows the poem to fulfill its own criteria of self-referentiality even as it addresses social relations by presenting poetry's autonomy as a nonrelevation that can—and, if it is to be fully meaningful, must—be shared.

The Academy of Fine Ideas: Stevens and de Man in the University

The implications of tautology are important for Stevens's relationship with one audience in particular: the academy. For in its abstraction and its seeming categorical definitiveness, tautology forms an exemplary part of Stevens's quasi-philosophical discourse, his manner of taking on the largest questions about reality, about the mind, about knowledge and belief. These questions belong to the academic domain of philosophy, but tautologies are exemplary for Stevens because,

---

34. Hi Simons received another tautological nonexplanation for this section: "I have in mind pure poetry. The purpose of writing poetry is to attain pure poetry." Letter to Simons, August 10, 1940, in *Letters*, 363–64.

in their logical vacuousness, they mark the *difference* between his discourse and philosophical discourse. More than that, they guarantee poetry's status as the academic equal of its philosophic rival. Stevens joins in the quarrel between poetry and philosophy, a quarrel in which the autonomy of poetry as a special kind of language—and as an independently funded academic unit—is at stake.

When in his later career he set foot on campus, Stevens bore the message of "The Irrational Element in Poetry" while still arguing for its philosophical significance. In the 1936 Harvard lecture of that title, Stevens prefaces his discussion with a disclaimer: "I am not competent to discuss reality as a philosopher." But he continues: "All of us understand what is meant by the transposition of an objective reality to a subjective reality" (*CPP*, 781). This casual invocation of a supposedly shared understanding closely resembles Stevens's tautological *Oxford Anthology* explanation that his poetry aims for "that which, without any particular definition, everyone recognizes to be poetry." In "The Figure of the Youth as Virile Poet," originally a paper given in 1943 at Mount Holyoke College, Stevens proclaims that there is a difference between "philosophic truth and poetic truth … and it is the difference between logical and empirical knowledge" (*CPP*, 676). He cites Bertrand Russell, a philosophical authority, only to demonstrate that "philosophers do not agree in respect to what constitutes philosophic truth" (676). His advocacy of poetry as an empirical knowledge attempts to steal the ground out from under analytic philosophy in particular. In a later work, "Imagination as Value," Stevens rather apprehensively alludes to the philosopher A. J. Ayer's scorn for metaphysics and its relegation to the realm of poetry; "we feel," he says, "without being particularly intelligent about it, that the imagination as metaphysics will survive logical positivism unscathed" (*CPP*, 727). In *Adagia*, he writes: "Perhaps it is of more value to infuriate philosophers than to go along with them."[35]

Nothing indicates Stevens's commitment to the idea of poetry as philosophy's academic rival so much as his project for a university Chair of Poetry, to be funded

---

35. Wallace Stevens, *Adagia*, in *Opus Posthumous*, rev. ed., ed. Milton J. Bates (New York: Knopf, 1989), 192. Stevens's readers did not always see the distinction. Randall Jarrell, writing in hostility to Stevens's philosophical leanings in a 1951 review, described his onomatopoeias as "those mannered, manufactured, individual, uninteresting little sound-inventions—how typical they are of the lecture-style of the English philosopher, who makes grunts or odd noises, uses homely illustrations, and quotes day in and day out from *Alice*, in order to give what he says some appearance of that raw reality it so plainly and essentially lacks." Jarrell describes one poem as "G. E. Moore at the spinet." "Reflections on Wallace Stevens," in *Poetry and the Age*, expanded ed. (Gainesville: University Press of Florida, 2001), 142, 144. Jarrell's comments work to maintain a discursive boundary, attempting to keep poetry cordoned off from the dry institutionality of Anglo-American philosophy.

by his friend Henry Church. Stevens hoped, he wrote to Church, that such a chair would disprove the idea that "universities do the Arts and Letters more harm than good."[36] Expanding on his idea in a draft "memorandum" in another letter to Church, Stevens asserts that "the knowledge of poetry is a part of philosophy, and a part of science"; "it must be an odd civilization," he adds jealously, "in which poetry is not the equal of philosophy, for which universities largely exist."[37] Crucially, the subject matter for the chair can be defined only tautologically: "What is intended is to study the theory of poetry in relation to what poetry has been and in relation to what it ought to be . . . . For this purpose, poetry means not the language of poetry but the thing itself, wherever it may be found. It does not mean verse any more than philosophy means prose."[38] Stevens then quotes one of his own lines as an example of the subject matter of poetry. His intention in theorizing poetry, in other words, is to theorize poetry and to study what everyone knows to be poetry. A Stevensian Chair of Poetry would probably give lectures consisting of the nonexplanations of which Stevens was master. Tautology becomes his way of imagining the autonomy of poetry within the university. That autonomy, however, would be not so much a transcendent philosophical principle as an investment of money in an institutional position independent from philosophy in its departmental form. Like verbal tautology, this position would work to corroborate the shared knowledge of poetry's distinctiveness that people already possess.[39]

Stevens's suggested candidate for a Chair of Poetry was Jean Paulhan (*Letters*, 375), but we might say that although Stevens and Church never realized the poet's plan, the chair was ultimately occupied by a different intellectual from Europe: Paul de Man. De Man's work constitutes a case for the distinctiveness of literary—especially poetic—language on the basis of its elusiveness and nonreferentiality; his career played a significant part in establishing, as Stevens hoped his Chair of Poetry might, a new academic formation that claimed equality with or even supremacy over philosophy. De Man's essays from the 1950s onward, with their themes of subjectivity, temporality, and ontology, insist on the relevance of literature to philosophy—in spite of the critic's emphatically literary, even aestheticist sensibilities. More than that, especially after his rhetorical turn, his writings frequently suggest that literature triumphs over philosophy on its own ground. By

36. Letter to Henry Church, May 28, 1940, in *Letters*, 358.

37. Letter to Henry Church, October 15, 1940, in *Letters*, 378. The memorandum is reprinted in *CPP*, 805–7.

38. *Letters*, 377.

39. "It would not be initiating the study of the true nature of poetry; it would merely be initiating its study in a high academic sense, certainly in America." *Letters*, 378.

the time of his last writings, de Man can confidently assert, in "The Epistemology of Metaphor," that "all philosophy is condemned, to the extent that it is dependent on figuration, to be literary and, as the depository of this very problem, all literature is to some extent philosophical."[40]

What took place in the intervening decades—to a considerable degree through de Man's own work—was the rise of "Theory" in American universities as a literature-based rival to philosophy. François Cusset has traced the history of this rise (and the subsequent fall) in *French Theory*; his account very usefully emphasizes the institutional structures through which radical French philosophy was translated into a syllabus for the American literature department.[41] Though I do not mean to reduce literary theory to a substitute philosophy, I do want to underscore the tactical dimension Cusset's history reveals: under the aegis of theory, literature departments defended their subject matter by mounting an assault on the precincts of philosophy. This tactic was the product of the declining viability of the New Critical defense of literary autonomy; the new movement was still concerned with literary autonomy, but it presented that idea in a new guise, as the grounds for a transcendent critique of philosophy.[42] According to Cusset, the departmental rivalry was exacerbated by the eclipse, in American philosophy, of the idealist, "Continental" tradition in favor of the analytic and ordinary-language traditions, with their orientation toward the sciences. As Cusset writes, "On one side are the specialists of the inquiry into truth … and on the other side are generalists invested with a mission, and, from Nietzsche to Sartre, ceaselessly opening a space in which their relation to truth is mediated by style, or by writing."[43] Stevens—who never lost

---

40. Paul de Man, "The Epistemology of Metaphor," in *Aesthetic Ideology*, ed. Andrzej Warminski (Minneapolis: University of Minnesota Press, 1996), 50. Other comparable statements include the celebration of "the mess of the *Critique of Judgment* and the breakdown of aesthetic theory" in the essay on Kleist ("Aesthetic Formalization: Kleist's *Über das Marionettentheater*," in de Man, *The Rhetoric of Romanticism*, 283); the remark that "the possibility of philosophy itself" rests on the aesthetic in another essay on Kant ("Phenomenality and Materiality in Kant," in de Man, *Aesthetic Ideology*, 73); and the assertion that Hegel's philosophy is an "allegory" of the disjunction between "literary experience and literary theory" ("Sign and Symbol in Hegel's *Aesthetics*," in de Man, *Aesthetic Ideology*, 104).

41. François Cusset, *French Theory: How Foucault, Derrida, Deleuze, & Co. Transformed the Intellectual Life of the United States*, trans. Jeff Fort with Josephine Berganza and Marlon Jones (Minneapolis: University of Minnesota Press, 2008).

42. "French theory, which did not yet bear this name, would thus be, for the young scholars interested in New Criticism, the figure of a third way between the dead ends of formalist criticism and the political blockages of a university institution subjected to the state as much as to the market." Ibid., 52.

43. Ibid., 97.

the impress of the philosophical idealism that dominated the Harvard of his student years—was already joining this conflict in his university lectures of the 1930s and 1940s, with his anxieties over logical positivism and his arguments for poetry's special relation to truth. American 'French Theory,' including the work of de Man, continues this conflict of the faculties between the sciences and the humanities, with philosophy as one of the most contested properties.[44]

De Man, Modernism, and the Correspondence Theory

Although a shared position in academic disciplinary conflicts unites Stevens and de Man, the latter is usually associated with a radical skepticism about referentiality, whereas I have been arguing that Stevens's tautologies construct a different, contextualized autonomy from reference: they seem to protect poetry's self-enclosure even as they project a sense of relation between speakers and audiences.[45] As a general theory of literature's autonomy from reference, de Man's rhetorical reading is unpromisingly absolute. Set against contemporary cognitive-scientific approaches like the theories of pragmatics I have been invoking, its account of language use appears simplistic, especially its treatment of the interpretive work of audiences.[46] When de Man takes up the figure of tautology, however, he creates a critical fiction of autonomy that resembles Stevens's much more closely than we might expect. Tautology brings de Man back to his own literary roots in modernism. And de Man's modernism, unlike his own general principles but like the fictions of other writers I have been discussing throughout this study, reconstructs autonomy as a way literature connects to its historical contexts—despite its resistance to external referentiality.

44. As John Guillory has written, the advent of French theory in literary studies "provided the literary professoriate with a powerful new weapon for contesting the epistemic superiority of the sciences." "The Sokal Affair and the History of Criticism," *Critical Inquiry* 28, no. 2 (Winter 2002): 503–4.

45. Fredric Jameson has argued that Stevens's version of autonomy from referentiality makes him a specific forerunner of literary Theory: in Stevens, says Jameson, "reference must be preserved at the same time that it is bracketed." Stevens's distinctive mode of self-reference, however, brings about "an unusual permutation ... and a new thing—theory itself—emerges." "Exoticism and Structuralism in Wallace Stevens," in *The Modernist Papers* (London: Verso, 2007), 218, 221.

46. For a useful contrast between the approaches, see Ian MacKenzie, *Paradigms of Reading: Relevance Theory and Deconstruction* (Houndmills, UK: Palgrave Macmillan, 2002).

De Man's turn to tautology comes in the course of his discussion of a central Romantic-modernist text, Baudelaire's sonnet "Correspondances," which de Man describes as fundamental to "the entire possibility of the lyric."[47] De Man seeks to show that Baudelaire's sonnet gives the lie to its own vision of a world in which humanity and nature, sensations and objects, words and ideas, are all interrelated—a world in which the poet has the privilege of uncovering the secret interconnections. De Man dwells on Baudelaire's use of the word *comme*, which, like the English *like*, can be used either for making similes or for listing particular examples of some general category. Whereas the middle two stanzas of the poem use *comme* in the former sense, the final tercet can be read as deploying *comme* in the latter sense:

> Il est des parfums frais comme des chairs d'enfants,
> Doux comme les hautbois, verts comme les prairies,
> —Et d'autres, corrompus, riches et triomphants,
>
> Ayant l'expansion des choses infinies,
> Comme l'ambre, le musc, le benjoin et l'encens,
> Qui chantent les transports de l'esprit et des sens.[48]

De Man sees in this piece of syntactic variation the implosion of Baudelaire's whole proto-symbolist apparatus:

> Considered from the perspective of the "thesis" or of the symbolist ideology of the text, such a use of "comme" is aberrant. For although the burden of totalizing expansion seems to be attributed to these particular scents rather than the others, the logic of "comme" restricts the semantic field of "parfums" and confines it to a tautology: "Il est des parfums ... / Comme (des parfums)." ("ATL," 249–50; ellipsis de Man's)

Tautology possesses, in this account, the power to nullify all the links between the poet's sense perceptions and his visions of "choses infinies." It is the de Manian trope to the highest power, the perfect example of the defeat of referentiality.

47. Paul de Man, "Anthropomorphism and Trope in the Lyric," in *The Rhetoric of Romanticism*, 262. Henceforth cited as "ATL" in the text.

48. Charles Baudelaire, "Correspondances," in *Les fleurs du mal*, 2nd ed., ed. Claude Pichois (Paris: Gallimard, 1996), 40. "There are perfumes cool like children's flesh, / Sweet like oboes, green like the prairie, / —And others corrupt, rich, overbearing, // With the expansiveness of infinite things, / Like ambergris, musk, spikenard, frankincense, / Singing ecstasy to the mind and to the senses." "Correspondences," in *The Flowers of Evil*, trans. Keith Waldrop (Middletown, CT: Wesleyan University Press, 2006), 14 (translation modified).

"The poem offers no explicit alternative," he goes on to emphasize, "to this language which, like perfumes enumerated by 'comme,' remains condemned to the repetition of its superfluity" (252).

Despite de Man's characteristically negative vocabulary—language is "condemned" or "confined" or "aberrant"—the thrust of the critical narrative is affirmative. He imagines a literary language radically autonomous from all the ends of predication or evocation, a language that absolutely refuses to produce knowledge. The note of freedom rings at the end of two paragraphs meditating on Baudelaire's "comme":

> Enumerative repetition disrupts the chain of tropological substitution at the crucial moment when the poem promises … to reconcile the pleasures of the mind with those of the senses and to unite aesthetics with epistemology. That the very word on which these substitutions depend would just then lose its syntactical and semantic univocity is too striking a coincidence not to be, like pure chance, beyond the control of author and reader. (250)

Tautology takes poetic language "beyond the control" of anyone, differentiating the effect of the poem from perception ("aesthetics") and knowledge ("epistemology"). Indeed, the poem's only real subject, in de Man, is the poem itself: the "theme" of the poem is, he concludes, "tropes" (252). The self-limiting, self-referring language of poetry—and its study in academic literary criticism—stands apart from, and indeed triumphs over, the discipline in whose purview aesthetics and epistemology fall: philosophy. Thus "Anthropomorphism and Trope," like many other de Man essays, offers to its scholarly readers both an affirmation of literary autonomy in the most absolute terms and the promise of a purely literary set of specialized tools of analysis with which to approach texts in the institutional setting of the university. It offers one more example of what John Guillory has described as the "symptomatic" character of de Man's work, its preoccupation with the autonomy of the literary academic within the university and the society as a whole.[49]

"Anthropomorphism and Trope" exhibits most clearly two of the symptoms Guillory discusses: an emphasis on tropes, both as theme and as technique, and an ominous motif of frustrated agency. Beyond these typical elements, however, de Man's choice of Baudelaire as a central example for his theory is telling. Though the essay denies the possibility of literary history, denouncing "pseudo-historical

---

49. See John Guillory, "Literature after Theory: The Lesson of Paul de Man," chap. 4 in *Cultural Capital: The Problem of Literary Canon Formation* (Chicago: University of Chicago Press, 1993).

period terms such as 'romanticism' or 'classicism'" ("ATL," 262), it treats a significant founding document of *modernism* as generative. Despite the predominance of Romanticism in de Man's theoretical work—Wordsworth, Hölderlin, Rousseau, Shelley—and the essay's framing of its topic as the predicament of "'Romantic' literatures" (239), de Manian themes like the autonomization of language, the release from external referentiality, and the free-standing material literary object all belong to an aesthetics of modernism which Baudelaire did much to establish in France and then internationally.

Of course Baudelaire, on any account, himself exemplifies the continuities between Romanticism and modernism at the level of aesthetic ideas. But it is equally important that he is, in Pierre Bourdieu's phrase, a "nomothete" for the autonomous literary field: someone whose particularly strenuous defense of "pure" art against both a moralizing, conservative literary establishment and a broader literary market establishes the norms for an autonomous literature.[50] Indeed, Baudelaire's trademark antimorality or amorality appears in de Man's essay, not in the analysis of Baudelaire himself but in the opening discussion of Nietzsche's "On Truth and Lie in the Extra-Moral Sense"; at the end of his essay, de Man evokes this extramorality when he says that the "power" which allows "Correspondances" to generate the lyric is the "sheer blind violence that Nietzsche ... domesticated by calling it, metaphorically, an *army* of tropes" (262). De Man invokes violence to suggest the power of literary language to defy "domestication." Though Satanic defiance of social norms is also a feature of Romanticism, Baudelaire's restatement of it, in the particular circumstances of his career, constituted one of the founding moments of modernism: especially after his 1857 prosecution for the alleged obscenity of *Les fleurs du mal*, Baudelaire embodied an oppositional literary and social stance that enduringly influenced the succeeding generations of decadents, symbolists, and modernists across Europe and North America.

De Man's literary-critical roots are in the Baudelairean version of modernism, with its heightened emphasis on the antimoral character of art for art's sake.[51] In

50. Pierre Bourdieu, *Les règles de l'art: Genèse et structure du champ littéraire*, rev. ed. (Paris: Seuil, 1998), 106, 108. Bourdieu's English translator renders *nomothète* as "founder." "Law-giver" would be better; the etymological point is that the nomothete establishes a *nomos*. Pierre Bourdieu, *The Rules of Art: Genesis and Structure of the Literary Field*, trans. Susan Emanuel (Cambridge: Polity Press, 1996), 60, 62.

51. Fredric Jameson offers a cogent account of de Man's modernism in his *Postmodernism*. Jameson describes de Man as a "nominalist," linking him to Adorno's theory of the nominalism of modern art. I diverge from Jameson's Adornian explanation of this nominalist tendency, however, because I prefer to emphasize how nominalism becomes a theory of aesthetic autonomy—and a way of recovering, rather than withdrawing from, literature's

a 1939 student newspaper essay, de Man defended André Gide's "amorality," his "refusal to accept a line of behavior, because it becomes an automatic rule and a limit to liberty."[52] More pertinently yet, in 1940 he celebrated Huxley for his neglect of "the most elementary modesty," Joyce for his "pure and simple scatology," and Lawrence for having "gotten himself treated as a pornographer by all the right-thinking souls of the empire."[53] De Man continued the theme in his writings for the collaborationist Le Soir[54]: "The least one can say is that the artistic values which rule the world of letters are not to be confused with those of the True and the Good and that anyone who borrowed his criteria from this region of human consciousness would be systematically wrong in his judgments."[55]

In such statements we find the same basic aesthetic position-taking as that of even de Man's latest essays, but he has not yet substituted Romantic authors and rhetorical terminology for his modernist points of reference. Nowhere is this clearer than in the young critic's interview with Paul Valéry. In the 1942 Le Soir article recounting this interview, de Man defends Valéry against any accusation of aestheticism. Instead, "symbolism" aspired to an art that spoke to all the "sectors of human activity"; but, as Valéry tells de Man, "the tool which we have—language—is not proper for attaining this goal." Thus, concludes de

context. See Postmodernism, or, The Cultural Logic of Late Capitalism (Durham, NC: Duke University Press, 1991), 250–51, 257. Jameson returns to de Man's modernism in A Singular Modernity: Essay on the Ontology of the Present (London: Verso, 2002), 106–13.

52. "Amoralité"; "refus d'accepter une ligne de conduite, parce qu'elle devient règle automatique et limite à la liberté." Paul de Man, "André Gide," Jeudi (Brussels), November 30, 1939, rpt. in Wartime Journalism, 1939–1943, ed. Werner Hamacher, Neil Hertz, and Thomas Keenan (Lincoln: University of Nebraska Press, 1988), 12. All translations of de Man from the French are my own, with the original in the notes.

53. "Huxley nous promène dans les mauvais lieux et semble oublier la pudeur la plus élémentaire. Joyce se permet de la scatologie pure et simple. Quant à Lawrence, ce fils de mineur, malade et misanthrope, il se fait traiter de pornographe par toutes les âmes bien pensantes de l'empire." "Le Roman anglais contemporain," Cahiers du Libre Examen (Brussels), January, 1940, in Wartime Journalism, 16.

54. Indeed, as Jameson remarks (Postmodernism, 258), even the infamous essay on "The Jews in Contemporary Literature" uses the occasion for a defense of literary autonomy—for the invidious purpose of claiming that such autonomy means that Jewish influences couldn't have affected the course of European literary history much. De Man, "Les Juifs dans la Littérature actuelle," Le Soir (Brussels), March 4, 1941, rpt. in Wartime Journalism, 45.

55. "Le moins qu'on puisse dire est que les valeurs artistiques qui régissent le monde des lettres ne se confondent pas avec celles du Vrai et du Bien et que celui qui emprunterait ses critères à cette région de la conscience humaine se tromperait systématiquement dans ses jugements." "Sur les possibilités de la critique," Le Soir (Brussels), December 2, 1941, rpt. in Wartime Journalism, 168.

Man, in language which in its martial imagery as well as its ideas anticipates "Anthropomorphism and Trope":

> The products of symbolist art appear as an incessant battle, a fight without result, to discover new possibilities and as yet unexploited riches in this capricious instrument which is language.[56]

De Man already knew how to celebrate the failures of literary language to extend beyond literature's autonomous domain in a style derived from post-Baudelairean French literature. In returning to Baudelaire near the end of his career, he was coming back to a source.

De Man's roots as a modernist aesthete are well known. I recall them because his personal history encapsulates the migration of modernist aesthetics into American academic literary criticism—and reminds us that deconstruction is itself a literary epigone of modernism. Yet de Man's modernism is curiously absent from Guillory's definitive account in *Cultural Capital*. For Guillory, the determining context for de Manian claims about literary language is the university literature department in the society of the technobureaucracy. De Man's insistence on the "rigor" of his method, with its apparatus of rhetorical terms, is symptomatic of an academic literary profession at an impasse, attempting to adapt itself to the ever more bureaucratized research university and its scientific norms for scholarship. This supposed rigor, according to Guillory, masks the crucial role of de Man's charisma as a master teacher, the very arbitrariness of whose tastes and arguments seem to his students to argue for the radical autonomy of his work.[57]

Though Guillory is certainly right about the extremely selective nature of the small canon of texts on which de Man bases his generalizations about literature and rhetoric, that selection is not so arbitrary as he implies. De Man dwells on a particular early modernism—the symbolist or late Romantic modernism of Proust, Rilke, Baudelaire, and Yeats—together with a group of nineteenth- and late-eighteenth-century Romantic precursors, to whom he imputes a canonically modernist aesthetics of impersonality, formal rupture, and nonreferentiality. Indeed, in 1983 de Man gestures to this modernist source when he describes a chapter on Yeats from his 1960 doctoral dissertation as an early work of "rhetorical

---

56. "Tous les secteurs de l'activité humaine"; "'l'outil dont nous disposons—le langage—est impropre à atteindre ce but'"; "les produits de l'art symboliste apparaissent comme une lutte incessante, un combat sans issue, pour découvrir des possibilités nouvelles et des richesses non encore exploitées dans cet instrument capricieux qu'est le langage." "Paul Valéry et la poésie symboliste," *Le Soir* (Brussels), January 10–11, 1942, rpt. in *Wartime Journalism*, 182.

57. Guillory, *Cultural Capital*, 259.

analysis of figural language *avant la lettre*."⁵⁸ He abandons only the claims of early twentieth-century modernism to literary-historical novelty, or, rather, he transfers the novelty onto his own scholarly method.⁵⁹ This move also serves the autonomy of literature and literary study, as de Man's other discussion of Baudelaire, the essay "Literary History and Literary Modernity," collected in *Blindness and Insight*, makes clear. According to this essay, Baudelaire's "Le Peintre de la vie moderne" exhibits the "discovery of his inability to be modern," which "leads him back to the fold, within the autonomous domain of literature."⁶⁰ Baudelaire, says de Man, knew the "curse" of a "compulsion to return to a literary mode of being, as a form of language that knows itself to be mere repetition, mere fiction and allegory, forever unable to participate in the spontaneity of action or modernity."⁶¹ The loss of the label "modern[ist]" is a small price to pay for this escape from history into the autonomy of literary language.

With the historical specificity of de Man as a modernist in mind, we can see that some of his deconstructive theoretical claims might be understood as fictions of autonomy. In the case of his theory of tautology, that fiction has a distinctive dialectical character: the failure of literary language to refer beyond itself nonetheless brings about the recovery of an extraliterary reality. The enigmatic conclusion to "Anthropomorphism and Trope" gestures to "the materiality of actual history," arguing that "Correspondances" "enumerate[s]" non-anthropomorphic, non-elegiac, non-celebratory, non-lyrical, non-poetic, that is to say, prosaic, or, better, *historical* modes of language power" (262; emphasis in original). "Enumeration" is the task of the tautological *comme* of Baudelaire's sonnet; de Man sees in this figure, which defeats metaphorical correspondence, the means by which history makes a genuine appearance in the poem. He produces, then, his own version of the correspondence theory: as with Stevens's "It is what it is as I am what I am," de

58. Preface to *The Rhetoric of Romanticism*, viii. He reprints the chapter in that volume as "Image and Emblem in Yeats" (145–238).

59. Cusset rightly remarks that de Man's deconstruction was "still imbued with the tragic and haughty ethos of high literary modernism." Cusset emphasizes the continuities between de Man and the New Critics in order to demonstrate the ways the American university structure domesticated "French theory" as above all a method of literary reading. In this domestication de Man was a crucial mediator. *French Theory*, 113.

60. Paul de Man, "Literary History and Literary Modernity," in *Blindness and Insight: Essays in the Rhetoric of Contemporary Criticism*, 2nd ed. (Minneapolis: University of Minnesota Press, 1983), 162. Normally de Man avoids the word *autonomy*, perhaps because of its status as a New Critical shibboleth.

61. Ibid., 161.

Manian correspondence exists between literary things and real things just because they are both self-sufficient.[62]

De Man anticipates a later reworking of Baudelaire's correspondences, just as exorbitant in its way, but far more promising as an explanatory model. In *The Rules of Art*, Bourdieu describes Baudelaire's theories as a version of pure art, a nomothetic standard for a nascently autonomous literature. Bourdieu quotes Baudelaire offering a Stevensian credo: "No poem would be so great, so noble, so truly worthy of the name of poem as that one which would be written for the pleasure of writing a poem."[63] But Bourdieu goes on to argue that this tautological insistence on writing poetry in order to write poetry does not preclude a correspondence with reality. "Parodoxically," he writes, "it is pure work on pure form, a formal exercise *par excellence*, which brings forth, as though by magic, a real more real than that which gives itself immediately to the senses." Against both Romanticism and the demand for objectivity in art,

> Baudelaire opposes a sort of mysticism of sensation broadened by the game of language: an autonomous reality, with no referent other than itself, the poem is a creation independent of creation, and nevertheless united with it by profound ties that no positivist science perceives, and which are as mysterious as the correspondences uniting beings and things with one another.[64]

Since, for Bourdieu, the "essential" consists in the artist's social relations, Baudelaire's "realist formalism" constitutes the germ of a properly sociological theory of literary form.[65] De Man, too, in describing Baudelaire's supposed inability to exceed the bounds of literary language itself, still wants to save modernist poetics for a deeper realism, a realism of "materiality" and "language power." Of course, de Man's real is not necessarily to be equated with Bourdieu's social reality of fields and positions. The sociologist's theory is itself a little willful: Baudelaire is not, despite Bourdieu's analogies, a Flaubertian realist, even if he was Flaubert's literary ally. But Bourdieu's general thesis remains provocative: the position-taking of literary modernism does not entail a straightforward denial of relations between language

---

62. Fredric Jameson notices de Man's reproduction of the correspondence theory in his discussion of the critical practice of homology: *Postmodernism*, 238.

63. Quoted in Bourdieu, *Rules of Art*, 106. Translation modified to reflect the original quoted in Bourdieu, *Les règles de l'art: Genèse et structure du champ littéraire*, 181.

64. Bourdieu, *Rules of Art*, 107; translation modified.

65. Bourdieu makes the same analysis of Flaubert; see my remarks on that analysis in chapter 3.

and the world; instead, it redescribes those relations in terms of autonomy. Out of the intention to write poetry comes the search for real correspondences. In this position-taking de Man, too, partook.

Whereas "Anthropomorphism and Trope" only gestures toward these correspondences under the signs of "materiality," "power," and "sheer blind violence," the final essay in *The Rhetoric of Romanticism*, "Aesthetic Formalization: Kleist's *Über das Marionettentheater*," hints at a more specific social relation. Once again, the figure of tautology plays a central role. De Man begins his essay by commenting on a commentary on Schiller's *Aesthetic Education*. The Oxford Schiller editors, Elizabeth Wilkinson and L. A. Willoughby, catch de Man's attention for speaking of "what they call the *tautology* of art, 'its inherent tendency to offer a hundred different treatments of the same subject'" (264). Wilkinson and Willoughby see this tendency in Schiller's image of society as an English dance, a highly formalized collective activity in which each individual seems to be acting spontaneously and freely. For de Man, this goes to show that "as a principle of formalization rigorous enough to produce its own codes and systems of inscription, tautology functions as a restrictive coercion that allows only for the reproduction of its own system, at the exclusion of all others" (265). If, says de Man, "aesthetic ideology" made Schiller blind to this coercive aspect of tautology, Heinrich von Kleist's "Über das Marionettentheater" permits some insight: we become aware that "aesthetic education by no means fails; it succeeds all too well, to the point of hiding the violence that makes it possible" (289). The violence de Man evokes in this essay is the symbolic violence of schooling, the means by which the teacher imposes certain ideas on the student. Indeed, "the politics of the aesthetic state are the politics of education" (273)—the politics, that is, of de Man's own profession. The tautological quality of literature acts on its contexts after all; specifically, it acts on the same academic field in which Stevens had blazed a trail for de Man. Through the contemplation of the apparently closed circle of tautology, de Man uncovers, though only in brief glimpses, a less mystified understanding of the ways literature remains *within* the game, or the dance, of culture.

The Sound of Autonomy

My argument that de Man's theory recovers a reality of social circulation for literature even as it defies linguistic reference might seem to have passed over a more obvious way in which his late work attempts to stage a recovery of the real:

his frequent appeals to what he calls "the prosaic materiality of the letter."[66] In particular, the sound of words, their ability to provoke punning or their latent capacity to be heard as mere noise, has often seemed to be the reality that deconstruction finds after it has disposed of signification. Punning is more Derrida's than de Man's trademark, but de Man was not averse to this rhetorical tactic, as the string of puns on the German *Fall* that concludes "Aesthetic Formalization" attests. Sound effects are, in fact, quite relevant to poetic tautology; as de Man says of Baudelaire's repeated, tautological "comme," the figure is like a "stutter" ("ATL," 259). In Stevens, the echoic, mantra-like quality of tautologies like "You as you are? You are yourself" makes it seem as though they predicate nothing about the world while still sounding like compelling assertions. Thus, they may seem to substitute autonomous sound for reference-dependent sense, in the way Stevens's more prominent sonic devices—his onomatopoeias, his rich phonetic patterning, his punning—do more emphatically.[67] But Stevens attempts to make the sounds of words do double duty as guarantors of poetic autonomy and tools for understanding the world; he combines tautological assertions with the *thematization* of poetic sound, in a self-referential circuit which does *not* disable all external reference. Rather, like de Man's Baudelaire—though in a lighter-hearted vein—Stevens uses the sound of tautology to recuperate reality.[68]

66. De Man, "Phenomenality and Materiality in Kant," 90. Indeed, I have given short shrift to de Man's effort to distinguish linguistic "materiality" from the aesthetic and "aesthetic ideology" and his claims for an ontological rather than an aesthetic autonomy for literature. These claims may seem to separate de Man from the modernist aesthetes. But such an argument depends on de Man's sense that the aesthetic, unlike the literary, is intimately tied to perception and hence to empirical knowledge. By contrast, I am speaking of the aesthetic as a social principle of classification, a rule for delineating the boundaries of the whole sphere of relations that constitute the literary field. As Guillory demonstrates so compellingly, de Man's version of the literary, ontological arguments notwithstanding, is very close to that of preceding generations. On this point see also Jameson, *Postmodernism*, 251–52.

67. For an exhaustive set of readings of Stevensian wordplay—and a further example of de Man–influenced scholarship on Stevens—see Eleanor Cook, *Poetry, Word-Play, and Word-War in Wallace Stevens* (Princeton, NJ: Princeton University Press, 1988).

68. My approach differs from the psychoanalytic-deconstructive one of Mutlu Blasing in her discussion of Stevens in *Lyric Poetry*: for Blasing, Stevens shows how "the human is realized in the 'otherness' of poetic language to meaning and to the mind that it objectifies as sounds of words." Mutlu Konuk Blasing, *Lyric Poetry: The Pain and the Pleasure of Words* (Princeton, NJ: Princeton University Press, 2007), 142. To a degree, Stevens invites readings like this, which take for granted the autonomy of poetic language; but I am arguing that he also reflects on the circumstances in which the invitation to believe in autonomy takes place, and the limits to the autonomy he invokes.

"The Man on the Dump" (*CPP*, 184–86) exemplifies Stevens's double sense of the sound of tautology. Its famous conclusion reprises the question-and-answer frame he had used for other tautological and enigmatic statements: "Where was it one first heard of the truth? The the" (186). The metaphysical question receives, as its trivial answer, a remark about words: one first heard of "the truth" in "the the" because "the truth" begins with "the." One can, of course, go on to infer a more philosophical meaning—some form of relativism, perhaps also a rider about language's role in making truth; such inferences are, as we have seen, normal to the operation of tautology. This particular stutter, however, looks odd enough on the page to call attention to the sound of the word and reemphasize the verb *heard*. To *hear* this repetition is, it seems, to hear words coming untethered from strong truth claims about the world, or at least to hear such claims being made only about the field of language use itself.

The intensely rhetorical finish does not mean, however, that Stevens has abandoned reference to the real world. On the contrary:

> That's the moment when the moon creeps up
> To the bubbling of bassoons. That's the time
> One looks at the elephant-colorings of tires.
> Everything is shed; and the moon comes up as the moon
> (All its images are in the dump) and you see
> As a man (not like an image of a man),
> You see the moon rise in the empty sky. (185)

The tautology "the moon comes up as the moon," sonorous and nearly meaningless though it seems, indicates that the real has returned. This redundant expression is as far as possible from the poem's opening anthropomorphization of the moon as "Blanche" making the sun "a corbeil of flowers" (184). The earthly correlate of this real, undescribable moon is a surprising sound: the comic, alliterative "bubbling of bassoons." In the next stanza, the dissonance continues, as "One sits and beats an old tin can, lard pail" (185). One might have expected that when the moon finally came up without any trailing images, it would have no musical accompaniment at all. But Stevens leaves room for artistic production—including poetic production—even in the face of a moon without images. The moon knows nothing of the chants of moon, but that does not mean an appropriately autonomized poetic response cannot be formulated. And this response is not limited to the tautologous recognition that the moon is what it is: Stevens's poem figures the whole context in which that tautology acquires its sense as the dump, a world of humanly made things that must be considered and surveyed before being rejected.

In place of the exaltation Stevens mocks in the final stanza—the exclamations "*aptest eve*," "*Invisible priest*"—the genuine poetic relation to the surrounding world lies in the "janitor's poems / Of every day" (186, 185). This definition of poetry is quite exact about the ambivalence of Stevens's refusal of reference. The janitor does not falsely imagine that he sings the sublimity of nature; on the contrary, his life is lived among the products of consumer society, where even fresh water comes in a can, and the flowers of spring live only in an offhand parenthesis, "(azaleas and so on)" (185), before joining the trash. But the poetic janitor comes into contact with the solid things of a consumer society in order to throw them away. His song of disgust consists in tautology:

> [H]ow many men have copied dew
> For buttons, how many women have covered themselves
> With dew, dew dresses, stones and chains of dew, heads
> Of the floweriest flowers dewed with the dewiest dew.
> One grows to hate these things except on the dump. (185)

The insistent repetition of "dew" focuses attention on the word's sound rather than its meaning—a kind of homeopathic cure for the decorative copying of dew hated by the speaker. Evoking "dewiest dew" enacts the disgust with which the man on the dump discards the dew-like artifacts. On the dump, though, these hated things are perfectly congenial: the dismissive verbal bubbling of bassoons, the sonic extravagance Stevens had practiced since *Harmonium*, gives the dew and its artifactual imitations their place in the poem while still allowing the poem to reject the cheap business (literally) of reference to a conventionalized nature.

These tautological usages can help make sense of sound in Stevens's 1941 defense of the qualified autonomy of poetry, "The Noble Rider and the Sound of Words." That essay might otherwise seem strangely evasive on the subject of sound; despite being featured in the title, sound gets only a cursory and inconclusive discussion in the essay's final section, where Stevens apologizes for having spent his time discussing the role of the poet instead of the axiom that "poetry is words; and … words, above everything else, are, in poetry, sounds" (*CPP*, 663). He is not really committed to poetry as a pure music of language sounds; he may simply be rummaging in the storehouse of aestheticist defenses of poetic autonomy. Still, his poetics does call attention to the linguistic medium. Tautology has this self-referential effect, while still giving us meaning—a meaning we already knew. "The mind has added nothing to human nature," says Stevens (665). The tautological effect of the mind turned back in on itself is a response to the "violence without." Stevens's embrace of escapism (662) and his denial of the social obligation of the poet (658) do not preclude his belief that poetry "help[s] people to live their lives" (661).

Alan Filreis has argued that the defense of escapism in "The Noble Rider" represents a "pre–Pearl Harbor" position of isolationism. Filreis contends that Stevens subsequently abandonded this position in favor of a "pact with national reality," in which the poet's commitment to facts accorded with America's new sense of responsibility toward Europe.[69] For Filreis, Stevens's next major prose statement, "The Figure of the Youth as Virile Poet"—when considered in its original context as a wartime conference paper given to French and American intellectuals—demonstrates this new nationalist commitment. But only a faint analogy exists between Stevens's secular aestheticism and the foreign policy position Filreis detects. In fact, Stevens resumes the thesis of "The Noble Rider" in almost the same terms in "The Figure of the Youth." In the earlier essay, "the mind has added nothing to human nature"; in the later work, yet more tautological definitions of poetry lead up to a similar conclusion:

> One is often tempted to say that the best definition of poetry is that poetry is the sum of its attributes .... Poetry is the scholar's art .... Like light, it adds nothing, except itself. (*CPP*, 681).

Filreis is quite right to see in the 1943 lecture a theory of poetry as situated in the world of facts and to underscore Stevens's description of the poet as creating "exchanges of speech" (685) rather than unresponsive soliloquies. But the power of tautology, in Stevens, is its capacity to make a plain matter-of-factness, conveyed in shared speech, itself the basis for poetry's autonomy. The youth as virile poet is certainly no longer the priest of a transcendental imagination; but having gotten "rid of the hieratic in everything," he still goes on to "create his unreal out of what is real" (679). The movement from "The Noble Rider" to "The Figure of the Youth," though it shifts the emphasis from "sound" to "speech," is far too slight to provide evidence for the major political shift Filreis claims.

Attending to tautology and its sounds also reveals a subtle connection between Stevens's two lectures and the final cantos of *Notes toward a Supreme Fiction* (1942). The seventh canto of "It Must Give Pleasure" prepares the ending of the poem by invoking an "Angel," only to shut it up: "Angel, / Be silent in your luminous cloud and hear / The luminous melody of proper sound" (*CPP*, 349). Having turned our attention to the medium of sound, as though we should expect purely musical poetry to conclude the poem, Stevens instead poses explicitly the largest question

69. Filreis, *Wallace Stevens and the Actual World*, 28, 39.

of the sequence: "What am I to believe?" (349). The answer caps a long rhetorical climax with tautology:

> Is it I then that keep saying there is an hour
> Filled with expressible bliss, in which I have
>
> No need, am happy, forget need's golden hand,
> Am satisfied without solacing majesty,
> And if there is an hour there is a day,
>
> There is a month, a year, there is a time
> In which majesty is a mirror of the self:
> I have not but I am and as I am, I am. (349–50)

This elaborated version of "I am that I am" even tends to make us forget that it is part of a rhetorical question: though it is supposed to be interrogative, it is the lone sentence of the canto that does not end with a question mark. Of course, tautology, more than any other figure, implies that to ask the question is to answer it. Denying the independent existence of the angel he contemplates earlier in the canto, Stevens's self-affirmation is itself rhetorically self-sufficient. Indeed, its form suggests, like the epigram "You are yourself" in "The Man with the Blue Guitar," that no revelation was necessary after all. In particular, if we have been listening only for "the luminous melody of proper sound," we need not have followed the sense at all. We only have to nod along to the music of tautology as it invites us to assent.

It is entirely appropriate to "argue" for a humanist credo in this way, since we ought to need only a reminder that the invisible world was something imagined in the first place. But this argumentative tactic means that the secular principle emerges out of an affirmation of the autonomy of poetry as "proper sound." Stevens's thesis takes the form of a highly echoic, nearly nonsensical chain of syllables: "I have not but I am and as I am, I am." The self-sufficiency of the "I" translates into the self-sufficiency of the poem. Indeed, Stevens makes it easier to believe in the poem than in the self: it is easier to express than to experience the expansion of the "hour / Filled with expressible bliss" into a day, a month, a year (349–50). The next canto reinforces the point by invoking the nonsignifying, repeating songs of the birds as kindred autonomous productions: "These things at least comprise / An occupation, an exercise, a work, // A thing final in itself and, therefore, good" (350). Stevens's repetition of "I am" is *both* a self-directed musical "exercise" *and* the means by which he makes himself and his readers at home in the natural world.

Even the sequence's coda, though it changes the object of its address to a comradely "Soldier," is entirely of a piece with the preceding cantos in its treatment of the sounds of autonomy—much as some readers have wished the coda were not part of the poem at all.[70] These last tercets describe the soldier's war and the poet's figurative "war between the mind / And sky" as "Two parallels that meet if only in / The meeting of their shadows or that meet / In a book in a barrack" (352). The patriotic gesture does not, however, get beyond tautology: "And after it [war] you return // With six meats and twelve wines or else without" (352). To say that either the soldier dies or he doesn't is to demonstrate how the soldier's efforts enter into the poem: with all the indifference conveyed by the tautological formula. Such a formula principally serves to show how the poem is capable of prolonging itself in "petty syllabi" and "sounds that stick." The "proper words" (352) evoked by the sequence's concluding stanza then turn from a *dulce et decorum est* into another version of the "proper sound" of canto III.vii. Such words do circulate, as books in barracks, but not because they speak directly of war.

On the contrary, the address to the soldier is a gesture *from within* poetic autonomy, an exhibition of both the capacities and the limitations with which a poetic supreme fiction responds to contemporary circumstances. That lines from this coda could serve as the decorative border on the back cover of the hand-printed Cummington Press first edition of *Notes toward a Supreme Fiction* makes this ambivalence clear.[71] In her recent *Planets on Tables*, Bonnie Costello pursues a similar argument with respect to Stevens's poems in the genre of still life in the 1942 volume *Parts of a World*. Stevens's still lifes, writes Costello, create an "imaginative and emotional connection to a world from which they are apart but also a part"; thus, he develops "a relational rather than a substantive or referential connection between art and history."[72] I have been arguing that Stevens strives for such a relational connection far more generally. The recurrence of tautology in his work demonstrates the persistence of his efforts in this mode of relation. But I would prefer not to presuppose art's position outside of history; instead, one aim and effect of Stevens's work is to continually renegotiate a *relatively* autonomous position for a poetry made out of the materials of his time. It is not the connection but the disconnection between art and history which needs to be conjured up; poetry, like everything else, is already *in* history.

70. Helen Vendler writes of this "anticlimax" that it "perhaps would not have been appended to *Notes* if the war had not made some external justification of poetry seem necessary." *On Extended Wings*, 205.

71. For a description of the Cummington Press *Notes*, see J. M. Edelstein, *Wallace Stevens: A Descriptive Bibliography* (Pittsburgh, PA: University of Pittsburgh Press, 1974), 46.

72. Bonnie Costello, *Planets on Tables: Poetry, Still Life, and the Turning World* (Ithaca, NY: Cornell University Press, 2008), 31, 35.

The Plain Sense of Tautology

In *The Rock*, Stevens relies one final time on tautology as a means of concluding a poem. "The Plain Sense of Things" (*CPP*, 428) evokes a desolate landscape; but, in its final two stanzas, even this waste of plainness is reclaimed for the imagination:

> The great pond and its waste of the lilies, all this
> Had to be imagined as an inevitable knowledge,
> Required, as a necessity requires.

Necessity requires, simply because that is the meaning of the word *necessity*. As a way of recuperating the imagination in the face of the run-down things of the world, this tautology seems particularly unemphatic. Its logical triviality takes the wind out of the declaration in the previous stanza, which Vendler calls "the central statement of Stevens's poetry"[73] "the imagination had / Itself to be imagined". The verbal and logical aridity of the poem's last phrase redoubles its implication of resignation to the necessity of the poem's bleak imaginings. Stevens hardly celebrates his demonstration that poetic imagination can prolong itself indefinitely in contemplating its own end, a droning "repetition / In a repetitiousness of men and flies." There is no happy recuperation of the failure of "a fantastic effort," not even in terms of a renewed perceptual clarity. Instead, the world of things and the poem each seem to carry on in separate, self-contained existence.

The connection between the world of the great pond and the poem lies in the tautological force of verbal definition, which dictates that a "necessity," any necessity, must require. But that force is actually the force of a connection between the poet and other people. In the first stanza, the speaker does not experience the end of the imagination alone: "we" come to it, not just a singular "I." The depopulated landscape of Stevens's poem is the scene of a social relation. A shared feeling forms the basis for that final tautology: faced with a natural world that neither needs nor accepts imaginative embellishment, the poet and his readers jointly experience the poem's self-perpetuating autonomy as a necessity that nonetheless depends on our consent. In the pragmatics of this ending, "we" are "required" to return as a self-aware collective of modernist readers.

This awareness is perhaps the most elemental of all fictions of autonomy. It combines the prospect of the most far-reaching aesthetic autonomy—freedom from the real—with the simplest possible artistic institution: an ongoing agreement among

---

73. Vendler, *On Extended Wings*, 112.

people about the meaning of a literary work. In dwelling on Stevensian tautology, we agree to allow the autonomous imagination free rein, but we are always brought back to a consciousness of the poet's need for our belief. Even de Man, whose efforts on behalf of literary and critical autonomy often swerve into the hyperbolic claim that language itself has unconstrained agency, makes the figure of tautology correspond to the power of autonomy's social mechanisms. Thus tautology is the type of the Stevensian style and of its grimmer, more ascetic academic younger sibling, the de Manian style. The philosophical propositions on the surface of their writings—about selves, about beliefs, about language—do not stand on their own, but neither are they merely expressions of a mood or a fleeting point of view. They forsake some, though not all, of the privileges of philosophical conceptualization in exchange for a rhetorically compelling evocation of literature's distinctiveness in ordinary social life. Stevens and de Man invite us to watch—or, when they emphasize sound, to listen—as they play on, modify, and elaborate our preexisting assumptions. For these two modernists, literary language is not permanently insulated from external reference, but it can temporarily suspend such referentiality in favor of a self-reference that can and must be embedded in relations among people: in conversations, in poetic performances, in the university and its warring faculties. Laying claim to such autonomy as those social relations permit, the poem is what it is because we are what we are.

Epilogue: Autonomy Now

Is autonomy an idea whose time has passed? To literary scholars it has seemed passé because it appears to deny literature's entanglements in history. But I hope the preceding chapters have made clear how some modernist affirmations of aesthetic autonomy came to grips with historical circumstances, self-consciously acknowledging the constraints that the system of class, the artist's personal life and lifestyle, and the writer's relationship to audiences place on literary works even as those works strive for independence. These autonomy fictions, I have argued, tell truths that the literary history of modernism cannot ignore. Still, relative autonomy is not a transhistorical feature of literary art but a specific modernist practice, integral to the development of new institutions for literature in the first half of the twentieth century. It may seem, then, that autonomy is only a matter of concern for scholars of the early twentieth century—or, at most, of a "long modernist period" opening in the 1880s and closing with de Man's late modernism. Indeed, my argument suggests that readers of other literatures or other periods should be cautious about translating modernist autonomy problems into nonmodernist domains.

Nonetheless, the significance of modernist autonomy is as great now as it was at the apex of modernist literature. Though modernism now belongs to history, it is historical not because it was overthrown or because its ideas are exhausted but because its institutionalization has progressed into new phases. In these final pages, I glance at two present-day institutions of literature that carry on modernism's conflicted, varied exploration of the problems of aesthetic autonomy: the university English department and the Nobel Prize in Literature. Even a brief look at these two institutions will make clear that modernist autonomy fictions have profound implications for contemporary scholarship and contemporary literature.

Autonomy, Literary Study, and Knowledge Production

The present-day university English department has modernist autonomy in its genetic code. As is well known, modernist autonomy ideas were important to the founding of the new disciplines of academic literary criticism in the first decades of the twentieth century.[1] These ideas link the founder of English practical criticism, I. A. Richards, to such iconic American New Critics as Allen Tate and Cleanth Brooks; all three admired the criticism and poetry of T. S. Eliot. We saw in the previous chapter how fictions of institutional and linguistic autonomy continued to shape academic literary study in the decades of de Manian theory. But autonomy aspirations in literary studies are not confined to the now-outdated practices of New Criticism and high theory. The very idea of higher education courses—and higher education professors—devoted to the specialist interpretation of select works of vernacular literature, including contemporary literature, owes much to modernist principles of autonomy. From the inauguration of the modern English department about a century ago to the present, the same basic notion of the autonomous literary subject matter has structured literature departments and their curricula. This institutional fact explains why, in the classroom, New and practical criticism have not entirely given up the ghost: every time today's English professors assign "close-reading" papers about a single novel or poem, they demonstrate that modernist autonomy fictions continue to ramify on a far grander scale than the modernists who wrote before the post–World War II expansion of higher education in the United States and elsewhere could have imagined.

The life of autonomy fictions in the college or university literature department has played an important part in the larger story of the literary field. In the United States the growth of creative writing programs in the second half of the twentieth century represented, to a considerable degree, the institutionalization of modernist aesthetics as a teachable program. According to Mark McGurl's *The Program Era*, the hegemony of the writing program represents nothing less than the fortunate "fall" into institutionality of modernist principles of impersonal craft, autonomous

---

1. As Gerald Graff puts it, the New Critics "reinterpreted and reevaluated earlier literature in the light of a modernist poetics that said poetry is neither rhetorical persuasion nor self-expression but an autonomous discourse." *Professing Literature: An Institutional History*, 20th anniversary ed. (Chicago: University of Chicago Press, 2007), 198.

expression, and writerly integrity—all versions, of course, of the commitment to aesthetic autonomy.[2] Operating in tandem with the promotion of related literary doctrines in literature courses, these imperatives of the writing workshop are so many invitations to produce fictions of autonomy. It is far beyond the scope of this epilogue to assess whether the postwar products of university-sponsored literary autonomy resemble modernist fictions of autonomy, though McGurl gives ample reason to suppose they do, tracing the modernist lineage of multiple kinds of postwar fiction. But whether there are widespread resemblances or not, we can be sure that the problems of autonomy will remain important to the history of literature in an era in which many writers are schooled in institutions with those problems woven into their curricula.

Still, although English professors may continue, with their creative writing colleagues, to encourage the supposition of aesthetic autonomy in their students' work, those professors would hardly write articles upholding autonomy themselves. Contextualism is the professional norm. As we have seen, however, many scholarly debates continue to turn on autonomy questions, even—or especially—when they appear to bypass autonomy and aesthetics altogether in favor of disputes about the political or cultural-critical content of literature. I have tried to show that reopening the question of literary autonomy need not mean ignoring the contributions of historically and politically informed scholarship. In the case of modernism, the writers themselves make the concept of relative autonomy necessary for understanding how historical circumstances like the decline of domestic service and political stances like cosmopolitanism are mediated in literary works.

Even in scholarship on literatures other than modernism, the widespread imperative to analyze the specifically literary features of literature—above all literary form—testifies to the influence of modernist autonomy practices on the procedures of the present-day scholarly discipline as a whole. The practice of close reading, well known to have many of its roots in modernist concepts of the autonomous literary work, continues to play an important role in the work of many literary academics. But the endurance of autonomy doctrine is even more visible in the fact that the most significant and productive *repudiation* of close reading in recent literary studies, the work of Franco Moretti and his collaborators in quantitative and large-scale literary analysis, insistently keeps questions of form and style in the foreground, treating them as relatively autonomous levels of literary history.[3]

---

2. Mark McGurl, *The Program Era: Postwar Fiction and the Rise of Creative Writing* (Cambridge, MA: Harvard University Press, 2009), 409.

3. Moretti justifies his work in *Graphs, Maps, Trees* in the name of "a materialist conception of form"; his discussion of "distant reading" proposes a new, large-scale model for

I do not reduce or dismiss the highly consequential divergences among the literary-scholarly practices of the last three-quarters of a century by linking them to early twentieth-century versions of autonomy. As we have seen again and again in the preceding chapters, attributing a role to autonomy ideas and practices is only the beginning, not the end, of an analysis. Participants in the academic and literary fields may adopt very different relations to this intellectual and institutional legacy.

I have been trying to show throughout this book, however, that for scholars two positions are particularly misguided: the complete embrace of autonomy as essential to the literary, and the complete denial of autonomy, which subordinates all literary investigations to extraliterary concerns. Denial rather than embrace has become the dominant note of literary scholarship when it comes to autonomy, but autonomy does have some defenders. Literary autonomy's advocates, like Charles Altieri and Richard Lansdown, tend to emphasize what they take to be the unique capacities of literary and artistic form; for them, the internal dynamics of literary works can ensure their distinction and independence from other discourses.[4] But modernist fictions of autonomy suggest that, on the contrary, a work's supposedly formal or internal dimensions are in fact social through and through; as cases like that of Wilde's butlers and valets suggest, affirmations of the "dominance of form" create ever-deeper ties between literary practice and social structures like the hierarchies of labor and class. It is in relation to these other fields of social life, and not because of some supposed internal necessity, that any kind of autonomy for literature is possible. Indeed, the arguments advanced by today's partisans of autonomy express a viewpoint made possible by the development, in the modernist period, of *institutional* foundations for a relatively autonomous literary subfield.[5]

---

formal analysis; and, as he has recently said, any new approach to literary study must "prove that it can do formal analysis." *Graphs, Maps, Trees: Abstract Models for Literary History* (London: Verso, 2007), 92; "Conjectures on World Literature," *New Left Review* 1 (January–February 2000): 54–68; "Style, Inc. Reflections on Seven Thousand Titles (British Novels, 1740–1850)," *Critical Inquiry* 36, no. 1 (Autumn 2009): 152.

4. Charles Altieri, "Why Modernist Claims for Autonomy Matter," *Journal of Modern Literature* 32, no. 3 (Spring 2009): 1–21; Richard Lansdown, *The Autonomy of Literature* (Houndmills, UK: Macmillan, 2001). In distinct ways, both writers are also skeptical about the empiricism they detect in historicist scholarship; literary autonomy, for them, with its antirepresentational or antirealist tendency, resists an empirical accounting. Here I diverge sharply from Altieri and Lansdown; my own aim has been precisely to give an empirical account of autonomy itself.

5. Among recent polemical statements on autonomy, my own view is more nearly in accord with that expressed in the title of Gregory Jusdanis's "Two Cheers for Aesthetic Autonomy," *Cultural Critique* 61 (Fall 2005): 22–54. Jusdanis makes the crucial distinction between false, ahistorical versions of autonomy and true accounts of the historical emergence of autonomous art institutions.

Once the institutions of literature come into view—and one of the virtues of high modernism for scholars is that it compels us to attend to those institutions—they make even the most sophisticated formalism seem too reductive. Like the opposing and somewhat more prevalent scholarly tendency to treat literature and culture as significant primarily in their ethical and political dimensions, the full-throated acceptance of autonomy leads literary scholarship to imagine a less complicated object of study than the one it actually has. Both extreme positions on autonomy foreclose the fundamental questions about the social life of literature: how do literary practice and the literary field engage with or modulate other practices and fields? What are the relationships between literary or symbolic forms of capital and other forms? How do literary institutions enable and limit literature's social engagements—or its relative autonomy? These questions, of course, require investigating literary production and literary reading as two distinctive social practices among many. Surprising though it may seem, taking the concept of autonomy seriously pushes literary study *not* in the regressive direction of a "return to the aesthetic" or a vindication of "close reading" in the narrow sense but rather toward the wide realms, and the empirical methods, of cultural history and the social sciences. Though the case studies in this book hardly stand on their own as empirical work by the standards of those fields, it is my hope that I have shown why the literary questions I have addressed lead down the sociological and historical roads I am pointing out for future work. I hope, too, that my arguments make clear why it would do no damage to the *disciplinary* autonomy of literary scholarship to take up this program of historical and sociological knowledge production, which in fact emerges out of demands internal to the literary field and literary studies. Instead, such a program bolsters the claims to legitimacy of a discipline sorely in need of it in the academy and in the wider culture.

Autonomy Abroad: Proliferation on the World Stage

The North American university English department might still seem to be a rather parochial domain for the continuing afterlife of modernist autonomy; though I believe understanding the changing fortunes of autonomy in literature and in scholarship is crucial to the work of literary history, autonomy lives on beyond the academic realm as well. As we saw in the discussion of Barnes and Joyce, modernism commands a more cosmopolitan perspective. Indeed, one of the grandest of all legacies of modernist autonomy is in our concept of global literature itself. After Joyce, Barnes, and their generation of transnational modernists, literary writers have frequently thought of themselves as part of a world community, whose global scope arises from the autonomy of the writer or her work from local ties. Whether political exiles, voluntary expatriates, or neither, such writers look beyond national borders in their aesthetic affiliations and rivalries as well as their social-political stances, and they invite their readers to do so as well. The modernist inflection to these practices of autonomy is particularly visible in one of world literature's most conspicuous institutions, the Nobel Prize in Literature. Though the Nobel Prize is not necessarily representative of all that world literature is or could be, it offers a meaningful glimpse of literary autonomy's presence on a global scale: in awarding the prize for literature, the Swedish Academy has become perhaps the most prominent institution consecrating authors of autonomy fictions from around the world.[6]

Autonomy's role in this version of world literature appears frequently in the Nobel laureates' lectures. The lectures abound in gestures toward autonomy, as in this Eliot-style declaration of impersonality: "The life, the opinions, are not the work, for it is in the tension between standing apart and being involved that the imagination transforms both." The author of this statement is the 1991 laureate Nadine Gordimer, famously committed to the antiapartheid movement and a member of the African National Congress long before the ban on the party was lifted; yet when she speaks as a Nobel writer, she emphasizes the relative autonomy of her work even from her own beliefs.[7] The committed writer turns out to have a modernist-like bent for impersonality—a tendency Gordimer shares with other laureates known for their political affiliations, like José Saramago, whose prize lecture in 1998 describes the author's education at the hands of his apparently autonomous characters, or Elfriede Jelinek, who, in a 2004 lecture delivered on video, describes herself as "sidelined" by her own language.[8] By the same token,

---

6. For a discussion of the symbolic economy of contemporary cultural prizes that includes an illuminating account of the Nobel Prize and world literature, see James F. English, *The Economy of Prestige: Prizes, Awards, and the Circulation of Cultural Value* (Cambridge, MA: Harvard University Press, 2005). English's work is an exemplary demonstration that struggles over literary and artistic autonomy remain very much alive in our own period, even as they are self-consciously circumscribed by institutions, economies, and politics.

7. Nadine Gordimer, "Writing and Being" (1991), http://www.nobelprize.org/nobel_prizes/literature/laureates/1991/gordimer-lecture.html (accessed July 17, 2012).

8. José Saramago, "How Characters Became the Masters and the Author Their Apprentice," trans. Tim Crosfield and Fernando Rodrigues (1998), http://www.nobelprize.org/nobel_prizes/literature/laureates/1998/saramago-lecture.html (accessed July 17, 2012); Elfriede Jelinek, "Sidelined," trans. Martin Chalmers (2004), http://www.nobelprize.

even a poet known for his devotion to form, Seamus Heaney, sees that work on form as an attempt to come to terms with a world of political strife and violence; turning to a modernist model, he cites Yeats's "Meditations in Time of Civil War" as "proof" that poetry can be both formally satisfying and true to a real-world dilemma. [9] These Nobelist statements indicate that in at least one prominent strand of contemporary world literature, the dilemmas of autonomy—the conflicts of a relatively independent literary practice that must account for its place in the world—remain an important theme in the literature of several continents.

Indeed, modernist-style autonomy concerns may be almost a requirement for admission to the Nobel pantheon. Such is the hypothesis suggested by Pascale Casanova in *The World Republic of Letters*. In her theory, writers, whatever their origins, garner "global" status and recognition in the European centers when they are understood to have synchronized their work with the "literary Greenwich meridian" defined by Joycean or Faulknerian style and a rejection of nationalist norms—which is to say, defined by modernism's version of cosmopolitan autonomy.[10] The Nobel Prize furnishes one of Casanova's most convincing examples of this operation of literary consecration—although Casanova herself does not take full account of the complexities of the modernist norms of autonomy the prize institutes, seeing them as thoroughly apolitical. In fact, the work of recent laureates includes lineal descendants of each of the particular autonomy themes I have surveyed in this book: domestic service is wrapped into the vicissitudes of literary form in J. M. Coetzee's *Foe* (1986); lateness and a newly ephemeral self inform Heaney's work in poems of the 1990s like "Postscript" (*The Spirit Level*, 1996); the nameless narrator's wanderings through China in Gao Xingjian's *Soul Mountain* (1990) evoke Gao's Joycean exile in France; and the spectacle of a nonreferential literary language nonetheless fraught with social significance appears in a striking form in Toni Morrison's first novel, *The Bluest Eye* (1970), which demolishes the language of Dick-and-Jane primers. Casanova's Paris-centered "world literary space" is in any case only a very partial view of the total literary production of the world, but the space she describes, like the practice of the recent Nobel laureates

---

org/nobel_prizes/literature/laureates/2004/jelinek-lecture-e.html (accessed July 17, 2012).

9. Seamus Heaney, "Crediting Poetry" (1995), http://www.nobelprize.org/nobel_prizes/literature/laureates/1995/heaney-lecture.html (accessed July 17, 2012).

10. See Pascale Casanova, *The World Republic of Letters*, trans. M. B. DeBevoise (Cambridge, MA: Harvard University Press, 2004), 4, 103.

who stand at or near its apex, carries modernist autonomy forward as one—or more than one—productive possibility in world literature.[11]

The Truth about Fictions of Autonomy

Modernist autonomy fictions continue to proliferate, but this proliferation may, like my account of modernist autonomy itself, not offer much comfort to those who would wish to keep literary art pure. Contemporary autonomy fictions, like their modernist predecessors, far from sealing the work into its own virtuous circle, constantly force literature to confront its embeddedness in the social world. There is no denying the loss that attends this confrontation for the believer in literature's essential autonomy. A literary work can no longer be a closed miniature cosmos, a zone of pure form and pure pleasure, a realm of complete freedom. For such loss, there is, in modernism at least, some recompense: modernist literature recaptures its capacity for telling the truth about its own situation, its own materials, its own nature as a human practice. But those truths have none of the exhilarating simplicity of the most uncompromising versions of aesthetic autonomy, nor do they offer the unadulterated satisfactions promised by the most zealous wings of the religion of art.

Though the modernist claim to relative autonomy is often justified, modernism's awareness of its own limits is, too. Literary aesthetes from Wilde through the latest modernists have codified the belief in aesthetic autonomy only to cut that autonomy down to size. We literary readers, who are shaped by modernism's institutions and follow in its path, must accept being cut down to size ourselves. A special sensitivity to the techniques and devices of modernism qualifies us to realize how much else we must become sensitive to. We do not escape into another world when we enter the literary work, least of all those modernist works, like Stevens's planets on tables or Joyce's magna opera, that promise to be worlds unto themselves. Nor can we expect the special properties of the literary work to provide comprehensive social visions or morally authoritative doctrines; the insight of

---

11. To be sure, now as in any other historical period, autonomy can never be the whole story of literary practice, and sometimes—in certain genres, certain places, certain times—it will hardly be part of the story at all. For an attempt to sketch alternative models of literary systems across a huge geographical and historical span, see Alexander Beecroft, "World Literature without a Hyphen: Towards a Typology of Literary Systems," *New Left Review* 54 (November–December 2008): 87–100.

the modernists I have examined depends on their ability to indicate the particular, historical, socially limited standpoint from which they operate.

In limitation, however, modernism reveals its own breadth. To pursue modernism's autonomy dreams is to explore the essential connections between literary art for art's sake and many other domains of culture, from domestic life to music theory, café lifestyle to academic funding. By showing that even modernism's most committed advocates of autonomy embraced their entanglements and dependencies, I hope I have given pause to would-be debunkers of all claims to aesthetic autonomy. For modernists from Wilde to de Man, those worldly entanglements included very real, though partial, forms of autonomy—relative freedoms that made possible some of the twentieth century's most distinctive and compelling literature. But I have not succeeded unless I have also convinced would-be celebrants of the religion of art, whether in modernist studies or elsewhere, to broaden their perspective—to pursue their devotion to art into all the complex reality of art's worldly relations. The best way for readers of modernist literature to stay true to its fictions of autonomy would be to look toward wider horizons.

Index

Portrait of the Artist as a Young Man, A. See
  Joyce, James, works of
position-taking. *See* field
postwar literature, 6, 188. *See also*
  modernism
Pound, Ezra, 20, 81, 81 n39, 133
pragmatics, linguistic, 153, 154 n9, 169, 184
  applied to tautology, 150, 153, 153 n8,
    162, 164 n32
  See also Grice, H. Paul; Relevance
    Theory; Sperber, Dan; Wilson,
    Deirdre
Proust, Marcel, 2, 19, 43, 52, 70, 111, 174
  relationship with servants. *See* Albaret,
    Céleste
Proust, Marcel, works of
  À la recherche du temps perdu, 53–67,
    131
  class in, 58, 58 n81, 60–61, 64
  Françoise (character) in, 53, 58–63, 67
  servants in, 15–16, 25–26, 43, 53–57
pure art. *See* aestheticism; autonomy

queerness, 27 n7, 81 n41, 107, 113–14,
  118–20, 138

Rainey, Lawrence, 6–7, 22–23, 81 n42,
  107 n100, 108 n101
Ransom, John Crowe, 3 n4
reaction, political. *See* conservatism
reading. *See* close reading; distant reading;
  literary studies
reading, rhetorical. *See* deconstruction
realism, 9, 27, 39, 42–43, 52, 163, 176
  rejection of, 4, 17–18, 29–31, 33, 54, 66
    n99, 119, 143–44, 189 n4
referentiality, 2, 4, 15, 17–19, 127, 153–59,
  161, 167, 169–72, 174–75, 178–80,
  183, 185, 192. *See also*
  self-referentiality
reflexivity. *See* self-referentiality
Relevance Theory, 84 n46, 153 n8, 169 n46
Remembrance of Things Past. See Proust,
  Marcel
revival, Celtic, 136, 138–39, 142, 142 n74,
  144, 144 n81
Richards, I. A., 187
Riddel, Joseph N., 155 n12
Rilke, Rainer Maria, 154, 174

Robbins, Bruce, 33, 52, 52 n72, 115, 115
  n8, 116
rococo, 122, 122 n23, 126. *See also*
  neobaroque
Romanticism, 12–13, 76, 86–87, 94–95,
  156, 158–59, 172, 174, 176
Rosner, Victoria, 36 n32
Rosu, Anca, 154 n9
Russell, Bertrand, 166

Said, Edward W., 75, 75 n16, 77, 112
Saramago, José, 191
Saussure, Ferdinand de, 153
Schiller, Friedrich, 12, 177
Schryer, Stephen, 3 n4
sciences vs. humanities (conflict of the
  faculties), 168–69, 185
secularism, 12, 83, 161, 181–82
self-referentiality, 9, 13, 16, 19, 23, 25, 43,
  80, 97, 106, 108, 111, 116, 120, 126,
  151–52, 158, 164–65, 176, 185
self-reflexivity. *See* self-referentiality
Seltzer, Mark, 51
servants, 30–31, 31 n20, 55, 67, 188
  and aestheticism, 15–16, 20, 24–28, 30,
    32–50, 65–67, 69, 143
  and closure, 50–51, 57–59
  dialectic of master and, 43–44, 63
  and form, 24–67, 189, 192
  in Huysmans, 16, 39–47, 66–67
  and illness, 41–42, 62–64
  in James, 16, 46–53, 66–67
  in modernism, 20, 25, 33, 52–53, 142–43
  in Proust, 15–16, 52–67
  resemblance to master, 35, 44, 52–53,
    60–62, 64–65
  in Victorian literature, 33
  in Villiers, 16, 28–30, 46, 67
  in Wilde, 15–16, 24–28, 33–39, 44–47,
    49 n68, 52–53, 65–67
  working conditions, 31, 55–56
  writings by, 31–32, 55, 55 n79, 56, 59,
    59 n84
service, domestic. *See* servants
sexuality. *See* queerness
Shakespeare, William, 54, 62, 149, 162
Shumway, David, 139
Simons, Hi, 160, 160 n23, 161